CLARENDON LIBRARY OF LOGIC AND PHILOSOPHY

General Editor: L. Jonathan Cohen, The Queen's College, Oxford

WITHOUT GOOD REASON

The Clarendon Library of Logic and Philosophy brings together books, by new as well as by established authors, that combine originality of theme with rigour of statement. Its aim is to encourage new research of a professional standard into problems that are of current or perennial interest.

General Editor: L. Jonathan Cohen, The Queen's College, Oxford

Also published in this series

Philosophy without Ambiguity by Jay David Atlas
Quality and Concept by George Bealer
Psychological Models and Neural Mechanisms by Austen Clark
Sensory Qualities by Austen Clark
The Diversity of Moral Thinking by Neil Cooper
The Logic of Aspect: An Axiomatic Approach by Anthony Galton
Ontological Economy by Dale Gottlieb
Experiences: An Inquiry into some Ambiguities by J. M. Hinton
The Fortunes of Inquiry by N. Jardine
Metaphor: Its Cognitive Force and Linguistic Stucture by Eva Feder Kittay
Truth, Fiction, and Literature: A Philosophical Perspective
by Peter Lamarque and Stein Haugom Olsen
A Model of the Universe: Space-Time, Probability, and Decision
by Storrs McCall
The Cement of the Universe: A Study of Causation by J. L. Mackie
The Nature of Necessity by Alvin Plantinga
Divine Commandments and Moral Requirements by P. L. Quinn
*Rationality: A Philosophical Inquiry into the Nature and the Rationale of
Reason* by Nicholas Rescher
Blindspots by Roy N. Sorensen
*Without Good Reason: The Rationality Debate in Philosophy and Cognitive
Science* by Edward Stein
The Coherence of Theism by Richard Swinburne
Anti-Realism and Logic: Truth as Eternal by Neil Tennant
Ignorance: A Case for Scepticism by Peter Unger
The Scientific Image by Bas C. van Fraassen
Chance and Structure: An Essay on the Logical Foundations of Probability
by John M. Vickers
Slippery Slope Arguments by Douglas Walton
What Is Existence? by C. J. F. Williams
Works and Worlds of Art by Nicholas Wolterstorff

WITHOUT GOOD REASON

The Rationality Debate in
Philosophy and Cognitive Science

EDWARD STEIN

CLARENDON PRESS · OXFORD
1996

Oxford University Press, Walton Street, Oxford OX2 6DP

Oxford New York
Athens Auckland Bangkok Bombay
Calcutta Cape Town Dar es Salaam Delhi
Florence Hong Kong Istanbul Karachi
Kuala Lumpur Madras Madrid Melbourne
Mexico City Nairobi Paris Singapore
Taipei Tokyo Toronto
and associated companies in
Berlin Ibadan

Oxford is a trade mark of Oxford University Press

Published in the United States
by Oxford University Press Inc., New York

British Library Cataloguing in Publication Data
Data available

Library of Congress Cataloging in Publication Data
Stein, Edward, 1965–
Without good reason : the rationality debate in philosophy and
cognitive science / Edward Stein.
— (Clarendon library of logic and philosophy)
Includes bibliographical references and index.
1. Man.   2. Reason.   3. Philosophy of mind.   4. Cognitive science.
I. Title.   II. Series.
BD450.S747   1996   128'.3—dc20   95–32650
ISBN 0–19–823574–7

1 3 5 7 9 10 8 6 4 2

Typeset by Graphicraft Typesetters Ltd., Hong Kong
Printed in Great Britain
on acid-free paper by
Bookcraft (Bath) Ltd.,
Midsomer Norton, Avon.

For Steve,
for many good reasons

Acknowledgements

THIS book began as my Ph.D. dissertation, 'Rationality and the Limits of Cognitive Science', for the philosophy programme in the Department of Linguistics and Philosophy at the Massachusetts Institute of Technology. From 1989 to 1991 I worked on this project with Ned Block, Bob Stalnaker, and David Brink as my formal advisers. They read many drafts and provided helpful comments. Among my fellow philosophy graduate students, Michael Antony, Susan Dwyer, Tracy Isaacs, Diane Jeske, Eric Lormand, Paul Pietrowski, Scott Smith, and Daniel Stoljar provided support and advice. Paul Bloom, Gary Marcus, William Snyder, and Karen Wynn were graduate students in MIT's Brain and Cognitive Sciences programme who also helped me in various ways; in particular, they helped me grapple with various aspects of linguistics and cognitive science. Friends and colleagues at other schools, most notably Alyssa Bernstein, Steve Greene, Peter Lipton, Paul Snowdon, and Rob Wilson, deserve mention as well. For much of this time, I received financial and in-kind support from MIT's Department of Linguistics and Philosophy as well as generous financial support from the Woodrow Wilson Foundation's Mellon Fellowships in the Humanities. My family helped me out as well.

After I graduated from MIT, I moved to New York University, where, for the first year, I took a break from issues concerning rationality, although I did revise a chapter of the dissertation for publication in *Synthese* as 'Rationality and Reflective Equilibrium' (*Synthese*, 99 (1994), 137–72; Chapter 5 of this book uses material from this article, which is reprinted by permission of Kluwer Academic Publishers). Two anonymous referees provided helpful suggestions, and L. Jonathan Cohen wrote an interesting reply ('A Reply to Stein', *Synthese*, 99 (1994), 173–6), which helped me get clearer on some important issues.

After working on other projects, I decided to write this book. Rob Wilson, Paul Bloom, and Peter Lipton each made important suggestions about the directions I should take. Their advice proved crucial to the current shape of this book. Paul Bloom, Frank Farrell, Tracy Isaacs, Diane Jeske, Noa Latham, Peter Lipton, John Richardson, Roy Sorensen, Steve Stich, and Rob Wilson read drafts of chapters and provided me with helpful comments at various stages of the process. Paul Bloom, Peter Lipton, Roy Sorensen, and Steve Stich read substantial portions of the penultimate version of the book and provided detailed comments. Two anonymous referees for Oxford University Press also made some helpful suggestions. In particular, Paul Bloom deserves singling out: if he had done much more to help with this book, I would have had to take him on as a co-author. Jonathan Cohen, in his capacity as editor of the Clarendon Library in Logic and Philosophy, provided important encouragement towards the end of the writing process. My editor at Oxford, Peter Momtchiloff, and others on the staff there, helped to make the final stages of manuscript preparation pleasant and efficient.

Many other friends and colleagues helped in ways less easy to specify but no less important. Particularly noteworthy among them are David Eppel, Morris Kaplan, and Chris Straayer. A significant portion of this book was written in Amsterdam in the first part of the summer of 1994. I owe a great debt to my friends and *kützwagen* there for their kindness and generosity. Finally, I thank Steve Lin for his love and support, especially during the final stages of work on this book.

Contents

List of Figures

List of Tables

1

Introduction

SUPPOSE a friend of yours is talking about his new friend Linda. He tells you that Linda is single, 31, bright, outspoken, and that, as a college student, she majored in philosophy and was concerned with issues of social justice. Given all your friend has told you about her, rank the following statements in order of the likelihood that they will be true of Linda:

(1) Linda is active in the feminist movement.
(2) Linda is a bank teller.
(3) Linda is a bank teller and is active in the feminist movement.

If you are like most people, you ranked (3) as being more probable than (2). This, however, is a mistake: (3) cannot be more probable than (2), because (2) is true whenever (3) is. Although this fact seems straightforward once I have pointed it out, people seem to avoid it systematically.[1] In so doing, they are making a mistake in reasoning. According to experiments done over the past few decades, humans make similarly significant errors in various realms of reasoning: logical reasoning, probabilistic reasoning, similarity judgements, and risk-assessment to name a few.[2] Together these experiments, which I will call *reasoning experiments*, are taken to show that humans are irrational.

The observation that humans are irrational is perhaps more commonplace than that humans have two legs, even though the latter seems more obvious. Even in the face of evidence from experiments like the *conjunction experiment* sketched above, many want to resist the thesis that humans are irrational. Some philosophers and psychologists have developed creative and appealing arguments that these experiments are mistaken or misinterpreted because humans *must* be rational. Any one

---

[1] This example is adapted from Amos Tversky and Daniel Kahneman, 'Extensional versus Intuitive Reasoning: The Conjunction Fallacy in Probability Judgment', *Psychological Review*, 90 (Oct. 1983), 293–315. For further discussion of this experiment, see Ch. 3, Sect. 2 below.

[2] A representative cross-section of the reasoning experiments can be found in Daniel Kahneman *et al*. (eds.), *Judgment under Uncertainty* (Cambridge: Cambridge University Press, 1982).

of these arguments, if successful would provide important insight into human nature. These arguments would also entail that there are limits to what science can show, namely science cannot show humans to be irrational. Finally, these arguments for human rationality have significant implications for epistemology, philosophy of science, philosophy of mind, and philosophy of language.

In what follows, I examine the various arguments for human rationality and for the existence of limits to cognitive science and science in general. I attempt to show that these arguments fail; cognitive science can and should play a role in determining whether or not humans are rational. My discussion has implications for the distinction between empirical and conceptual knowledge, the proper relationship between philosophy and science, and for the project of epistemology. In particular, I will suggest that the traditional approach to knowledge errs by ignoring the important role science should play in epistemology.

1. What is it to be Rational?

1.1. Three Ways to be Rational

There are two truisms that seem in tension but, at the same time, seem to coexist happily in our common-sense view of humans and rationality. On the one hand, we agree with Aristotle that man is a rational animal, while on the other hand, we agree with Freud that humans are irrational. This apparent tension can be resolved by distinguishing among several different senses of 'rational'. First, when talking about rationality, one might simply be referring to reasoning ability; humans are rational in the sense that we consciously and explicitly reason, we give arguments for the things we believe, and so on. Perhaps this is what Aristotle meant when he said that man is a rational animal. Second, one might use 'rational' to denote *perfect* reasoning; humans are thus *ir*-rational in the sense that we frequently make mistakes in reasoning due, more often than not, to the vicissitudes of the human condition. For example, we make mistakes in reasoning because our behaviour is influenced by repressed sexual desires. Perhaps this is what is behind the Freudian truism that humans are irrational. Glossed in these ways, the two truisms are perfectly compatible. It is consistent with the fact that humans reason that sometimes humans make mistakes in reasoning; in fact, the truth of the second fact depends on the truth of the first.

There is a third sense of 'rational' that is used when talking about humans. This sense of rational allows that humans can make reasoning errors, but attributes these mistakes to forces that interfere with human reasoning rather than to mistakes internal to our reasoning process. There is a quite intuitive distinction at work here. To simplify matters, consider the following observation: there are two different explanations behind a person's inability to, say, answer a question. Typically, I have no trouble telling you precisely how old I am, but, on certain occasions, say when I am quite tired, under the influence of mind-altering substances, or preoccupied, I may have difficulty reporting my age, that is, I may hesitate, blurt out the wrong answer, or the like. In contrast, if you ask a total stranger how old I am, she will not know the answer; at best, she could guess, but, if she has never laid eyes on me and knows next to nothing about me, her guess will be a wild one. The stranger lacks knowledge of my age, while I have the knowledge but, under certain circumstances, I am unable to deliver it because of interfering factors. In terms that I will explain at some length below, when she gets my age wrong, she is making a *competence* error, but when I get my age wrong, I am making a *performance* error. The third sense of rationality appeals to this distinction. According to this sense of rationality, humans are rational if the only mistakes in reasoning we make are attributable to interferences with human reasoning rather than to human reasoning ability itself. This sense of rationality is particularly interesting and it is this sense that philosophers and psychologists have in mind when they debate whether or not humans are rational, and in particular, it is this sense of rational that is involved when psychological experiments (like the one about Linda sketched above) are cited as 'hav[ing] bleak implications for human rationality'.[3]

[3] Richard Nisbett and Eugene Borgida, 'Attribution and the Psychology of Prediction', *Journal of Personal and Social Psychology*, 32 (1975), 935. Others who have claimed that such experiments support the conclusion that humans are irrational include: Daniel Kahneman and Amos Tversky, 'Subjective Probability: A Judgment of Representativeness', *Cognitive Psychology*, 3 (1972), 430–54; repr. in Kahneman *et al.* (eds.), *Judgment under Uncertainty*, 46: 'for anyone who would wish to view man as a reasonable intuitive statistician, such results are discouraging'; Paul Slovic, Baruch Fischhoff, and Sarah Lichtenstein, 'Cognitive Processes and Societal Risk Taking', in John Carroll and John Payne (eds.), *Cognition and Social Behavior* (Hillsdale, NJ: Erlbaum, 1976), 173–4: 'people's judgments of important probabilistic phenomena are not merely biased but are in violation of fundamental normative rules'; and Richard Nisbett *et al.*, 'The Use of Statistics in Everyday Inductive Reasoning', *Psychological Review*, 90 (1983), 340: 'people commit serious errors of inference'.

1.2. The Standard Picture of Rationality

I call the claim that humans are rational the *rationality thesis* and the claim that humans are irrational the *irrationality thesis*. Both of these claims are typically based on what I call the *standard picture of rationality*. According to this picture, to be rational is to reason in accordance with principles of reasoning that are based on rules of logic, probability theory, and so forth. If the standard picture of reasoning is right, principles of reasoning that are based on such rules are *normative principles of reasoning*, namely they are the principles we *ought* to reason in accordance with.

The standard picture of rationality is not the only possible picture of rationality. In Chapter 7, I will consider others. As described, however, the standard picture of rationality is intuitively very plausible. It seems certain that the principles which we think are the normative principles of reasoning are in fact the normative principles of reasoning. To appreciate the appeal of the standard picture, compare the principles of reasoning with mathematics. Consider the statement 'Two plus two equals four'. This statement seems intuitively plausible. A theory of mathematics that says two plus two does not equal four would be highly implausible. Principles of reasoning based on rules of logic, probability, and so forth seem equally well established.

Assuming that the standard picture of rationality is the right picture, we might wonder why it is. There are various theories, some of which I will return to in subsequent chapters. For now, consider what makes mathematical facts true. According to Platonism, which is perhaps the standard view of mathematics, mathematical facts are true independent of cognitive operations and independent of any relation to human minds. Two plus two equals four regardless of whether humans believe it or not and even before humans existed. Although Platonism has been criticized on various grounds, there is at least the quite strong appearance that it is true. A non-Platonist theory must at least explain the strong intuitive appeal of Platonism. Platonism seems equally strong with respect to the rules of logic. The mathematical statement 'Two plus two equals four' seems of the same status as the logical statement ' "Bill Clinton and Hillary Clinton live in the White House" entails "Bill Clinton lives in the White House" '. The rule of mathematics that says multiplication of x by y is equivalent to the sum of y x's is of the same status as the following rule of logic:

> AND-ELIMINATION RULE: The truth of the conjunction of two statements entails the truth of each statement in the conjunction.

The standard picture of rationality does not require the truth of Platonism; for example, the standard picture, as described, is compatible with the view that the principles of rationality are whatever we think they are. The standard picture of rationality does, however, fit nicely with Platonism's intuitive appeal when it is combined with the view that we are equipped to access mathematical facts, logical truths, and the normative principles of reasoning. The principles that we think are the normative principles of reasoning match the principles that are the normative principles of reasoning because we have the capacity for determining what the normative principles are. For now, I will assume that the standard picture of rationality, or an account roughly like it, is true. As I proceed, however, I will raise several problems for this view.

Note that the principles of logic do not, on their own, provide an account of how we ought to reason. Reasoning involves beliefs and the rules of logic say nothing about beliefs. According to the standard picture of rationality, the principles of reasoning that we ought to follow are based on rules of logic. Consider the statement

(*a*) Bill Clinton is the President and Al Gore is the Vice-President.

This statement entails both the statement

(*b*) Bill Clinton is the President

and the statement

(*c*) Al Gore is the Vice-President.

This example is an instance of the and-elimination rule of logic. The and-elimination rule gives rise to the following principle of reasoning:

AND-ELIMINATION PRINCIPLE: If you believe the conjunctive statement *A* **and** *B*, you should believe both the statement *A* and the statement *B*.

According to this principle, if you believe the statement (*a*) then you should also believe the statement (*b*) and the statement (*c*). Note that I have distinguished between rules of logic and principles of reasoning that stem from them. Rules of logic apply to statements and determine the logical relations among them; principles of reasoning that stem from rules of logic apply to beliefs and determine the relations among them. Some, but certainly not all, principles of reasoning are based on rules of logic. According to the standard picture of rationality, principles of reasoning based on rules of logic are normative principles of reasoning.

As another example, consider the following rule of logic:

MODUS PONENS: A and **if** A, **then** B together entail B.

This gives rise to the following normative principle of reasoning:

MODUS PONENS PRINCIPLE: If you believe A and you believe **if** A, **then** B, you should believe B.

So, for example, if you believe

If unemployment rate goes up, then the stock-market will fall

and you believe

The unemployment rate will go up

then you should also believe

The stock-market will fall.

Not all principles of reasoning are based on rules of logic; some normative principles of reasoning are based on the rules of probability theory. Consider the following rule of probability:

CONJUNCTION RULE: The probability of some event A occurring cannot be less than the probability of A and some other event B both occurring.

This rule of probability gives rise to the following normative principle of reasoning:

CONJUNCTION PRINCIPLE: You should not attach a lesser degree of probability to an event A than you do to both the event A and the (distinct) event B occurring.

For example, the conjunction principle says that if you believe

There is a 50 per cent chance that, tomorrow, the temperature will be 40 degrees and it will rain

then you should *not* believe

There is a *less* than 50 per cent chance that it will rain tomorrow.

It was the conjunction principle that was violated by subjects in the experiment involving Linda. It cannot be more likely that Linda is a bank teller and a feminist than it is that she is a bank teller because in every case in which Linda is a bank teller and a feminist she is also a bank teller.

So far, I have just enumerated a couple of principles of reasoning that are plausibly normative and seemingly important. It would be nice, however, if I could give a complete list of the normative principles of reasoning. Enumerating the normative principles of reasoning is a notoriously difficult task that goes back to the early days of epistemology. Producing a complete list of the norms of reasoning would go quite far towards developing a complete and true theory of knowledge (the remaining task—itself a rather difficult one—would be to explain why these principles are the norms and not some others—that is, to *justify* these principles). Developing a complete list of the norms of reasoning is, however, beyond the scope of this project. Given the difficulty of this task, it is fortunate that I do not need to have a complete list of the norms of reasoning in order to determine what kind of question it is to ask whether or not humans reason according to the norms or to determine the proper relationship between epistemology and cognitive science, and, more generally, epistemology and science. Instead, it will suffice to enumerate a couple of principles of reasoning that are plausibly normative and seemingly important.

1.3. *Reasoning in accordance with the Normative Principles*

Having sketched what the normative principles of reasoning are, the next obvious question concerns what it is to reason in accordance with these norms. A tempting answer to this question is that to reason in accordance with the norms of reasoning is *always* to do what the norms would dictate, for example, always to believe B when you believe A and **if** A, **then** B, always to believe that the probability of A is greater than or equal to the probability of A **and** B, and so on. This quick answer cannot be what friends of the rationality thesis have in mind; always doing what the norms of reasoning dictate is clearly not a necessary condition for counting someone as rational since a person can make all sorts of mistakes in reasoning without being disqualified as rational. Suppose I know George is in his office, I believe that if George is in his office, then it must be Friday, and, further, suppose I have not had enough sleep last night. When you ask me what day it is and I say 'Thursday', you do not, even if you know my beliefs about George and his office hours, accuse me of being irrational; rather, you accuse me of making a mistake, of being forgetful, or the like, as a result of not having had enough sleep. You would remind me that I know George is in his office and that I know George is in his office only on Fridays, and then expect me to admit my mistake and confess that it must be Friday. Assuming I did this, when you look back on my behaviour, you would *not* say that I was being irrational. If, however, I agree that George is in his office and that George is in his office only on Fridays, but continue to deny that today is Friday and do so without any attempt to reconcile my beliefs (for example, by saying that it is not *always* true that George is in his office only on Fridays, for instance, this week he is going to be in Paris on Friday so he came in on Thursday), *then* you might go so far as to call me irrational. This suggests that more is involved in failing to be rational than just failing always to do what the norms dictate; sometimes failing to behave in a way that matches the norms is not a sign of irrationality, but rather is just due to having made a mistake (or, in terms that I will explain below, sometimes failing to behave in a way that matches the norms is a performance error rather than being indicative of having an irrational reasoning competence). It seems that to reason in accordance with a rule of reasoning is to reason in such a way that your behaviour is typically best explained by your following this rule even if you sometimes make mistakes.

Behind the notion of a mere mistake is the idea that making a mistake involves a *momentary lapse*, a divergence from some typical behaviour. This is in contrast to attributing a divergence from a norm to reasoning in accordance with principles that diverge from the normative principles of reasoning. Behaviour due to irrationality connotes a *systematic* divergence from the norm. It is this distinction between mere mistakes and systematic violations (between performance errors and competence errors) that is implicitly assumed when the reasoning experiments are cited as evidence for the irrationality thesis. It is also implicitly assumed by friends of the rationality thesis when they *deny* that the reasoning experiments are relevant to whether or not the rationality thesis is true.

Consider, by way of example, the conjunction experiment. Subjects in this experiment are given a description of Linda and asked whether they think it is more likely that Linda is a bank teller or that Linda is both a bank teller and a feminist. The conjunction principle dictates that my assessment of the probability that Linda is a bank teller should be greater than or equal to my assessment of the probability that Linda is both a bank teller and a feminist. The conjunction experiment shows that the conjunction rule is frequently violated by individuals and across the human population in general. Friends of the irrationality thesis say that the best explanation of these results is that humans follow some principle other than the conjunction principle; interpreted in this way, the results count in favour of the irrationality thesis. This explanation supports the picture of humans as making systemic errors in reasoning rather than making mere mistakes: we do not generally reason in accordance with the conjunction rule but sometimes make mistakes; rather, we systematically violate the conjunction rule because we reason in accordance with some other principle of reasoning that is not a normative principle of reasoning.

The distinction between mere mistakes and systematic errors underscores the point that what is at issue between the rationality thesis and the irrationality thesis has to do with *capacities*. I can have the capacity to do something (for example, ride a bike or apply modus ponens) and yet not display that capacity on a particular occasion (for example, because I am tired or drunk). The rationality thesis claims that humans have an underlying capacity to reason in accordance with the norms; the irrationality thesis denies this. Talk of capacities leads nicely to an even better way of describing what is at issue between the rationality thesis and the irrationality thesis that involves borrowing the linguist's distinction between competence and performance.[4]

A person's linguistic competence is her underlying knowledge of language, her ability to understand and utter grammatical sentences. People, however, often make mistakes and, for example, utter or write ungrammatical sentences. These errors are not, however, due to any deficiencies in a person's linguistic competence. Rather they are due to some sort of *interference* with this competence, an interference that prevents a person from engaging in linguistic behaviour that is in accordance with linguistic competence. These interferences involve non-linguistic factors like insufficient memory, lack of attention, high amounts of alcohol in the bloodstream, and so on. Failing to apply properly a rule of one's linguistic competence is a performance error. The application of this distinction allows linguists to focus on the essential features of human linguistic capacity and ignore the static of performance errors that often affect actual linguistic behaviour.

---

[4] See e.g. Noam Chomsky, *Aspects of the Theory of Syntax* (Cambridge, Mass.: MIT Press, 1965); *Reflections on Language* (New York: Random House, 1975); *Rules and Representations* (New York: Columbia University Press, 1980); *Language and Problems of Knowledge* (Cambridge, Mass.: MIT Press, 1980); and *Knowledge of Language* (New York: Praeger, 1986).

Defenders of the rationality thesis say that *all* divergences from the norms of reasoning are performance errors and, as such, these divergences are not indicative of an underlying ability to reason. Defenders of the irrationality thesis agree that the competence–performance distinction is applicable to the realm of reasoning, but they deny that our *reasoning competence*[5] matches the norms of reasoning; they offer alternative accounts of human reasoning competence, accounts according to which we are not rational. For example, friends of the irrationality thesis would claim that the conjunction experiment shows that following the conjunction rule is *not* part of our reasoning competence; in general, they would argue that our reasoning competence does not match the norms of reasoning and that therefore humans are irrational. The notion of competence is crucial to getting the debate between the rationality thesis and the irrationality thesis off the ground; it is especially crucial to reconciling the rationality thesis with the results of the reasoning experiments. I will explore the analogy between linguistic competence and reasoning competence at length in Chapter 2. I argue that there are some important similarities between linguistic competence and reasoning competence, but there is one important difference—linguistic norms (that is, principles of grammaticality) are clearly indexed to linguistic competence while principles of reasoning are not obviously indexed to reasoning competence. For now, I adopt the following terminology for discussing the two theses about human rationality: the rationality thesis says that human reasoning competence matches the normative principles of reasoning (that is, the rules embodied in our reasoning competence are the same as those that we ought to follow), while the irrationality thesis says that human reasoning competence diverges from the norms (that is, the rules embodied in our reasoning competence are different from those we ought to follow).

---

[5] John Macnamara, *A Border Dispute* (Cambridge, Mass.: MIT Press, 1986), uses the term 'mental logic', Stephen Stich, *The Fragmentation of Reason* (Cambridge, Mass.: MIT Press, 1990), uses the term 'psycho-logic', and L. Jonathan Cohen, 'Can Human Irrationality be Experimentally Demonstrated?', *Behavioral and Brain Sciences*, 4 (1981), 317–70, uses the term 'cognitive competence', for roughly the same concept that I call 'reasoning competence'. I opt for 'reasoning competence' because it emphasizes the importance of the notion of competence as borrowed from linguistics but does not suggest as broad a notion as 'cognitive competence'. 'Cognitive competence' seems as if it would include linguistic competence while 'reasoning competence' does not. For my purposes, I want to avoid suggesting that linguistic competence is part of our underlying ability to reason while at the same time suggesting an analogy with linguistic competence.

1.4. Whose Rationality?

Thus far, I have been talking about human rationality as if it is clear whose reasoning abilities I am talking about. One might reasonably ask whether the rationality thesis requires that *all* humans reason in accordance with the normative principles of reasoning, that *most* humans reason in accordance with the normative principles, that *more than half* of us do so, or just that *one* person reasons in accordance with the norms. By talking about human rationality in terms of human reasoning competence, the rationality and irrationality theses concern the reasoning *capacities* of all *normal* humans. The rationality thesis says that all normal humans have the capacity to reason in accordance with the normative principles of reasoning. I am assuming that normal humans have basically the same type of reasoning competence in the same way that normal humans typically have the same digestive system or visual capacity.

Given this, there are various ways in which the rationality thesis is compatible with an individual human not reasoning in accordance with the norms. First, she might not be a normal human in terms of reasoning capacity. One can talk about human reasoning capacity while allowing that there may be people with impaired reasoning capacities in much the same way as one can talk about human vision and human visual capacity while allowing that there are blind, colour-blind, and other visually impaired people. This means that the rationality thesis is compatible with there being some humans who are not normal because they have a reasoning competence that does not match the normative principles of reasoning. Second, a person might have a certain capacity for reasoning but fail to make use of this capacity. A normal child who is not exposed to any language by puberty will not develop a full-fledged natural human language,[6] in spite of the fact that, as a normal human, she has the capacity for language. Similarly, it is compatible with the rationality thesis that a normal person might not reason in accordance with the normative principles if she has the capacity for reasoning but does not make use of it. Human reasoning competence might, for example, be like human linguistic competence in that certain environmental inputs are required for the competence to develop to its capacity. The rationality thesis is compatible with there being a normal human who does not reason in accordance with the norms because she failed to get the appropriate environmental inputs. The rationality

---

[6] Steven Pinker, *The Language Instinct* (New York: Morrow, 1994), 290–4.

thesis, thus clarified, says that all normal humans have a reasoning competence that gives us the capacity to reason in accordance with the normative principles of reasoning, even though some normal humans may not attain their full capacity.

Conversely, the irrationality thesis says that all normal humans have a reasoning competence such that we do not have the capacity to reason in accordance with the normative principles. The irrationality thesis is compatible, however, with the claim that *sometimes* people reason in the way that they would if they were following the normative principles of reasoning. Consider the following non-normative principle of reasoning:

ASYMMETRICAL AND-ELIMINATION PRINCIPLE: If you believe the conjunctive statement A **and** B, you should believe A but not B.

A person who has this principle in her reasoning competence would infer

(*b*) Bill Clinton is the President

from the statement

(*a*) Bill Clinton is the President and Al Gore is the Vice-President.

In so doing, she would be reasoning in the same way that she would if she were following the and-elimination principle. From (*a*), she would also infer

(*d*) Al Gore is not the Vice-President.

In so doing, she would not be reasoning in the same way that she would if she were following the and-elimination principle. This explains how the conjunction experiment (the one involving Linda) can be taken to support the irrationality thesis even though some subjects in the experiment correctly say that Linda is more likely to be a bank teller than she is to be a bank teller and a feminist.

What if only one person (or just a few people) always follows the normative principles of reasoning? Would this be enough to establish the truth of the rationality thesis? This depends on the details of the situation. There are three ways that only one person might reason in accordance with the normative principles of reasoning. First, every human might have the capacity to reason in accordance with the normative principles of reasoning, but only one person might fulfil this capacity. If this were the case, on my understanding of rationality, humans would be rational. Second, every human might not have the normative principles of reasoning in their reasoning competence but one person might simply be lucky in that her reasoning behaviour matches the reasoning behaviour of a person who has the normative principles of reasoning in her reasoning competence. In this case, humans would be irrational. Third, all humans but one might lack the normative principles of reasoning in their reasoning competence. In this case, the person with the normative principles in her reasoning competence would be non-normal in the way that a person without a stomach or who cannot see is non-normal. In this case, humans would be irrational.

1.5. Why is this Interesting?

Whether or not humans are rational is an interesting and important question about human nature. My discussion in subsequent chapters will emphasize the connections between human rationality and epistemology, philosophical psychology, and philosophy of language, on the one hand, and between human rationality and cognitive science, evolutionary theory, neuroscience, and theory of computation on the other. Human rationality is interesting and important for many other reasons as well. Aristotle thought that rationality is part of our human essence and a feature of human excellence. Is he right on either score? Some political theorists have argued that the viability of democracy depends of the rationality of humans as political agents. If humans are irrational, is democracy a bad form of government? Economics, on the most widely accepted view of the field, requires the assumption that humans are rational. If humans are irrational, is all of economic theory undermined? In this book, I will not attempt to develop the connections between my project and these other issues. I will not even attempt to offer a defence of the relevance of my project to these issues. I mention them here to point to various reasons why we should care whether humans are rational that fall outside epistemology, philosophy of science, and philosophy of psychology.

I should also mention that the sort of irrationality that interests me in this book is at least a bit different from another kind of irrationality, what I call *irrational action*, that is, action that seems to go against an agent's goals, best interests, and so forth.[7] An example of an irrational

---

[7] Irrational action has been the subject of numerous recent philosophical inquiries, for example, David Pears, *Motivated Irrationality* (Oxford: Oxford University Press, 1984); Alfred Mele, *Irrationality: An Essay in Akrasia, Self-Deception and Self-Control* (Oxford: Oxford University Press, 1987); and Brian McLaughlin and Amélie Rorty (eds.), *Perspectives in Self-Deception* (Berkeley: University of California Press, 1988).

action is continuing to smoke even though you want to live as long as possible and you know that smoking decreases life expectancy. You might continue to smoke without violating a normative principle of reasoning; your irrational action might be attributable to a physical addiction to nicotine, a weakness of the will, or something other than a deviation from a norm. Irrationality in the sense of irrational action is my concern in this book in so far as it relates to irrational reasoning.

2. Traditional, Naturalized, and Descriptive Epistemology

Epistemology is the study of knowledge: what it is, how it is attained, and who has it. Typically, knowledge is understood to be a species of belief; if I *know* Bill is in Washington, then I must *believe* Bill is in Washington. The reverse is not true; each of us has many beliefs that do not count as knowledge. One way you can have a belief that is not knowledge is if you believe a statement that is false. If I *believe* that the moon is made of green cheese, I do not *know* the moon is made of green cheese (even if I feel quite confident about my belief), because my belief is false (the moon is not made of green cheese). Another way that I can have a belief that is not knowledge is if I believe something that I am not justified in believing. Suppose you ask me what the first name of the Prime Minister of England is. Thinking that 'John' is a common name for Englishmen and that most prime ministers are men, I form the belief that 'John' is the Prime Minister's first name; accordingly, I can be said to believe that the Prime Minister's first name is John. As John Major is the Prime Minister, my belief would be true. My belief would not however be *justified* (roughly because my belief is not appropriately connected to the fact that John Major is the Prime Minister) and hence would not be an instance of knowledge. At a minimum, then, to know something is to have a true belief that is justified.[8]

In order to gain knowledge, one has to have beliefs. Beliefs can be

---

[8] Edmund Gettier, 'Is Justified True Belief Knowledge?', *Analysis*, 23 (1963), 121–3, argues that a belief can be true and justified but still not an instance of knowledge. A veritable cottage industry in philosophy developed in response to Gettier's article to attempt to fill in the additional condition(s) for knowledge in addition to truth and justifiedness. Some of the discussions of this article, as well as the article itself, are reprinted in Paul Moser (ed.), *Empirical Knowledge* (Savage, Md.: Rowman & Littlefield, 1986), pt. II, pp. 231–70. Addressing Gettier's challenge to the task of defining knowledge is beyond the scope of the present project. I mention it here to indicate that it is not completely clear what the criterion for knowledge is.

acquired in various ways including directly through the senses (I believe that it is raining outside because I see rain falling when I look outside), through testimony (I believe that it is raining outside because a trusted friend tells me that it is), and through reasoning (I believe that it is raining because I see that my mother has taken out her umbrella, and I believe that she only takes out her umbrella when it is raining). Because reasoning is an important way that we manipulate beliefs and acquire knowledge, the study of human rationality is an important part of epistemology.

René Descartes started his meditations on human knowledge by noting that, in the past, he believed many things that later proved false.[9] Given this fact, he endeavoured to reflect on various principles for the acquisition of beliefs, rejecting those that had led him astray in the past or that might lead him astray in the future and embracing only those principles that would lead him to the truth. In order to do this, Descartes looked for a firm and immobile point, a truth or truths on which he could ground principles of belief acquisition and maintenance that would ensure that all his beliefs were knowledge. Descartes's project was to develop an account of how we should arrive at our beliefs. He tried to do so independently of experience and without looking at the world because experiential access to the world is fallible and thus not firm ground on which to develop an account of how we should arrive at our beliefs. The Cartesian project is central to what I call *traditional epistemology*.

Some, most notably Willard V. O. Quine,[10] think that the normative project of traditional epistemology should be rejected because it is hopeless. They say that there is no way to ground our beliefs on a firm and immobile point. If this is right, the traditional project of epistemology might be replaced by the project of describing how we come to believe things. Traditional epistemology would, on this view, be replaced by 'the science of belief', what might be called *descriptive epistemology*. The project is *descriptive* rather than *normative* in that it tells us how we proceed with respect to beliefs but *not* how we *should* proceed. Normative epistemology, a part of philosophy as traditionally construed, is to be replaced by descriptive epistemology, a part of science that is connected to psychology, biology, and neuroscience.

---

[9] René Descartes, *Meditations Concerning First Philosophy* (1641).
[10] Willard V. O. Quine, 'Epistemology Naturalized', in *Ontological Relativity and Other Essays* (New York: Columbia University Press, 1969); repr. in Hilary Kornblith (ed.), *Naturalizing Epistemology*, 2nd edn. (Cambridge, Mass.: MIT Press, 1994).

What I call descriptive epistemology is often referred to as 'natural-ized epistemology'. There is, however, another project for which I want to reserve that term. This project preserves a normative component for epistemology (like traditional epistemology) but at the same time it draws from science (like descriptive epistemology). *Naturalized epi-stemology* uses scientific evidence as part of the process of determining how we ought to acquire beliefs. Perhaps the best way to illustrate this project is Otto Neurath's metaphor of the ship. Imagine that we are on a ship that has some rotten planks. We want to repair the ship's planks. The best way to do this would be to bring the ship into dock, disem-bark, and, standing on firm ground, repair the ship's planks. But suppose that we are far from any dock. We can still repair the ship by standing on some planks while repairing the others. This project is not guaranteed to succeed because the planks that we choose to stand on while making repairs on some others may themselves be rotten. Still, if we carefully chose the planks we stand on, we can be somewhat hopeful of success. Our beliefs are like the planks on the ship. Just as some of the ship's planks are rotten, some of our beliefs are false. We want to rid our-selves of false beliefs in the same way that we want to rid the ship of rotten planks. Traditional epistemology says that we can get rid of false beliefs by finding firm ground on which to base our beliefs. The argu-ments for descriptive epistemology say that the human epistemological condition is like a ship permanently at sea: there is no firm ground from which we can repair our epistemological ship. Naturalized epistemo-logy says that, just as we can repair a ship at sea, we can get rid of some false beliefs by assuming the truth of some of our beliefs, typically the truth of some of our scientific beliefs.[11]

[11] Others have draw this distinction in different ways and using different terms. Jaegwon Kim, 'What is "Naturalized Epistemology"?', in James Tomberlin (ed.), *Philosophical Perspectives*, ii: *Epistemology* (Atascadero, Calif.: Ridgeview, 1988); repr. in Kornblith (ed.), *Naturalizing Epistemology*, uses the phrase 'Quine's naturalized epistemology' for the theory of knowledge that I call 'descriptive epistemology' and the term 'naturalism' for what I call 'naturalized epistemology'. Hilary Kornblith, 'Introduction: What is Natur-alistic Epistemology?', in Kornblith (ed.), *Naturalizing Epistemology*, uses 'naturalized epistemology' for the conjunction of what I call 'descriptive epistemology' and what I call 'naturalized epistemology'. What Kornblith calls 'the strong replacement thesis' would be a thesis entailed by descriptive epistemology and what he calls 'the weak replacement thesis', 'psychologism', and 'ballpark psychologism' would, in my termino-logy, be versions of naturalized epistemology. Philip Kitcher, 'The Naturalists Return', *Philosophical Review*, 101 (1992), 53–114, uses the phrase 'radical naturalism' for what I call 'descriptive epistemology' and the phrase 'conservative naturalism' for what I call 'naturalized epistemology'. Two problems with my terminology should be indicated. First, some people would deny that what I call 'descriptive epistemology' is epistemology

Like traditional epistemology, naturalized epistemology has a normative component—it tells us which of our beliefs count as knowledge (in terms of the ship, it tells us which planks are rotten)—but, like descriptive epistemology, it has at least a partially empirical character. The empirical contribution to naturalized epistemology can come in various forms. For example, a naturalized epistemology, rather than explaining the justification of beliefs in terms of the logical properties of beliefs or the logical relations of contents of beliefs (which is what traditional epistemology does) might explain the justification of beliefs in terms of causal or lawlike connections among psychological states or processes. The naturalized epistemologist can do this without requiring that justification must be spelled out in naturalistic terms.[12] Or, the naturalized epistemologist can see empirical facts as constraining or providing a useful way of testing epistemological theories formulated in non-empirical terms (that is, in terms of the logical properties of beliefs or the logical relations of contents of beliefs).[13]

The nature of the question 'Are humans rational?' is related in interesting ways to these three different ways (traditional, descriptive, and naturalized) of doing epistemology. Rationality is usually seen as a normative notion; to say that someone is rational is roughly to say that she reasons in the way she ought to. The traditional epistemologist agrees with this traditional picture of rationality as normative. Because reasoning is one of the ways we manipulate beliefs and because the traditional epistemologist thinks that there are particular ways that beliefs ought and ought not to be manipulated, the traditional epistemologist sees rationality as normative. He would add that determining what is rational involves reflection rather than empirical investigation because he thinks that it is not an empirical project to determine what are the particular ways that beliefs ought to be manipulated. Whether or not humans reason in the way that they ought to could, in so far as the traditional epistemologist is concerned, be an empirical question.

The descriptive epistemologist, because she denies the normative character of epistemology, is committed to denying the normative

at all. For the moment, at least, I am open to the possibility that this is a misnomer. Second, my terminology makes the title of Quine's seminal article 'Epistemology Naturalized' a misleading one; according to my terminology, 'Epistemology Descriptivized' would have been preferable (though less felicitous). I take it that neither of these problems is particularly serious.

[12] Kim, 'What is "Naturalized Epistemology"?', and Kitcher, 'The Naturalists Return'.
[13] Kornblith, 'Introduction', 10–12.

character of the theory of how we manipulate beliefs. The descriptive epistemologist might suggest that, instead of assessing human rationality, we can study how we in fact reason. This empirical study will not tell us whether humans reason in the right way, but it will give us an account of how we reason. The descriptive epistemologist would suggest that we should not want anything more than this.

The naturalized epistemologist agrees with the traditional epistemologist that rationality is a normative notion, but thinks that empirical considerations could be relevant to determining what counts as rational. The naturalized epistemologist thinks this because he thinks that to be rational is to manipulate our beliefs in the right way through reasoning and because he thinks that empirical considerations are relevant to how our beliefs ought to be manipulated. It does not bode well for naturalized epistemology if whether or not humans are rational is a conceptual matter. If human rationality is a conceptual issue, then empirical knowledge is not relevant to a major portion of the way we acquire knowledge. Still, naturalized epistemology would not be refuted; empirical evidence might be relevant to ways we acquire knowledge besides reasoning.

Throughout the chapters that follow, I will be engaging in epistemology, more often than not, through an examination of reasoning. In Chapter 7, I will return specifically to these issues and consider what implications the conclusions of earlier chapters have for epistemology in general. In particular, I will argue these considerations count in favour of naturalized epistemology.

3. Coming Attractions

Before one can give and defend an answer to the question 'Are humans rational?', one must understand what kind of question this is. In the remainder of this chapter, I sketch various options. Along the way, I offer a guide to the arguments I will be discussing in chapters to come.

The main reason for believing the irrationality thesis is that the results of the reasoning experiments show that the principles that characterize human reasoning competence diverge from the normative principles of reasoning. Evidence that humans fail to reason in accordance with the normative principles of reasoning seems to be evidence for the irrationality thesis. For example, experimenters ask subjects whether they think Linda is more likely to be a bank teller or whether she is more likely to be a bank teller and a feminist. If they find that subjects think that the second possibility is more likely than the first (as they in fact do[14]), then they cite this as evidence for the irrationality thesis. This counts as evidence that humans are irrational because it is irrational to believe that a statement A is more likely than another statement B, which is true whenever A is and sometimes when A is not. The conjunction experiment will be discussed in more detail in Chapter 3 along with another experiment, called the *selection task*, which investigates our ability to apply rules of deductive logic.

That the reasoning experiments establish the truth of the irrationality thesis is based on the following straightforward way of understanding the nature of the question 'Are humans rational?' In order to figure out whether humans are rational, we start with a criterion for being rational, and we determine whether humans fit this criterion. Without going into any of the details, whether a creature is rational involves the sorts of reasoning processes it uses. To determine, then, whether humans are rational, we must study how humans reason. If humans reason in the right way, then we are rational; if we do not, then we are irrational. To determine how humans reason, we need to look at the world, in particular, at human psychology. Human psychology is an empirical discipline; it involves looking at the behaviour and the brains of humans. To study human psychology, we observe human behaviour, perhaps by performing experiments like the reasoning experiments, and we look at how humans are constructed, perhaps by cracking open the skull to have a look at the human brain. The details aside, the question of human rationality requires determining how humans reason and this requires doing some psychology, an empirical discipline. If this line of thought is right, then the question of human rationality is empirical and this could be the end of this book, a book so short and trivial that you would be reading it without good reason.

Matters are far from this simple. In reaction to these experiments and the pronouncements that humans are irrational which are based upon them, philosophers and others have defended the claim that humans are rational with a diverse set of interesting and plausible arguments that draw from epistemology, philosophy of science, philosophy of mind, philosophy of language, linguistics, computational theory, and evolutionary theory. In Chapters 3 to 7 of this book, I will develop these arguments with an eye towards understanding and evaluating the claim

---

[14] Tversky and Kahneman, 'Extensional versus Intuitive Reasoning'.

that humans are rational. These arguments try to show that even in light of the reasoning experiments, humans are rational. Most of the arguments for this conclusion a 2 conceptual (the argument about interpretation discussed in Chapter 3 and the evolutionary arguments discussed in Chapter 6 are the exceptions) and most of them accept the standard picture of rationality (two of the arguments discussed in Chapter 7 are the exceptions). My discussion will also explore the implications of this inquiry to the project of epistemology. Before I map out the structure of the rest of the book, I want to say something about what it means for a question to be empirical or conceptual.

3.1. Empirical and Conceptual Matters

An empirical question asks about the particular details of the world we live in. Typically, to answer a question of this sort, one must have a look at the world. To determine how much an electron weighs or how tall my sister is, one must examine the way things are. This is done by performing experiments, taking measurements, and so on. Conceptual questions do not require this sort of examination of the actual world. A conceptual question is answered by reflection on the relevant concepts. To determine whether all bachelors are unmarried, one does not systematically survey all bachelors to see whether or not each of them is married; instead, one can figure out that all bachelors are unmarried by analysing the concepts involved. A bachelor *just is* an unmarried man; therefore, by definition, all bachelors are unmarried. Part of my project in this book is to determine whether the question 'Are humans rational?' is an empirical question, and, if so, what sort of empirical facts are relevant to it.

Some might argue that this part of the project is based on a mistake because the distinction between empirical and conceptual statements is less clear than it may seem. In his classic article 'Two Dogmas of Empiricism', Quine discredits some of the traditional assumptions relating sensory experience to the status and truth-values of our beliefs.[15] According to Quine, even such seemingly straightforward empirical statements as 'There are brick houses on Elm Street' can be insulated from sensory data that would normally be taken to verify or falsify them; such a sentence 'can be held true come what may . . . [for example] by pleading hallucination or by amending . . . logical laws'.[16] If I

---

[15] Willard V. O. Quine, 'Two Dogmas of Empiricism', in *From a Logical Point of View* (Cambridge, Mass.: Harvard University Press, 1961).   [16] Ibid. 43.

were taken on a thorough tour of Elm Street and shown that each house
I encounter is made of wood, I could still, if I wanted to, hold on to the
statement 'There are brick houses on Elm Street' by insisting that I
must have missed a house or that I must have mistaken as wooden at
least one house that is in fact made of brick. An ingenious person can
take any statement that prima facie seems to require looking at the
details of the world and show that it actually does not require such
evidence. Similarly, even those statements that seem completely immune
from empirical refutation might be revised in the face of some empirical evidence. If this is right, then the distinction between empirical and
conceptual statements may be in trouble. Above I characterized a statement as empirical if its truth depends on the way the world is. If Quine
is right that the truth of 'There are brick houses on Elm Street' may not
depend on the way the world is and that statements like '*A* **and** *B*
implies *A*' may be rejected if the world turns out in a particular way,
then the question of whether human reasoning is conceptual or empirical may be uninteresting.

A response to this line of thought would be to try to salvage the
conceptual–empirical distinction by appeal to Quine's own idea that
beliefs can be thought of as located in conceptual space at 'varying
distances from the sensory periphery'.[17] The idea is to see each person
as having a 'web of belief',[18] an interlocking set of beliefs in which
beliefs that are revisable in the face of experience are close to the
border of the web and beliefs that are highly unlikely to be revised in
the face of experience are in the centre of the web. The idea would be
to recast the question about human rationality as follows: is the belief
that humans are rational likely to be revised in the face of evidence, in
particular, evidence concerning how humans in fact reason? Someone
who thinks that the reasoning experiments can do nothing to undermine
our belief in human rationality would see the belief that humans are
rational as being in the centre of the web, while someone who thinks
the reasoning experiments might have 'bleak implications' for human
rationality would see the belief that humans are rational as close to the
edge of the web.

This attempt to recast the debate about the nature of the question
whether humans are rational might seem vulnerable to a deeper Quinean
worry. Quine does not simply substitute 'near the edge of the web' for

[17] Ibid.
[18] This idea is developed in Willard V. O. Quine and J. L. Ulian, *The Web of Belief*
(New York: Random House, 1970).

'empirical' and 'in the centre of the web' for 'conceptual'; the point of his invocation of the web is that beliefs we take to be empirical can be held constant come what may and beliefs we take to be conceptual can be revised in the face of certain kinds of evidence. For example, in pre-Copernican times, the belief 'The earth is the centre of the universe' was in the centre of most people's webs. Over time, this belief, which seemed unrevisable, was rejected in the face of astronomical and other scientific evidence.[19] If this is right, then it might seem that there is nothing special about a belief that is currently at the centre of most people's webs of belief beyond the fact that such a belief is *at present* well insulated from empirical refutation. This gives rise to the deeper worry that the issue of whether the belief 'Humans are rational' is at the periphery or in the centre of the web is roughly equivalent to an opinion poll of how strongly people hold the belief that humans are rational and thus would be a matter for sociology rather than for philosophy or psychology.

I want to suggest that this deeper worry need not be taken very seriously, even if one is persuaded to reject the standard distinction between empirical and conceptual truths. While Quine does argue that there is no such thing as an intrinsically unrevisable belief or an intrinsically 'revisable-in-the-face-of-sensory-evidence' belief, he does not argue for and is not committed to the view that a belief's status (as unrevisable or revisable by sensory experience) is arbitrary or unimportant. In fact, since Quine is a holist, namely, he thinks that our beliefs about the world 'face the tribunal of sense experience not individually but as a corporate whole',[20] he sees all our various beliefs as extensively interconnected and their location in the web of belief as dependent on the sorts of interconnection that hold among them. If this is right, then where the belief 'Humans are rational' fits in the web is constrained by its connections to other beliefs and their position in the web. Further, given that humans share roughly the same sensory apparatus and roughly the same principles of belief revision, it follows that the placement of a particular belief in the web is not at all arbitrary or uninteresting. When I inquire whether 'Humans are rational' is a conceptual or empirical statement, according to the web of belief picture, I am inquiring about how beliefs about human rationality relate to other beliefs, in particular beliefs about human psychology and

---

[19] Thomas Kuhn, *The Copernican Revolution* (Cambridge, Mass.: Harvard University Press, 1957).   [20] Quine, 'Two Dogmas of Empiricism', 41.

neurophysiology and beliefs about epistemology, philosophy of language, and the like. If the arguments against the traditional distinction between conceptual and empirical facts are strong, then the question about the status of human rationality might be less clear, but it remains of interest in so far as we are interested in the relations among the various disciplines and among different kinds of knowledge. I am not here embracing the Quinean criticism of the conceptual–empirical distinction or his web of belief picture. My point is that even if this criticism is right, assessing the nature of the question of human rationality is still a worthwhile project.[21]

Even with a clear picture of the distinction between what is conceptual and what is empirical, it is not at all clear what to say about the question 'Are humans rational?' There are two kinds of argument to the effect that the reasoning experiments are not relevant to the issue between the rationality thesis and the irrationality thesis: arguments that accept the standard picture of rationality and arguments that reject this picture. I discuss diverse versions of each of these arguments in turn.

3.2. Arguments for the Rationality Thesis within the Standard Picture

The first two arguments for the rationality thesis that accept the standard picture of rationality involve issues about how to interpret human behaviour and human cognitive mechanisms in general and the reasoning experiments and human reasoning competence in particular. In Chapter 3, I discuss a general interpretative strategy of importance to friends of the rationality thesis. The strategy is to interpret every instance of a person failing to reason in accordance with the normative principles of reasoning as a performance error. This interpretative strategy, if justified, would have some significant ramifications for my inquiry. The first ramification would be that, so interpreted, the results of the reasoning experiments would fail to suggest that humans are irrational. Second, without the evidence of the reasoning experiments, the irrationality thesis would lose its primary source of support and, as a result, the rationality thesis would be in good shape. The third ramification would be that empirical considerations would not be relevant to the question of human rationality because this interpretative strategy would discount any evidence in favour of human irrationality. Note that

---

[21] A more extensive discussion of some of these issues in Quine can be found in Christopher Hookway, *Quine* (Stanford, Calif.: Stanford University Press, 1988), ch. 2.

this argument is empirical; it implies that, because of the many performance errors we make, we can never have access to human reasoning
competence. In Chapter 3, I explain why this strategy has these ramifications and why this strategy must be justified before it can be used.

In Chapter 4, I consider an argument based on the principle of charity.
The principle of charity is a guide for translating utterances of other
speakers; the idea is that translation should be charitable to the person
being translated.[22] This principle can be extended to the interpretation
of people's reasoning competence and more generally to the interpretation of people's cognitive mechanisms.[23] One general argument for
the principle of charity is that you must assume that the person you are
trying to understand is at least somewhat rational, because you will not
be able to make sense of a truly non-rational person. The principle of
charity argument for the rationality thesis is that cognitive scientists
must be mistaken in interpreting subjects in the reasoning experiments
as being irrational because doing so would violate the principle of
charity. Interpreters of the reasoning experiments (including the experimenters who perform them) attribute non-normative principles of
reasoning to subjects and, based on these experiments, to humans in
general. The principle of charity argument for the rationality thesis says
that such attributions are mistaken: the principle of charity should be
applied to subjects in the reasoning experiments. Properly done, this
would show that the reasoning experiments are fully consistent with the
rationality thesis and do not provide any support for the irrationality
thesis. I distinguish between a strong and weak version of the principle
of charity applied to people's reasoning competence—the weak version
of the principle of charity is defeasible (it says that people should be
interpreted as rational *unless* there is strong evidence to suggest otherwise) while the strong version of the principle of charity is not (it says
that people should *always* be interpreted as rational). I argue that the
weak principle of charity is justified, but it does not provide an argument
for the rationality thesis. The strong principle of charity, if justified,
would provide an argument for the rationality thesis, but I argue that it
is not justified.

[22] Willard V. O. Quine, *Word and Object* (Cambridge, Mass.: MIT Press, 1960); and
'Ontological Relativity', in *Ontological Relativity and Other Essays*.
[23] See the works of Daniel Dennett, esp. *The Intentional Stance* (Cambridge, Mass.:
MIT Press, 1987); the works of Donald Davidson, esp. *Inquiries into Truth and Interpretation* (Oxford: Oxford University Press, 1984); Elliott Sober, 'Psychologism', *Journal
of Social Behavior*, 8 (1978), 165–91; and Cohen, 'Can Human Irrationality be Experimentally Demonstrated?'

The remaining arguments for the rationality thesis that accept the standard picture of rationality are not specifically about the interpretation of the reasoning experiments. In Chapter 5, I turn to the *reflective equilibrium* argument for the rationality thesis. The general idea behind this argument is that since both our norms of reasoning and our actual reasoning behaviour are based on our intuitions about what counts as good reasoning, reasoning behaviour and the norms cannot diverge; in so far as the reasoning experiments seem to prove that reasoning behaviour diverges from the norms, they do so only in virtue of detecting the performance errors we make.[24] The most interesting version of this argument involves the theory of reflective equilibrium, an epistemological theory that says a set of principles is justified when it is modified to fit with first-order intuitions about its domain of application.[25] The idea is that both the normative principles of reasoning and the description of reasoning competence come from a process of reflective equilibrium with our intuitions about what counts as good reasoning as input. As such, the two sets of principles cannot diverge. This is a conceptual argument for the rationality thesis; if it succeeds, the question of human rationality is not empirical.

This argument is usually criticized by saying that the normative principles of reasoning are not the result of a process of reflective equilibrium.[26] I defend the reflective equilibrium account of where the norms come from and suggest that critics of this account underestimate its resources. The reflective equilibrium argument for the rationality thesis fails, I think, for another reason. Even if the empirical process of giving a complete description of human reasoning competence is a process of reflective equilibrium, the inputs to a reflective equilibrium process to determine our reasoning competence would differ from the inputs to such a process to determine the norms of reasoning. Certain kinds of biological, computational, and neuroscientific evidence are relevant to developing an account of our reasoning competence, but not to determining what the norms of reasoning are. Further, even if the input to the two reflective equilibrium processes were the same—

---

[24] Cohen, 'Can Human Irrationality be Experimentally Demonstrated?'; Macnamara, *A Border Dispute*; and Sober, 'Psychologism'.
[25] The concept of reflective equilibrium comes from Nelson Goodman, *Fact, Fiction and Forecast*, 4th edn. (Cambridge, Mass.: Harvard University Press, 1983), 63–4; it was taken up in John Rawls, *A Theory of Justice* (Cambridge, Mass.: Harvard University Press, 1971), and baptized 'reflective equilibrium' in John Rawls, 'The Independence of Moral Theory', *Proceedings and Addresses of the American Philosophical Association*, 48 (1974–5), 5–22.   [26] e.g. Stich, *The Fragmentation of Reason*, ch. 4.

perhaps because epistemology should be naturalized and thus scientific evidence would be relevant to the normative principles of reasoning—different parts of the input would be weighted in different ways as part of the two reflective equilibrium processes. Reflective equilibrium may be the right process for determining what the norms of reasoning are, but the reflective equilibrium argument for the rationality thesis still fails.

The final argument for the rationality thesis that accepts the standard picture of rationality is not, like most of the arguments that precede it, a conceptual argument. The argument says that evolutionary theory, but not the reasoning experiments, is relevant to settling the issue between the rationality and the irrationality theses. The idea of this argument, which I consider in Chapter 6, is that evolution, through natural selection, produces organisms with mechanisms that select true beliefs (what I call *truth-tropic mechanisms*) and that organisms with such mechanisms would be rational ones. Humans, being the result of natural selection, have truth-tropic cognitive mechanisms and such mechanisms give rise to a reasoning competence that instantiates truth-tropic principles of reasoning. This argument provides a prima facie reason for not interpreting the results of the reasoning experiments as showing that humans are irrational. The evolutionary argument is supposed to show that the reasoning experiments can*not* establish the truth of the irrationality thesis because the evolutionary history of our reasoning competence provides a strong reason for interpreting it as rational.[27] This argument has an important empirical premiss—the truth of the theory of natural selection—but it has an affinity with conceptual arguments for the rationality thesis because the evolutionary argument says that, given a rather well-established empirical premiss, the nature of the question of human rationality does not require any further examination of the world. From the point of view of psychologists who perform the reasoning experiments, for example, the result of the evolutionary

---

[27] Daniel Dennett, 'Making Sense of Ourselves', in *The Intentional Stance*; Jerry Fodor, 'Three Cheers for Propositional Attitudes', in *Representations* (Cambridge, Mass.: MIT Press, 1981); Alvin Goldman, *Epistemology and Cognition* (Cambridge, Mass.: MIT Press, 1986); William Lycan, 'Epistemic Value', in *Judgment and Justification* (Cambridge: Cambridge University Press, 1988); Ruth Millikan, 'Naturalist Reflections on Knowledge', *Pacific Philosophical Quarterly*, 65 (1984), 315–34; David Papineau, *Reality and Representation* (Oxford: Blackwell, 1987); Karl Popper, 'Evolutionary Epistemology', in J. W. Pollard (ed.), *Evolutionary Theory* (London: Wiley, 1984); W. V. O. Quine, 'Natural Kinds', in *Ontological Relativity and Other Essays*; repr. in Kornblith (ed.), *Naturalizing Epistemology*; and Elliott Sober, 'The Evolution of Rationality', *Synthese*, 46 (1981), 95–120.

argument for the rationality thesis is basically the same as either the reflective equilibrium argument for the rationality thesis or the principle of charity argument for the rationality thesis—namely, that the reasoning experiments are irrelevant to the rationality thesis.

The evolutionary argument for the rationality thesis has typically been criticized for adopting a simplistic picture of evolution.[28] Steven Jay Gould and Richard Lewontin use the adjective 'Panglossian' to describe the knee-jerk practice of appealing to natural selection as the evolutionary force that explains every trait; the term comes from Voltaire's Dr Pangloss, who said, for example, that the reason humans have noses is to hold up our eyeglasses.[29] Gould and Lewontin correctly point out that there are other forces of evolution besides natural selection. A critic of the evolutionary argument for the rationality thesis could point out that these forces might be behind the evolution of our reasoning competence. If this is the case, then there is no guarantee that our reasoning competence will be truth-tropic; the evolutionary argument for the rationality thesis would thus fail. I defend the evolutionary argument against this criticism. Natural selection is the only evolutionary force that can explain functionally complex structures.[30] Since our reasoning competence is functionally complex, if it evolved, then it did so through natural selection.

The evolutionary argument for the rationality thesis fails, I think, for another reason. Even though our reasoning competence must be the result of natural selection, the operation of natural selection does not guarantee that all of our principles of reasoning will be truth-tropic. The criterion for natural selection is reproductive success, and sometimes being truth-tropic and leading to reproductive success come apart. Because natural selection cannot guarantee truth-tropicity, natural selection cannot guarantee rationality; the evolutionary argument for the rationality thesis thus fails.

There are two modifications to the evolutionary argument that I also consider. The first modification is to attempt to connect evolution and rationality through reproductive fitness rather than through truth. This evolutionary argument begins with the claim that evolution involves

[28] e.g. Stich, *The Fragmentation of Reason*, ch. 3.

[29] Steven J. Gould and Richard Lewontin, 'The Spandrels of San Marcos and the Panglossian Paradigm: A Critique of the Adaptationist Programme', *Proceedings of the Royal Society of London*, 205 (1978), 281–8; repr. in Elliott Sober (ed.), *Conceptual Issues in Evolutionary Biology* (Cambridge, Mass.: MIT Press, 1984).

[30] George C. Williams, *Adaptation and Natural Selection* (Princeton: Princeton University Press, 1966).

selection for reproductive success and the claim that having principles of reasoning and mental mechanisms that lead to reproductive success is all it takes to count as rational. Putting these two claims together, we get the argument that, since humans have evolved, they will have mechanisms and principles of reasoning that lead to reproductive success and, hence, they will be rational. This argument only works by rejecting the standard picture of rationality; maximizing reproductive success is rational in a very different sense than reasoning in accordance with rules of logic.

The second modification to the evolutionary argument for the rationality thesis draws from an approach to theory of knowledge known as evolutionary epistemology.[31] The two versions of the evolutionary argument considered thus far involve innate mental mechanisms. But perhaps the principles that guide reasoning are *not* innate.[32] If this is the case, then biological evolution and natural selection cannot be the driving forces behind the development of our reasoning competence. This is where evolutionary epistemology is supposed to be relevant. According to this view, the development of human knowledge is governed by a trial-and-error process *analogous* to biological natural selection. If the principles that govern human reasoning come from a process analogous to biological natural selection (what I call *epistemic natural selection*), then the evolutionary argument for rationality might be successful. This argument would proceed as follows: epistemic natural selection would select principles that produce true beliefs; having such truth-tropic principles makes an organism rational; because, according to evolutionary epistemology, humans acquire their principles of reasoning through epistemic natural selection, humans are therefore rational. The argument for human rationality based on conceptual evolution fails because natural selection will not select only truth-tropic principles of reasoning. This is similar to the reasons the argument based on biological evolution failed, but the conceptual evolution argument fails independent of the details of biology. This shows that even the general structure of evolutionary theory cannot guarantee rationality.

[31] See e.g. Donald Campbell, 'Evolutionary Epistemology', in Paul Schilpp (ed.), *The Philosophy of Karl Popper*, i (LaSalle, Ill.: Open Court, 1974); Michael Bradie, 'Assessing Evolutionary Epistemology', *Biology and Philosophy*, 1 (1986), 401–59; Bradie, 'Epistemology from an Evolutionary Point of View', in Sober (ed.), *Conceptual Issues in Evolutionary Biology*; and Edward Stein, 'Evolutionary Epistemology', in Jonathan Dancy and Ernest Sosa (eds.), *A Companion to Epistemology* (Oxford: Blackwell, 1992).

[32] See e.g. Stich, *The Fragmentation of Reason*, 71–4, for arguments on this point. I criticize such arguments in Ch. 2 below.

3.3. Arguments for the Rationality Thesis that Reject the Standard Picture

For the irrationality thesis to be true, the normative principles of reasoning and human reasoning competence must diverge. The preceding arguments for the rationality thesis accepted the standard picture of rationality and tried to show that human reasoning competence does not diverge from the normative principles of reasoning. Friends of the rationality thesis might proceed in another manner: rather than argue that the reasoning experiments are not about reasoning competence, they can attack the irrationality thesis in the other direction, by arguing that the standard picture of rationality is mistaken with respect to the normative principles of reasoning. Assuming, for example, that the rationality thesis is wrong and that the conjunction principle is not a normative principle of reasoning, subjects in the Linda experiment may well be reasoning in accordance with the norms. If we are mistaken in our account of what the normative principles of reasoning are, then humans might turn out to reason in accordance with the norms of reasoning and, hence, be rational even in the face of the reasoning experiments. In Chapter 7, I consider three attempts to undermine the irrationality thesis in roughly this way.

For humans to inquire whether humans are rational is a quite different thing than for us to inquire what the mass of an electron is or whether humans are mammals. Whether humans are rational may be more like the question of whether humans have a good aesthetic sensibility and the question of whether humans have a good sense of humour. Suppose, for example, experimenters showed subjects works of art (some beautiful and some not beautiful), asked them to say whether each work of art is beautiful or not, and, on the basis of whether the subjects correctly distinguished the beautiful works of art from the non-beautiful ones, thereby determined whether or not humans have a good aesthetic sensibility. Or suppose that experimenters told subjects some jokes (some funny and some not), asked subjects to identify whether each joke was funny or not, and, on the basis of whether the subjects correctly distinguished the funny from the unfunny jokes, thereby determined whether humans have a good sense of humour. What do you think of these proposed experiments? Would such experiments actually determine whether humans have a good aesthetic sensibility or a good sense of humour? It seems quite odd to say that they would. In fact, it is tempting to say that whether or not humans have a good aesthetic

sensibility or a good sense of humour is not the sort of question about
which an empirical inquiry can be undertaken.

A few different intuitions are at work here. First, these experiments
assume that there are standards of funniness or aesthetic valuation that
apply to all humans, but it is not obvious that there are any such general
standards. Relativism, the view that the standards in some realm are
relative to an individual—or a small group of people—is true for some
realms, for example, ice-cream flavours. When I say that Fudge Swirl
is the best kind of ice-cream, I mean that it is the best ice-cream from
my point of view, *not* that it is true for all humans. Roughly the same
may be true with respect to sense of humour and aesthetic evaluation.
When I say that the joke about what you get when you cross a Mafioso
and a literary theorist (someone who makes you an offer you can't
understand) is funny, I mean that *I* think it is funny, but I do not mean
that everyone else ought to find it funny. If I tell the joke, this indicates
that I suspect that some other people might think it is funny, but I allow
that there are others who have a sense of humour that differs from
mine. On some views, the same is true for aesthetic valuations. When
I say that a particular work of art is beautiful, I am just expressing my
own opinion. I leave open the possibility that others will disagree with
me and that their opinion could be as reasonable as mine. Relativism
is true for ice-cream flavours and at least plausible with respect to
funniness and aesthetics. If relativism is true for funniness, then the
experiment I describe above would rest on a mistake: the experiment
mistakenly assumes that it is an empirical question whether humans
have a good sense of humour. In fact, the question may be conceptual.
Each of us may have our own sense of humour and, associated with it,
our own standard of funniness.

Another reason why the proposed experiments about aesthetic sensibility and sense of humour seem odd is that such experiments assume
there is some standard of aesthetic valuation (or funniness) that exists
independent of the human aesthetic (or 'amusement') faculty. It seems
plausible, however, that even if there are standards that apply to all
humans, there are no standards that exist independent of humans because the only standards that exist are indexed to us. Our human aesthetic faculty makes it the case that the features that make things seem
beautiful to us—say, certain colour combinations, the right mix of unity
and variety, and so on—are in fact the features that make things beautiful.
Things that seem beautiful to us are unlikely to seem beautiful to
creatures with sensory faculties dramatically different from ours. If this

is right, then no experiment could possibly show that humans have a poor aesthetic sensibility because the standards of aesthetic evaluation come from our own aesthetic capacities. Further, no empirical investigation into our particular aesthetic faculties is required to determine that humans have a good aesthetic sensibility because the standards of aesthetic valuation come from our aesthetic capacities. This shows that humans have a good aesthetic sensibility and it does so independent of any empirical facts about our particular aesthetic capacities because the normative standards come from whatever aesthetic capacities we have.

Finally, even if there is a standard of aesthetic valuation (or funniness) that is independent of human capacities and that applies to all humans, the proposed experiments might seem odd because they are based on the assumptions that experimenters have access to which works of art are and are not beautiful and that they can use this knowledge to assess the aesthetic abilities of the subjects. But what gives the experimenters this special access? They could decide for themselves that artworks *A*, *B*, and *C* are beautiful and artworks *D*, *E*, and *F* are not or they could consult art experts to make this sort of determination. But on what basis do the experimenters' or the experts' assessments count as the *right* judgements of what is beautiful while the subjects' assessments do not? Further, if we grant this special status to the experimenters or the art experts, we thereby *assume* that humans (at least some of us) have good aesthetic judgement. The problem is that even if there are standards of aesthetic valuation that are independent of us, there is no guarantee that we have access to such standards. Without such a guarantee, experimenters are not able to determine whether the principles that guide our aesthetic judgement are the right principles for aesthetic judgement. Empirical considerations will not help matters—even if we can determine what aesthetic principles we follow, we are in no position to assess them against the standards of what is beautiful. The experiment to determine whether humans have a good aesthetic sensibility seems odd because such an experiment depends on our having access to the very standards that the experiment is supposed to tell us whether or not we can access.

There are thus three worries that arise with respect to the proposed experiments to determine whether humans have a good aesthetic sensibility and whether humans have a good sense of humour:

1. There might be no objective or general standards of aesthetic valuation (or funniness)—that is, beauty (and funniness) might be

relative to the tastes of individual humans and, thus, there might
be no general standards of beauty (or funniness).
2. There might be objective standards of aesthetic valuation (or funniness), but these standards might be indexed to human faculties
   —that is, there might be no standards of beauty (or funniness) that
   are independent of humans.
3. Although there might be general, human-independent standards of
   aesthetic valuation (or funniness), we might not have access to
   them.

To return to reasoning, many philosophers and some other people are
suspicious of those who claim that the reasoning experiments are relevant to the question of whether humans are rational, and, more generally, whether any empirical considerations are relevant to human
rationality. Some of this suspicion comes from the same sort of intuitions
that counted against the imagined experiments concerning aesthetic
judgement. In particular, whether or not we are rational would not be
straightforwardly empirical if any of the following situations held true:

1. Relativism is true about reasoning. There are no normative principles of reasoning that apply to all humans. Whether a principle
   counts as good for reasoning is indexed to each person.
2. What counts as good reasoning is indexed to human reasoning
   ability in general; there are no normative principles of reasoning
   independent of our reasoning abilities against which to compare
   these abilities.
3. There are normative principles of reasoning independent of our
   reasoning abilities but we have no way of getting outside our own
   reasoning faculties to compare them to the normative principles
   of reasoning.

Each of these possibilities will be discussed at length in the course of
this book. For now, I want to say something brief about each.

First, consider the possibility that there are no general standards of
what counts as good reasoning that apply to humans in general. While
relativism is plausible in certain realms (taste, funniness, and perhaps
aesthetics), prima facie, relativism seems implausible with respect to
reasoning. It seems crazy to say that reasoning in accordance with
principles based on rules of logic is a good thing for some people but
not for others. Violating principles based on rules of logic seems wrong
for everyone, not just for some folks. Since (1) is false, it fails to show

that human rationality is not an empirical issue. Relativism is not, however, this straightforwardly implausible with respect to reasoning.

One way to make relativism about reasoning more plausible is to point to the finite computational resources that each human has. We each have a limited amount of memory, a limited life-span, a limited brain-size, and a limited amount of resources to devote to the project of reasoning.[33] Given these limitations, we need to develop *efficient* reasoning strategies. Different people, because of their different intellectual resources, their different interests, their different needs, and their different environments, will develop and follow different rules of reasoning. Looked at this way, relativism about the principles of reasoning is not so implausible.

The truth of this sort of relativism does not entail that the question 'Are humans rational?' is a conceptual question. How many calories a person should consume in a day is indexed to her height, her age, her rate of metabolism, and the like. This shows that different people should consume different amounts of calories, but it does not prove that how many calories a person should eat is a conceptual manner. For relativism about human rationality to entail that human rationality is a conceptual issue, one must show either that there are no normative principles of reasoning at all (the existence of the human finitary predicament does not establish this—relativism does not entail nihilism) or one must show that the way a person should reason is necessarily the same as how that person in fact reasons. The truth of relativism would entail that the question 'Are humans rational?' is a conceptual question only if there was some further argument to show that all the divergences that a person makes from the principles that are the normative principles of reasoning for that person must be performance errors. This argument has affinities to the argument (sketched above and discussed in Chapter 3) that accepts the standard picture of rationality and says that all divergences from the normative principles must be performance errors. Just as the Chapter 3 argument fails, so too, I argue in Chapter 7, does the relativistic argument for the rationality thesis.

Second, consider the possibility that the normative principles of reasoning are indexed to human reasoning ability in general. If this is the case, it is hard to see how we could fail to reason in accordance with the norms because the norms are based on us. If the normative principles

---

[33] Christopher Cherniak, *Minimal Rationality* (Cambridge, Mass.: MIT Press, 1986), discusses the implications of the human finitary predicament for issues related to human rationality.

of reasoning just come from our reasoning capacity, then humans must be rational. If this is right, then human rationality is a conceptual question, and the answer to the question is that we *are* rational. This argument might seem similar to the reflective equilibrium argument that I discuss in Chapter 5, but there is an important difference. The reflective equilibrium argument accepts the standard picture of rationality and attempts to show that our normative principles of reasoning must be the same as the principles embodied in our reasoning competence. The present argument attempts to reach the same conclusion but by rejecting the standard picture of rationality. In Chapter 7, I argue that this attempt fails.

Finally, consider the possibility that we have no way of getting outside our reasoning faculties. In the case of the proposed experiment about human aesthetic sensibilities, the problem was how the experimenters could determine for themselves which artworks were beautiful and which were not. The parallel problem with respect to reasoning is that experimenters who wish to determine whether humans are rational need to start with an account of which principles of reasoning are rational and which ones are not. Unless they already assume that they themselves are rational, they will be unable to do so.

There is a more specific version of this possibility that applies to reasoning. In order to inquire whether we are rational, we need to use our reasoning faculties, the very faculties that we are trying to assess. The problem is this: suppose we are irrational and that our reasoning faculties cannot be relied upon to work properly. If this is the case, when we inquire into the matter of whether or not we are rational, we cannot be relied on to get the right answer; even if we conclude that we are rational, we might well be wrong, because at least some of our methods for reaching this conclusion are, by stipulation, irrational. Now suppose, as is the case, that we do not know whether we are rational or not and, further, that we want to determine whether or not we are. If we are truly in doubt about our reasoning abilities, then we cannot trust the results of our inquiry because if we are irrational, then our methods of inquiry may be unreliable. This suggests that the irrationality thesis cannot be established by empirical methods. It does not show, however, that the issue of human rationality is a conceptual one. A question can be empirically unanswerable yet not conceptual if an answer to the question is empirically inaccessible. An example of this is the problem of other minds, namely, how can I know there are minds in the world besides my own when the only evidence I have for other minds is based on the behaviour of other bodies? For all I can observe, everybody else in the world might be a robot. According to this analysis, it is possible that there are other minds, but the question may not be empirically answerable because there might not be any empirical evidence that I could have that would bear on the question of whether there are other minds. The question whether humans are rational might also be an empirical question with an epistemologically inaccessible answer. This is consistent with the suggestion that we cannot get outside our reasoning abilities. The first possibility thus does not establish that the issue of human rationality is a conceptual question, although it does undermine the idea that human rationality is a straightforwardly empirical matter. I will criticize this argument in Chapter 7.

3.4. Assessing the Standard Picture

These three possibilities—there might be no normative principles of reasoning that apply to all humans; there might be such principles, but they might not be independent of our reasoning abilities; and there might be such independent principles, but we might not be able to compare our reasoning abilities against some extra-human normative principles of reasoning—attempt to defend the rationality thesis by undermining the standard picture of rationality. In Chapter 7, I argue that they fail to establish the rationality thesis. This leaves open the possibility that, even though they do not successfully establish the rationality thesis, these arguments successfully undermine the standard picture of rationality, and that some alternative pictures of rationality— for example, what I call the *pragmatic picture of rationality* and the *relativistic picture of rationality*—might be the proper account of what rationality is.

In the rest of Chapter 7, I turn my attention to the standard picture of rationality. Up to this point, I will have assumed that the standard picture of rationality is true but I will not have said much in its defence. In Chapter 7, I will discuss the virtues of the standard picture of rationality and consider two arguments against it. The first argument has to do with the human finitary predicament. The worry is that some of the principles of reasoning that are deemed norms by the standard picture of reasoning are not feasible for humans to reason in accordance with. If so, then the standard picture of rationality must be mistaken because an unfeasible principle cannot be a norm. The second argument accuses friends of the standard picture of rationality of what Stephen Stich calls *epistemic chauvinism.*[34] The idea is that the only reason we have for embracing the standard picture's account of what the normative principles of reasoning are is that these principles are favoured in our culture, our language, and our way of thinking. This is not, however, a good reason for accepting an account. I develop responses to both of these arguments, but the standard picture is, I think, still in trouble. In the remaining sections of Chapter 7, I develop an alternative to the standard picture that I call the *naturalized picture of rationality.* According to this picture, various empirical facts about humans and our environment must be taken into consideration in determining what the normative principles of reasoning are. I argue that this account has the virtues of the standard picture of rationality while avoiding the problems that face the standard picture.

3.5. The Punch Line

In Chapter 8, I conclude my discussion by returning directly to the central questions that began this inquiry: 'Are humans rational?', 'Is this a conceptual or empirical question?', and 'If this is an empirical question, what kind of evidence will it answer?' I here explain how the preceding discussion establishes that the question whether humans are rational is primarily an empirical question, the sort of empirical question that the reasoning experiments help answer. Further, I suggest that the reasoning experiments give us some reason to think that humans are irrational, although there is more empirical work to be done, not just in psychology proper, but in evolutionary theory, computational theory, and neuroscience. My conclusion here is based on the naturalized picture of rationality developed in Chapter 7. I conclude by discussing the broader morals of this inquiry, in particular the project of naturalizing epistemology.

[34] Stich, *The Fragmentation of Reason*, 94, and *passim*.

2

Competence

IN Chapter 1, I described the rationality thesis as the view that human reasoning competence matches the normative principle of reasoning. This way of characterizing the rationality thesis draws the idea of competence from linguistic theory. In Section 1 of this chapter, I will discuss the notion of linguistic competence with an eye towards whether an analogous notion of competence can be developed in the realm of reasoning. Along the way, I will discuss related theses in contemporary linguistic theory; these details will be useful to the rest of this inquiry. In Section 2, I discuss the nature of human reasoning competence.

1. Language

1.1. Linguistic Knowledge

A language is an abstract system that relates signals (for example, in particular contexts, certain-shaped collections of ink, certain sounds, or certain hand gestures) to meanings. Linguistics is the study of human languages. As characterized by contemporary linguists working in the paradigm of cognitive science, the central project of linguistics is to develop an account of the linguistic knowledge of humans.[1] By linguistic *knowledge*, I do not mean knowledge in the sense that I know how much an electron weighs and I do not mean knowledge in the sense of having conscious beliefs. Further, by knowledge of language, I mean something more than the capacity to speak a language. My

---

[1] See Noam Chomsky, *Aspects of the Theory of Syntax* (Cambridge, Mass.: MIT Press, 1965); *Reflections on Language* (New York: Random House, 1975); *Rules and Representations* (New York: Columbia University Press, 1980); *Language and Problems of Knowledge* (Cambridge, Mass.: MIT Press, 1980); and *Knowledge of Language* (New York: Praeger, 1986). By focusing on Chomskian linguistics, I am painting a skewed picture of the discipline of linguistics. Many practising linguists do not concern themselves with the questions that Chomsky focuses on (for example, some of them do much less abstract work) and some of those who do disagree with Chomsky. To be more precise, instead of using just the term 'linguistics', I should say 'Chomskian linguistics' or 'generative linguistics' throughout.

linguistic behaviour includes uttering English sentences, understanding English sentences, being able to identify ungrammatical sentences, being able to judge whether two sentences are related to each other in various ways, and so on. Underlying and governing this behaviour is a set of unconscious rules. The cognitive structures that underlie these rules constitute my linguistic knowledge, the sort of knowledge that linguists study.

As I mentioned in Chapter 1, philosophers typically think of knowledge as a kind of justified true belief, but it is far from clear in what sense our linguistic principles are justified. Noam Chomsky in some places tries to avoid this confusion by talking about *cognizing* linguistic principles rather than having knowledge of them.[2] Chomsky has dispensed with this admittedly awkward term but does not, when he talks of knowledge of language, mean to use 'knowledge' in the justified true belief sense of the term.

Two features of our knowledge of language are that it is unconscious and abstract. One might initially be tempted to say that my knowledge of English consists in only knowing that some very long list of sentences—including, for example,

> The dog chased the cat,
> Paula hit the ball with the bat

—are grammatical English sentences. The problem with this view is that linguistic behaviour is creative (or productive) in the sense that we each create and understand novel sentences. (Odds are that you have never encountered this sentence before, but you have no problem whatsoever understanding it.) There are, in fact, an infinite number of grammatical English sentences; we cannot memorize (or know) them all. Rather, we know certain abstract linguistic rules that enable us to produce and identify a wide range of sentences, even ones that are completely novel. This accounts for why linguistic knowledge consists of rules rather than particular facts.

As a concrete example, consider a study of children's knowledge of the rule for making compound words out of regular and irregular plural nouns.[3]

---

[2] See e.g. Chomsky, *Reflections on Language, passim.*
[3] Peter Gordon, 'Level-Ordering in Lexical Development', *Cognition*, 21 (1986), 73–91. The study is nicely summarized in Steven Pinker, *The Language Instinct* (New York: Morrow, 1994), 146–7.

[C]ompounds can be formed out of irregular plurals but not out of regular plurals. For example, a house infested with mice can be described as *mice-infested*, but it sounds awkward to describe a house infested with rats as *rats-infested*. We say that it is *rat-infested*, even though by definition one rat does not make an infestation. . . . [T]hree- to five-year-old children obey this restriction fastidiously. Showing the children a puppet . . . [Gordon] first asked them, 'Here is a monster who likes to eat mud. What would you call him?' He then gave them the answer, a *mud-eater*, to get them started. Children like to play along, and the more gruesome the meal, the more eagerly they fill in the blanks. . . . A 'monster who likes to eat mice', the children said, was a *mice-eater*. But a 'monster who likes to eat rats' was never a *rats-eater*, only a *rat-eater*. (Even the children who made the error *mouses* in their spontaneous speech never called the puppet a *mouses-eater*.) The children, in other words, respected . . . subtle restrictions on combining plurals . . . [to make] compounds . . .[4]

Children seem to know something like the following rule:

> To make a compound word using a plural noun, use the singular form of a noun when the noun has a regular plural, but use the plural form of the noun when it has an irregular plural.

How, we might wonder, do 3-year-old children come to know such a rule? You might think that they learn it by listening to speakers of their language use compound words of the relevant sort. Gordon showed that compounds containing plurals are rather uncommon. Adult speech provides children with insufficient evidence (basically, no evidence) that English follows this rule. Further, the rule is too complex for children to have *consciously* learned it. In any event, few (if any) parents have explicitly tried to teach their children this rule, and even if they did, children would not understand what their parents were talking about. This example shows that knowledge of language is unconscious— children do not *consciously* know the rules for making compound words, but, since they clearly know the rules, they must know them unconsciously. The example further shows that knowledge of language is knowledge of complex rules rather than particular linguistic facts—children clearly cannot have memorized which compound words are grammatical since they will not have encountered them before and the rule that would enable them to make the various distinctions without the relevant linguistic evidence is complex.

Given what I have said so far, it is tempting to say that linguistic knowledge is an ability, a capacity, or a set of dispositions. Chomsky,

---

[4] Pinker, *The Language Instinct*, 146–7.

however, explicitly discourages thinking about knowledge of language as a capacity, an ability, or a disposition towards certain linguistic behaviours. He describes the imaginary case of Juan, who temporarily suffers from aphasia, the impairment of language ability due to brain damage.[5] After a period of time, Juan's condition goes away and he can speak and understand language again. Juan does not, Chomsky notes, have to relearn his native language. This means that something must have remained when Juan lost the capacity for speech. That something which remained is his knowledge of language. For this reason, Chomsky wants to underscore that knowledge of language is not simply a capacity. He writes:

it does not seem to me quite accurate to take 'knowledge of English' to be a capacity or an ability, though it enters into the capacity or ability exercised in language use. In principle, one might have the cognitive structure that we call 'knowledge of English', fully developed, with no capacity to use the structure; and certain capacities to carry out 'intellectual activities' may involve no cognitive structures but merely a network of dispositions and habits, something quite different. Knowledge, understanding or belief is at a level more abstract than capacity. . . . The notions of 'capacity' and 'family of dispositions' are more closely related to behavior and 'language use'; they do not lead us to inquire into the nature of the 'ghost in the machine' through the study of cognitive structures and their organization.[6]

Knowledge of language is, thus, constituted by the abstract, unconscious, and complex rules that underlie our linguistic abilities.

Given its nature, linguists do not have direct access to linguistic knowledge. Our underlying linguistic knowledge is accessible primarily by observing actual linguistic behaviour such as speech, comprehension, and various linguistic judgements such as whether a sentence is grammatical and whether a sentence is an answer to a particular question. In the course of our everyday linguistic behaviour, we often utter ungrammatical sentences. Sometimes these mistakes are due to a lack of attention on the part of the speaker or listener because of an inadequate amount of sleep, excessive drug use, or excitedness (call these *situational* factors). Other times, these mistakes are due to basic facts about the human condition such as constraints on processing-time and memory (call these *psychological* factors). For example, there are grammatical sentences that would take centuries to utter that no human

---

[5] Chomsky, *Language and Problems of Knowledge*, 10–11.
[6] Id., *Reflections on Language*, 23.

could judge to be grammatical because of our finite life-spans. Mistakes due to either of these types of factor are called *performance errors*; they do not reflect an underlying lack of knowledge of the language by the speaker or hearer. Linguistic performance—that is, actual linguistic behaviour—is contrasted with linguistic competence, the underlying linguistic knowledge, knowledge which manifests itself as linguistic ability. What linguists want to describe is underlying knowledge—the knowledge that underlies language use and understanding—that interacts with abilities, capacities, mechanisms, and the like, so they need to idealize, to abstract away from these other abilities, in order to 'home in' on linguistic competence. The competence–performance distinction in linguistics will be discussed in detail below (Section 1.4).

1.2. Linguistic Nativism

Nothing I have said so far about linguistic knowledge addresses how we get this knowledge. Prima facie, we learn how to speak a language in much the same way we learn how to play chess or drive a car with standard transmission, that is, we are taught, partially by example, partially by explicit rules, and partially by trial and error. Over the past few decades, Chomsky has persuasively argued that linguistic knowledge is primarily innate. According to Chomsky, there are universal principles that are genetically programmed in us, as humans, that dramatically restrict the range of possible languages we can learn. These principles allow for some variation; hence the differences among languages. Acquiring a language, according to Chomsky, involves the setting of parameters which account for the differences in languages. The differences between languages are not particularly significant; acquiring a language, according to Chomsky, is roughly equivalent to developing an adult arm: although some environmental inputs are required, the course of development is to a great extent predetermined and constrained.[7] The debate between nativists and their opponents is not so much over whether our knowledge of language is innate, but rather is over whether the innate components of our linguistic knowledge are specific to language or whether they are instances of general knowledge that is involved in learning almost anything. Everyone agrees that innate capacities are involved in learning a language (otherwise, a tennis shoe could acquire a language) and that the environment makes some contributions beyond our innate capacities (whether a child learns

---

[7] See e.g. Chomsky, *Knowledge of Language*.

to speak Portuguese rather than Swahili is determined by the environment in which she grows up). At issue is *how much* is contributed by the innate stuff rather than by the environment and *what form* this contribution takes. The nativist says that quite a lot of our linguistic knowledge is innate and further that this innate knowledge is *language-specific*, rather than general; the non-nativist says that quite a lot is either environmental or the result of general learning mechanisms. There are four different kinds of evidence for nativism about language: developmental evidence, evidence of the universality of language, neurological evidence, and genetic evidence. I will consider each in turn.[8]

1.2.1. Developmental Evidence

The main argument for linguistic nativism has to do with the fact that children learn language without enough exposure to the relevant linguistic input to teach them what they clearly know. The idea, called the *poverty of stimulus argument*, is that a young child in an English-speaking environment encounters a small and idiosyncratic set of English sentences—some of them ungrammatical (not to mention the random collection of *non*-English sentences to which she will be exposed)—during the period when she is developing a language. By the time she has developed into a mature language speaker, the child will be able to recognize, understand, and produce novel English sentences. The English sentences she encounters grossly underdetermine the rules of the language that produced them. It would be impossible, in fact, for a child to infer the linguistic rules that adult speakers know from the data she will encounter in, say, the first three years of her life. From this fact, linguists conclude that a child's linguistic development must be guided by a rich set of language-specific rules that restrict the class of possible natural human languages.

As this point is somewhat tricky, I need to proceed carefully. Recall that our linguistic knowledge is *creative*: each of us is capable of producing an infinite number of grammatical sentences. Further, we are capable of distinguishing grammatical sentences from ungrammatical ones. As children, each of us developed our linguistic abilities despite the fact that we were only exposed to a finite number of grammatical sentences. These facts alone do not establish linguistic nativism. Learning that 'dog' applies to hairy four-legged creatures that bark (but not to

---

[8] Linguistic nativism is clearly and persuasive defended in Pinker, *The Language Instinct*.

furry ones that purr) involves being able to move from a finite number of instances of hearing 'dog' associated with barking, hairy four-legged creatures to an ability to distinguish dogs from non-dogs in an infinite number of circumstances. The difference between the generalization involved in learning what 'dog' means and in learning a linguistic principle is that, in the case of learning linguistic principles, children do not make simple generalizations but instead make generalizations that require positing language-specific knowledge.

Recall the example of children's knowledge of compound words made out of irregular plurals. If children were simply generalizing on the basis of examples like

A monster that eats mud is a mud-eater,
A monster that eats people is a people-eater,

and so on, they would utter sentences like

A monster that eats rats is a rats-eater,

but they do not. In fact, children know the right rule without any evidence from which they could make these sorts of generalizations. Children do not typically encounter any instances of compound words that make use of irregular plural nouns (like 'teethmarks') but they know that these sorts of words are grammatical while compound words that make use of regular plural nouns (like 'fingersprints') are not. The rule that distinguishes between irregular and regular plural nouns must be language-specific. This supports linguistic nativism.[9]

The general point is that the data children are exposed to do not completely determine what the language underlying that data is. For all the data that little Bobbie has encountered show, the language that is behind that data might be English, but it also might be one of an infinite number of other languages that share with English the property of being consistent with the data that Bobbie has encountered in the few years of his life. In the example above, a child might well have no evidence that favoured English over a possible language (call it Schminglish) in which compound words could be formed using regular plural nouns, that is, a language in which words like 'fingersprint' would be grammatical. Not only couldn't a child infer English over Schminglish on

---

[9] For other discussion of developmental evidence, see ibid. and Steven Pinker, 'Language Acquisition', in Daniel Osherson and Howard Lasnik (eds.), *Language: Invitation to Cognitive Science*, i (Cambridge, Mass.: MIT Press, 1990).

the basis of the data she has encountered, even a sophisticated linguist could not infer a grammar from the evidence a child has.[10] The sort of innate knowledge that could, in association with the limited linguistic input, enable children to learn English (rather than Schminglish and the infinitely many other languages that are consistent with children's data) in the relatively short time that they do must be quite *specific* principles of language learning. The facts of how children learn language show not only that a great deal of our knowledge of language is innate, but further that this knowledge is language-specific.

1.2.2. Universality

Contrary to what one might think prima facie, the range of possible human languages is constrained. In fact, there are various features, called *linguistic universals*, that all human languages (at least the ones we know about) have in common.[11] Most linguistic universals take the form of conditionals, that is, they are of the following form: if a language has some feature *a*, then it will have some feature *b*.[12] The existence of linguistic universals might be thought to count as evidence that certain principles of language are innate. There are two reasons why this might not be the case. First, the existence of such universals could be accounted for if all human languages stemmed from the same language. Second, the existence of such universals could be due to more general constraints besides linguistic ones, namely constraints on human thought. As I will argue in the following two paragraphs, neither of these is a good explanation for actual linguistic universals. As a result, the existence of linguistic universals does count as evidence for linguistic nativism.[13]

There are two main reasons why the existence of linguistic universals cannot be explained by the claim that all languages stem from a single ancestor. First, this view depends on it being the case that new languages come into existence when gradual changes are made to a single

---

[10] See Stephen Stich and William Ramsey, 'Connectionism and Three Levels of Nativism', *Synthese*, 82 (1990), 177–205, esp. 183–7, for further discussion of this point.

[11] See Joseph Greenberg *et al.* (eds.), *Universals of Human Language*, 4 vols. (Stanford, Calif.: Stanford University Press, 1978); and Bernard Comrie, *Language Universals and Linguistic Taxonomy* (Chicago: University of Chicago Press, 1981).

[12] Pinker, *The Language Instinct*, 234.

[13] The discussion that follows borrows extensively from Pinker, ibid. 32–3 and 234–6. Pinker's discussion of creoles draws from Derek Binkerton, *The Roots of Language* (Ann Arbor, Mich.: Karmona, 1981).

parent language. New languages can, however, come into existence in various ways. A striking example of this is known as *creolization*. When speakers of different languages have to communicate but cannot learn each other's languages, they speak to each other in a *pidgin*, a sort of proto-language that uses choppy strings of words with no standard word order and no basic grammatical structure. When children are exposed to a pidgin at the time when they would typically be acquiring a native language, they will develop their own grammar to go with the pidgin, thereby producing a *creole* language. Creole languages are full-blown languages that are as expressive and grammatically complex as any other language, but they are not the result of simple alterations to the structure of any pre-existing language. Creoles are counter-examples to the view that all human languages evolve from a single ancestral language. Second, conditional linguistic universals (that is, universals of the if–then form), the most common type of universal, cannot be explained by the single-ancestor model of language change. Nothing that a child could learn from listening to a language could teach him that if a language has feature *a*, then it has feature *b*. A child could learn that a language has feature *a* and feature *b* or that a language has neither feature *a* nor feature *b*, but not a counterfactual truth about a language, namely that if it had feature *a*, then it would have feature *b*. Both of these observations suggest that the evolution of language does not and did not occur in a way that fits with the view that there is a single ancestral language. This leaves open the possibility for linguistic universals to be due to linguistic nativism.

The second possibility that might undermine the support that the existence of linguistic universals provides for linguistic nativism is that linguistic universals might be due to more general constraints, for example, on learning or cognition. The problem with this possibility is that most of the linguistic universals that hold are so specific that it seems impossible for them to be due to more general constraints. Consider the following example. There are two types of suffixes, *derivational* and *inflexional*. A derivational suffix is one that makes a new word out of an old one (for example, 'Marx' gets made into 'Marxist' by the addition of the derivational suffix '-ist'). An inflexional suffix is one that modifies a word so that it fits the appropriate role in a sentence (for example, 'car' gets made into 'cars' by the addition of the inflexional suffix '-s'). Joseph Greenberg discovered the following linguistic universal: if a language has both of these sorts of suffix, then the derivational suffix always occurs closer to the stem of the word being modified than the inflexional suffix.[14] This explains why we can use the word 'Marxists' to refer to several people who adhere to Marx's political philosophy but cannot use the word 'Marxesist' to refer to a person who adheres to the collective comedic style of Groucho, Chico, and Harpo Marx. As Steve Pinker points out, 'It is hard to think of how . . . [Greenberg's] law could be a consequence of any universal principle of thought or memory . . .'.[15] How could it be that the concept of three people embracing a political philosophy based on the work of one Marx is thinkable while the concept of one person embracing a comedic style based on the work of three Marxes is unthinkable? Such very specific universals seem explicable only by constraints stemming from the universal nature of our linguistic knowledge, not by the universality of some more general kind of constraints. Given this, the existence of linguistic universals seems to count as evidence for the innateness of specific linguistic knowledge.

1.2.3. Neurological Evidence

A third possible source of evidence for linguistic nativism involves damage to specific areas of the brain that leads to the impairment of particular language functions while leaving other cognitive abilities intact. Such evidence suggests that our knowledge of language is innate and language specific rather than the result of general learning mechanisms and thus provides support for nativism about language. There is, for example, a condition known as Broca's aphasia, which is caused by damage to Broca's area, a particular area of the left front lobe of the brain. People with Broca's aphasia often have serious problems speaking (or signing, if they communicate through sign language) even though they do not have trouble with language comprehension, they can control their throat-muscles perfectly well, and their general intelligence is unaltered.[16]

Cases of brain injuries that lead to language impairment but no other cognitive impairment do not show, on their own, that there is a language-specific cognitive mechanism. This evidence is consistent with it being the case that we learn language through some general learning mechanism. It is logically consistent that the entire brain might be

---

[14] Joseph Greenberg (ed.), *Universals of Language* (Cambridge, Mass.: MIT Press, 1963).   [15] Pinker, *The Language Instinct*, 236.
[16] Ibid. 46–54. For a more detailed discussion, see Howard Gardner, *The Shattered Mind* (New York: Basic Books, 1974).

required for language comprehension, while other cognitive functions only require part of the brain to do whatever it is that they do. This would explain why Broca's aphasics perform well on intelligence tests but have trouble verbally answering a simple question. There are many reasons why this explanation, though logically possible, is empirically wrong; I will discuss just two. First, neurological evidence shows that very specific parts of the brain are used in language comprehension. Techniques such as CAT (computerized axial tomography), MRI (magnetic resonance imaging), and PET (positron emission tomography), which allow an active brain to be studied, reveal that language processing typically occurs in specific regions of the left side of the brain.[17] Second, and more importantly, there are people who have seriously impaired non-linguistic cognitive functions but have linguistic abilities that are intact. Some people who have too much pressure in the cerebrospinal fluid that fills their brain's ventricles (the condition known as hydrocephalus) have some cognitive disabilities but have unimpaired language abilities. Some people with Alzheimer's disease, autism, and certain aphasias fit a similar cognitive profile—fluent in language, but incompetent at many other cognitive tasks.[18] That language can be impaired without affecting other cognitive functions and vice versa seems to show that there are language-specific portions of the brain.

Neurological evidence alone does not establish linguistic nativism. It might be that, over time, parts of the brain can come to have specific functions that are not innate but are the result of how information about language gets stored in the brain. Linguistic ability has to be coded for in the brain somewhere. That place, wherever it is, could be damaged and linguistic ability could be impaired. This does not explain, however, why there is a *specific* place in the brain that is responsible for language ability in most people; if it is just a matter of language being coded for *somewhere* in the brain, why do most people have their language ability in the same place? Perhaps language processing is typically localized in specific regions of the left side of the brain because these regions are close to the parts of the brain where certain motor control mechanisms relevant to language use are located. For this to be plausible, these motor control mechanisms would have to be somewhat abstract because people who use sign language seem to do

[17] Pinker, *The Language Instinct*, 300–2.
[18] Ibid. 50–3 and Richard Cromer, 'The Cognition Hypothesis of Language Acquisition', in *Language and Thought in Normal and Handicapped Children* (Cambridge, Mass.: Blackwell, 1991).

their language processing in the same part of the brain as those who use spoken language.[19] Whether or not this particular account is true, there are several models of how language ability could be localized in specific parts of the brain without linguistic nativism being true.[20] Neurological evidence shows that there are language-specific portions of the brain, but it does not establish that linguistic ability is innate.

1.2.4. Genetic Evidence

I turn next to genetic evidence for linguistic nativism. The existence of genetic conditions that lead to language impairment but not to the impairment of other cognitive faculties would support the view that humans have language-specific capacities. In fact, there is evidence that an alteration in a specific gene impairs linguistic ability (although this does not show that a specific gene *controls* linguistic ability). The evidence comes from a disorder known as specific language impairment (SLI). People with SLI find it very difficult to speak and they frequently make serious and rather specific grammatical errors (for example, they misuse pronouns, they make mistakes with plurals, they get confused about simple differences in tense), but much of their language ability, their overall intelligence, and their cognitive faculties seem normal. This disease runs in families and is distributed in such a way that environmental factors have nothing to do with whether a family member develops it or does not (for example, there is an instance of the fraternal twin of a person with SLI who has unimpaired language skills). A single gene seems responsible for the condition because SLI is an all-or-nothing condition—either one has 'full-blown' SLI or one has no such impairment at all. This condition does not show that a single gene is responsible for linguistic capacities (partly because people with SLI can communicate to a certain extent); it does show that our genes do cause our brains to develop (or not, in the case of SLI) in a way that is specifically designed for language. This provides strong evidence for linguistic nativism as well.[21]

---

[19] See Howard Poizner *et al.*, *What the Hands Reveal about the Brain* (Cambridge, Mass.: MIT Press, 1990).

[20] See e.g. Martha Farah, 'Neuropsychological Inference with an Interactive Brain: A Critique of the "Locality" Assumption', *Behavioral and Brain Sciences*, 17 (1994), 43–104.

[21] M. Gopnik, 'Dysphasia in an Extended Family', *Nature*, 374 (1990), 715; and M. Gopnik and Martha Crago, 'Familial Aggregation of a Developmental Language Disorder', *Cognition*, 39 (1991), 1–50. This evidence is nicely summarized in Pinker, *The Language Instinct*, 48–50 and 297–331, on which the preceding discussion is based.

1.3. The Language Organ

The evidence discussed in the previous section suggests that humans have innate language-specific capacities. This nativist claim that our linguistic knowledge is language-specific is sometimes talked about in terms of a *mental organ*. A mental organ is a cognitive system that performs a specific function. A mental organ is analogous to a bodily organ like the heart or the liver. Chomsky says:

> We may usefully think of the language faculty, the number faculty, and others as 'mental organs,' analogous to the heart, or the visual system or the system of motor coordination and planning. There appears to be no clear demarcation line between physical organs, perceptual and motor systems, and cognitive faculties. . . . [T]here seems little reason to insist that the brain is unique in the biological world in that it is unstructured and undifferentiated, developing on the basis of uniform principles of growth or learning . . . that are common to all domains.[22]

Chomsky's analogy between our linguistic knowledge and, say, the visual system is illustrative of several claims. First, the basic structure of both is genetically determined. Second, both will develop in different ways (within various constraints) according to environmental inputs—for example, if a child is not exposed to a certain amount of light in her formative years, she will not develop normal visual capacities; similarly, if a child is not exposed to linguistic input, she will develop impoverished language capacities. Third, the ontogenetic development of both will happen without conscious attention to the process—a child does not have to learn consciously to develop eyes or to develop linguistic abilities (in contrast, say, to learning to ride a bike or to write, which do need to be learned consciously). Fourth, both the visual system and the language faculty constitute functional units—the visual system is for seeing and the language faculty is for producing and understanding meaningful signals. This last point is worth dwelling on a bit because it seems central to the notion of an organ.

Not every capacity that humans have is appropriately seen as a stemming from a mental organ. The capacity that humans have for swinging a baseball bat does not constitute a 'batting organ'. The various parts of the body involved in hitting a baseball have their own separate uses (vision, locomotion, etc.). In contrast, though the eye is made up of many parts that do different things, all or most of these parts do not

---

[22] Chomsky, *Rules and Representations*, 39.

play other roles; they are useful in so far as they play a role in enabling the eye to perform its function. Our linguistic capacity is like our visual capacity and unlike our batting capacity. Though our linguistic capacity has various 'parts', they are useful only in so far as they play a role in language. The difference between swinging a bat and using language that I am pointing to here suggests that there is a language organ but not a batting organ. This difference dovetails nicely with the claim that learning a language is constrained by specific innate principles; in contrast, learning to bat is constrained by general learning mechanisms.

Jerry Fodor, in *The Modularity of Mind*, points out an important difference between mental organs and anatomical organs that Chomsky glosses over: 'When Chomsky says that there is an innately specified "language organ", what he means is primarily that there are truths (about the structure of possible first languages) that human beings innately grasp.'[23] There are, however, no such truths (not even any beliefs) that humans innately grasp in virtue of having a heart. In other words, mental organs involve unconscious knowledge, specifically, in the case of the language organ, knowledge about the structure of languages, while organs of the non-mental sort do not involve any innately grasped truths or even any propositional attitudes. This is not an argument against the mental-organ picture of linguistic competence, but a warning against potential misunderstandings of it.

It is useful to contrast the view that our capacity for language is a mental organ with the view that our capacity for language is a *module*. Fodor says that a cognitive mechanism is modular if it is domain-specific, innately specified, hardwired, autonomous, and not assembled (that is, instantiated in such a way as not to require any mediating computational steps; in other words, a cognitive mechanism is not assembled if it performs its function through some *primitive* mechanical process).[24] As the terms 'mental organ' and 'module' are often used, however, the distinction between them is far from clear; some people, in fact, use the terms as if they are synonymous. Despite the differences in usage, everyone seems to agree that a module is a mental organ, but not vice versa. If there is a language *module*, then there is a language *organ*; there might, however, be a language organ but not a language module. For my purposes, I will adopt Fodor's definition of a module, and count as a mental organ a cognitive mechanism that is, at a minimum,

---

[23] Jerry Fodor, *The Modularity of Mind* (Cambridge, Mass.: MIT Press, 1983), 7.
[24] Ibid., *passim*, esp. 37.

domain-specific and innately specified. Given these definitions, the argument that I have sketched above for there being innate, domain-specific constraints on language learning entails that there is a language organ. Whether there is a language module is a question that I leave unsettled.

1.4. Linguistic Competence

As I have indicated above, there is something about the competence–performance distinction in linguistics that must be right. For example, we can make sense of the idea of a 'slip of the tongue': it is a case of someone making an utterance that was different from what she meant to say. When a person makes a genuine grammatical slip, we do not think that it is indicative of a lack of linguistic ability or knowledge; we distinguish between her underlying competence and her performance. This notion of a competence is, at one level, an intuitive one. We might say, for example, that Albert has a competence for playing the piano if he knows how to play the piano well or if, under the right circumstances, he plays the piano well. Perhaps when certain conditions hold (for example, if he has a broken arm or is under the influence of LSD), we would expect that he would be unable to play to his usual high standards. We would allow for this and even for Albert's just having an occasional bad day, yet still think that he has a competence for piano playing. The idea is that sometimes Albert's actual piano-playing behaviour is not up to par with his capacity for playing the piano. It is roughly this intuitive sense of competence that is formalized in linguistic theory.

Giving an account of a person's linguistic competence explains something different from giving an account of a person's linguistic performance. One such difference, for example, is that the explanations are in different terms. Giving an account of a person's linguistic *performance* explains all of her utterances, linguistic intuitions, and so on, including false starts, spoonerisms (for example, when she says 'a twenty-one sun galoot' when she meant 'a twenty-one gun salute'), hiccups, and drunken babbling. Such an explanation will involve appeals to her knowledge of language and the language-specific mechanisms that make use of this knowledge, but it will also make frequent and significant appeal to lots of other things, including her memory, her diet, her drug use, and many features of her psychology. Giving an account of a person's linguistic competence is a narrower task. It involves accounting for a person's linguistic behaviours when non-linguistic factors do not interfere with linguistic output. Such an explanation involves referring to a person's knowledge of language, perhaps as embodied in her language organ. Giving an account of a person's linguistic *competence* goes a long way towards giving an account of her linguistic *performance*.

Even this more detailed account of the distinction between competence and performance leaves somewhat unclear what linguistic competence *is* and thus what, at some level, linguistics is about. I will explore three different views of what competence is. First, there is the view that competence is an idealization, a way of abstracting away from interfering factors; call this the *idealization view of competence*. Second, there is the view that competence is the functioning of the language organ (or of whatever mechanism it is that underlies linguistic behaviour); call this the *mechanism view of competence*. Third, there is the view that competence is the knowledge of language; call this the *knowledge view of competence*. Thus far, I have not bothered to distinguish these three different senses of competence. In the next several paragraphs, I will look at the difference senses of the term.[25]

1.4.1. The Idealization View of Competence

First, turning to the idealization view of competence, Chomsky, in one of his earlier major works, says: 'Linguistic theory is concerned primarily with an ideal speaker-listener, in a completely homogeneous speech-community, who knows its language perfectly and is unaffected by such grammatically irrelevant conditions as memory limitations, distractions, shifts of attention and interest, and errors (random or characteristic) in applying his knowledge of language in actual performance.'[26] Here he sounds as if he is favouring the idealization view of competence. On this sense of the term, a person's competence is her linguistic behaviour under ideal conditions. This characterization is, as put, ambiguous; it conflates two different ways idealization could take place. On one reading, ideal conditions would be those conditions under which the language mechanism functions properly. On this reading, however, competence as an idealization of behaviour just amounts to competence as the operation of the language organ (the mechanism

---

[25] For some interesting relevant discussion about philosophical issues concerning the competence–performance distinction, see Jerry Fodor and Merrill Garrett, 'Some Reflections on Competence and Performance', in John Lyons and Roger Wales (eds.), *Psycholinguistic Papers: Proceedings of the 1966 Edinburgh Conference* (Edinburgh: Edinburgh University Press, 1966); and the eight essays in Ned Block (ed.), *Readings in Philosophy of Psychology*, ii (Cambridge, Mass.: Harvard University Press, 1981), pt. 4: 'Innate Ideas'.   [26] Chomsky, *Aspects of the Theory of Syntax*, 3.

view of competence). On the other reading, the idealization would be guided by simplicity considerations, the desire for a unified theory, and so forth. On this view (the one that I henceforth have in mind when I talk about the idealization view), linguistic competence is linguistic behaviour under ideal circumstances, abstracting away from the particulars of individuals and their linguistic situations. According to this view, a rule of linguistic competence is like a law of physics that ignores interfering factors like friction and air resistance and favours developing the simplest, most unified account of our linguistic ability.

1.4.2. The Mechanism View of Competence

Second, one might see competence as the operation of a mental organ, the underlying mechanism that embodies our linguistic knowledge and is responsible for our language capacities. On the mechanism view of competence, linguistic competence is the unfettered operation of the language organ, that is, it is the behaviour of the language organ if it were attached to the best possible input–output devices, memory, and the like. You might think of extracting a 'normal' language organ from somebody's brain and implanting it into a very powerful computer that would simulate the computational environment that would enable the organ to operate at its optimal capacity. This is roughly comparable to determining the horsepower of an engine. To do so, you do not focus on the engine's performance under the various non-optimal performance conditions in which it might be found (for example, having poorly fitted hoses, having rusted connections to the spark-plugs, having watered-down gasoline in it, and so forth). Instead, you imagine extracting it from its resting-place in an automobile or lawnmower and placing it under optimal conditions. The mechanism view of competence is supposed to work in roughly the same fashion. Among the virtues of this way of looking at competence is that, unlike the idealization view, this view focuses on the actual mechanism behind linguistic behaviour. At the same time, it captures what seems right about idealization, namely that competence has to do with the holding of the right conditions.

One worry about this view of competence is that it seems dependent on the existence of a mental organ and this seems to be an overly restrictive notion of competence in general. It makes perfect sense to talk about Albert's competence for piano playing even though it is unlikely that there is a piano-playing organ underlying Albert's competence. This is not a serious objection to this view of competence. Although there is no piano-playing organ behind a person's piano-playing ability, there is a set of cognitive mechanisms behind Albert's piano-playing ability, mechanisms that are lacking in incompetent piano players like myself. The fusion of these mechanisms, even if it is comprised of a hotchpotch of organs and mechanisms, can still be conceptually isolated from interfering factors that constitute performance errors. In a similar fashion, if there is not a language organ, we can still make sense of the mechanism view of competence in linguistics by focusing on the mechanism(s) that underlies our linguistic ability.

Seeing competence as an idealization of behaviour is different from seeing it as the operation of the language organ. To see this, consider the auditory system and what might be thought of as auditory competence. Suppose that the auditory system was constructed in such a way that there was a 'deaf spot', a specific sound frequency, within the range that humans can *actually* hear, that (counterfactually) humans could not hear. On the mechanism view of competence, human auditory competence would, in the imagined case, be characterized as having a deaf spot because, even under ideal conditions, humans cannot hear sounds of that particular frequency. In contrast, on the idealization view of competence, the deaf spot would not be seen as part of competence, but would be seen as the result of performance errors (or something like them) and would be abstracted from because of simplicity and unity considerations; human auditory competence would thus be characterized as continuous, that is, without any deaf spots. The same sort of difference would hold between the idealization and the mechanism view of *linguistic* competence.

Given the deaf-spot example, the idealization view of competence seems as if it is not a view of competence after all. The linguist sets out to develop an account of the actual human capacity for language; the idealization view, because it places a premium on simplicity and the like, will, at best, produce an idealized approximation to competence rather than actual competence. The problem with the idealization view stems from the fact that the linguist is trying to characterize an actual existent mechanism in our brains, a mechanism that is partly responsible for the production of linguistic behaviour. Idealization moves away from the mechanism that undergirds our linguistic behaviour.

Friends of the behaviour idealization view might, however, argue that idealization is the best hope we have for developing a theory of competence given our epistemological situation. Linguists must rely on what is accessible, namely linguistic behaviour, because they cannot directly access the language mechanism or our knowledge of language. Due to the existence of performance errors, behaviour will not deliver an account of competence. That is why we need to make idealizations. Through considerations like simplicity, unity, and so forth, we can, say friends of the idealization view, move from behaviour to a theory of competence.

I have two replies to this defence of the idealization view. First, it confuses the metaphysical question of what our competence *is* with the epistemological question of how we can *know* about our competence. I am here concerned with what linguistic competence is, not with how we can access it. The argument made by friends of the idealization view of competence focuses on problems with access, not on the nature of competence itself. Second, even if we turn to epistemological issues, there are other ways of getting access to linguistic competence than behaviour and idealizations of it. Psychological, neurological, and genetic evidence can help us understand performance errors (for example, when they occur and what effects they have), the functioning of the language organ, and so on, thereby giving us access to linguistic competence. The argument in defence of the idealization view of competence thus fails on two counts. The idealization view of behaviour is not a good way to look at linguistic competence.

1.4.3. The Knowledge View of Competence

The third way of talking about linguistic competence is as a person's knowledge of language.[27] Above, I described linguistics as the study of our knowledge of language. Accepting this picture of linguistics, it is tempting to say that linguistic competence just is a person's knowledge of language. This may sound like a strange way of talking, but consider Albert's competence at playing the piano. It makes perfect sense to say that his competence consists in his knowledge of how to play the piano. To say that Albert knows how to play the piano is just to say that he knows what to do to make certain sounds, under the right sort of circumstances, come out of a piano. Similarly, to say something about a person's linguistic competence is to say that she has the knowledge to make certain sounds (or hand movements, if she is a speaker of a sign language), under the right sort of circumstances, that communicate things.

How does the knowledge view of competence differ from the mechanism view of competence? The language mechanism (which, on some views, is the language organ) includes our knowledge of language, but it also includes language-specific mechanisms that make use of our

---

[27] See e.g. Chomsky, *Knowledge of Language*.

knowledge of language to produce linguistic output. For example, there is a part of the language mechanism responsible for parsing, namely for breaking apart sentences into units that match the form of our knowledge of language. This parsing machinery is dedicated to language, but it is not part of our knowledge of language. Such devices, to simplify matters a bit, are the object of study of *psycholinguistics*, not linguistics. Psycholinguists are interested in the psychological mechanisms that implement linguistic knowledge; linguists are interested in the nature of linguistic knowledge rather than the mechanisms that implement it. The knowledge view of competence is associated with linguistics while the mechanism view of competence is associated with psycholinguistics. As an example, recall Chomsky's story, discussed above, about Juan, whose language ability is temporarily impaired due to brain damage. When Juan's brain heals, he does not need to relearn language. Juan did not lose his knowledge of language even though he may have temporarily lost the ability to use language. If the damage was localized to his language organ, then it was some language-specific comprehension or parsing mechanism that was damaged. According to the knowledge view of competence, Juan's injury did not affect his linguistic competence; according to the mechanism view of competence, it did. These two views of competence are not incompatible; they are interrelated. The problem is that it is easy to slide back and forth between these two different notions of competence. The ambiguity is sometimes insignificant, but other times it matters.

Whether you favour the mechanism view or the knowledge view of linguistic competence, the distinction between competence and performance should be clear. Linguistic performance is actual linguistic behaviour. On the knowledge view of competence, linguistic competence consists in our knowledge of language. According to this view, a performance error is any divergence from the rules that make up our knowledge of language. A performance error could be due to various psychological factors including the operation of language-specific psychological mechanisms that do not embody our knowledge of language. On the mechanism view of competence, linguistic competence consists in the rules embodied in our language organ (or whatever mechanisms underlie our linguistic ability). According to this view, a performance error is any divergence from the rules embodied in our language organ due to psychological factors including the operation of the non-language-specific psychological mechanisms and other factors that have a psychological impact.

What both accounts leave out is the details of which particular cognitive structures count as part of linguistic competence and how, in particular, we are to distinguish those cognitive structures that are genuine parts of linguistic competence from those that have an effect on linguistic performance but not as part of competence. Both sorts of structure are psychological; the problem is to identify which are uniquely linguistic. This problem will not go away simply; a full account of human cognitive psychology is required to solve this problem.[28] I will return to this problem in the context of my discussion of reasoning competence in Section 2 below.

1.5. A Simple Objection to Linguistic Competence

Consider now an objection to the notion of linguistic competence.[29] Since performance errors do occur, linguists cannot read an account of competence directly off linguistic behaviour. Rather, while they begin their inquiry with a study of actual performance, they must abstract from performance to develop a theory of competence. Some actual utterances will be attributed to psychological factors (for example, limits on short-term memory) and situational factors (for example, drunkenness) and not counted as data to be explained by a theory of competence. If, for example, I utter the ungrammatical sentence 'I are sitting at my desk', a linguist need not alter her general competence theory or her competence theory of English; rather, she would explain my uttering an ungrammatical sentence as a performance error, for example, as due to my not having had enough sleep. This use of the competence–performance distinction may, however, seem suspect. A similar sort of distinction could be employed in such a way that would have the effect of making a theory unfalsifiable. Consider, for example, how an astrologer might use an analogue of the competence–performance distinction to block evidence from counting against astrological theory. Suppose, for example, that an astrologer claims that the position of the planet Venus indicates that Scorpios will experience romantic trauma

---

[28] Jerry Fodor, 'Introduction: Some Notes on what Linguistics is About', in Block (ed.), *Readings in Philosophy of Psychology*, ii, makes roughly the same point. He says, '[It is not a small problem] which is the correct parsing of the speaker/hearer's psychology into "linguistic mechanisms" and "others"' (203).

[29] The objection is similar to one made by Jay Rosenberg, 'About Competence and Performance', *Philosophical Papers*, 17 (1988), 33–49, esp. 41–4. For a reply to Rosenberg, see John Tienson, 'About Competence', *Philosophical Papers*, 19 (1990), 19–36.

on 11 November. A sceptic of astrology might offer testimony from dozens of Scorpios who experienced no such trauma on the indicated date. The astrologer might respond that this prediction failed due to some 'performance' error, such as interference in the orbit of Venus caused by a comet, or interference due to the fact that several of the Scorpios in question had Jupiter as their rising star. As a result of this performance error, the sceptic's evidence does not constitute an objection to astrological theory. Astrology would thereby remain untainted by such supposed counter-evidence. Something should, however, seem suspicious; the astrologer's original prediction made no mention of comets or rising stars. Though the details of the example are obviously contrived, the point is that some astrologers behave as if they believe nothing should be taken as a falsification of astrological theory.

The general issue here is a standard one in philosophy of science. Karl Popper notes that 'it is always possible to find some way of evading falsification [of a particular theory], for example by introducing *ad hoc* an auxiliary hypothesis or by changing *ad hoc* a definition. It is even possible without logical inconsistency to adopt the position of simply refusing to acknowledge any falsifying experience whatsoever.'[30] These 'immunization strategies'[31] allow any empirical evidence against a theory to be discounted. In the case of astrology, nothing would count as evidence against astrological theory in the eyes of many 'practising' contemporary astrologers. A general problem for the use of the competence–performance distinction is to make sure that the distinction does not act as an immunization strategy.

Popper characterizes an immunization strategy as an unjustified modification of a theory (in the sense that there is no justification for the modification other than that it would prevent the theory from being falsified by the data) in such a way that some particular data will not falsify. In a sense, this characterization just pushes the question back—what distinguishes such an *ad hoc* adjustment to a theory from a motivated, reasonable one? Answering this question is beyond the scope of this project; instead, I will implicitly appeal to the intuitive difference between an *ad hoc* and an appropriately motivated modification of a theory.

There are three reasons why using the competence–performance distinction is a legitimate strategy. First, the performance errors that

---

[30] Karl Popper, *The Logic of Scientific Discovery* (New York: Basic Books, 1959), 42.
[31] Id., *Objective Knowledge* (Oxford: Oxford University Press, 1972), 30.

linguists appeal to have plausible explanations; they fit a pattern and have a structure. That linguistic competence is not exhibited in atypical situations is unsurprising—chemical changes in the brain due to situational factors such as LSD in the bloodstream should affect linguistic behaviour in virtue of the fact that linguistic utterances are initiated in the brain. That linguistic competence is also not exhibited due to psychological factors like memory limitations is similarly predictable. Linguistics, like other sciences, should be expected to make use of *ceteris paribus* clauses, perhaps ineliminable ones.[32] (This suggests a natural way to look at performance errors: they are what happens when *ceteris* is not *paribus*.) Performance errors in linguistics thus fit into a general picture of human psychology; the application of the competence–performance distinction is not unmotivated like an immunization strategy.

A further reason for thinking that using the competence–performance distinction is a legitimate strategy is that linguists do not typically appeal to this distinction when the data does not fit with their favourite theory. Chomsky, for example, has made major changes to his preferred theory of linguistic competence over the years, changes that he could well have avoided making if he had used the competence–performance distinction as an immunization strategy. That Chomsky chose instead to modify in great detail his theory of competence to fit the data suggests that the competence–performance distinction is not a linguist's 'vaccine'. More generally, linguists are always offering counter-examples to each other's theories and they almost never reply by using the competence–performance distinction as an immunization strategy.[33] More typically, they respond by modifying the criticized theory to handle the example or by showing that the proposed counter-example does not in fact count against the theory under consideration.

Finally, the competence–performance distinction is important to linguistics because, even if people never made any performance errors, a theory of linguistics would need to go beyond actual linguistic behaviour to develop a full theory of human linguistic knowledge. There are an infinite number of sentences that will never be uttered. A complete

---

[32] On the ineliminability of *ceteris paribus* clauses, see e.g. Nancy Cartwright, *How the Laws of Physics Lie* (Oxford: Oxford University Press, 1983).

[33] For a suggestion to the contrary (and a few laughs), see Geoffrey Pullum, 'The Revenge of the Methodological Moaners', in *The Great Eskimo Vocabulary Hoax and Other Irreverent Essays on the Study of Language* (Chicago: University of Chicago Press, 1991).

linguistic theory needs to include these possible utterances as part of our linguistic knowledge. A theory of performance based only on actual utterances would be unable to do so. A theory of competence is thus required for a complete linguistic theory. The competence–performance distinction is, thus, quite important for the development of linguistic theory. As such, it does not seem to be an immunization strategy. Some version of the competence–performance distinction seems a legitimate and perhaps necessary tool for linguists to use.

2. Reasoning Competence

The dispute between friends of the rationality thesis and friends of the irrationality thesis is over whether our reasoning capacity measures up to the normative principles of reasoning; the rationality thesis says that we reason in accordance with the norms while the irrationality thesis says that we reason in accordance with principles that diverge from the norms. Friends of the rationality thesis are not, however, committed to the view that we never make mistakes in reasoning; they admit that we may make such mistakes quite frequently. They claim, rather, that when we do make mistakes in reasoning—when we diverge from the norms—we are not reasoning in accordance with our underlying ability to reason. The competence–performance distinction fits quite naturally here. The rationality thesis implies that a divergence from the normative principles of reasoning constitutes a performance error. To put the point another way, the rationality thesis says that our reasoning competence, our underlying capacity for reasoning, can be characterized by rules that match the normative principles of reasoning.

The idea here is a straightforward one at first gloss. Just as it makes sense to talk about Albert's piano-playing competence, it makes sense to talk about a person's reasoning competence. Friends of the rationality thesis, however, want to deploy a more robust sense of reasoning competence, more on a par with linguistic competence than with piano-playing competence. The comparison with linguistics seems apt given the intimate connection between language and cognition. There are, however, several potential difficulties for applying the competence–performance distinction to reasoning. I begin this section by trying to spell out in greater detail what reasoning competence is. I then consider arguments for the innateness of our reasoning competence. Finally, I turn to a discussion of a significant difference between reasoning competence and linguistic competence.

2.1. What is Reasoning Competence?

The general idea of applying the competence–performance distinction to reasoning is to distinguish between inferences made in accordance with a person's reasoning competence and those resulting from various interfering factors that constitute performance errors. On this view, actual human reasoning behaviour is explained by appeal to the operation of our reasoning competence in combination with performance errors caused by situational or psychological factors. Reasoning competence can be seen either as our underlying knowledge of principles of reasoning or as our ability to reason under the right circumstances. Like linguistic competence, reasoning competence can be viewed as a kind of knowledge or as the operation of a mechanism. Turning first to the knowledge view of competence, just as linguistic competence includes knowledge of language, reasoning competence includes principles of reasoning like the and-elimination principle. Saying that the and-elimination principle characterizes human reasoning competence is compatible with the fact that humans sometimes fail to reason in accordance with this principle. To say that the and-elimination principle is part of human reasoning competence is to say that humans reason in accordance with this rule in the absence of performance factors that interfere with its application.

Turning next to the mechanism view, just as our linguistic competence can be thought of as the unfettered functioning of the mechanism underlying our linguistic capacities, our reasoning competence can be thought of as the unfettered functioning of the mechanism(s) underlying our reasoning capacities. The question for the mechanism view of reasoning competence is what the mechanism behind our reasoning ability is. To answer this, we need to know whether there are good reasons for thinking there is a mental organ (or some other innate mechanism) underlying reasoning competence in something like the way there is in the case of linguistic competence. It is clear that reasoning competence is in some way instantiated in the brain. What is not clear is whether it is innate, and if so, what form this innateness takes (in particular, whether the innate machinery is reasoning-specific or more general). Particular answers to these questions are not crucial to the task at hand or to my overall project, but exploring this issue is of intrinsic interest and is warranted as it will come up in future chapters. That a full and clear picture of the mechanism underlying reasoning competence is not crucial to this inquiry is good news because the discussion that follows fails to produce any strong conclusions about the nature of reasoning competence.

In any event, in the case of reasoning, there is nothing incompatible about there being two ways of looking at competence. Recall that, in the case of linguistic competence, there is a difference between the knowledge and the mechanism view of competence: the mechanism view includes as part of linguistic competence language-specific psychological machinery that is not part of our knowledge of language, while the knowledge of language view does not. It is not obvious in the case of reasoning whether there are reasoning-specific mechanisms that are not part of our knowledge of reasoning. If there are not, then the mechanism and the knowledge view of reasoning competence are equivalent. If there are such mechanisms, then the two views would differ in the same way that they do with respect to linguistic competence. These issues will return when, in Chapter 3, I consider some problems encountered when trying to draw borders around reasoning competence.

2.2. Nativism Applied to Reasoning Competence

To begin, I will sketch some reasons for thinking that our reasoning competence is innate. I will first consider the various sorts of evidence that counted in favour of linguistic nativism to see if similar evidence will count in favour of nativism concerning reasoning. A natural place to start, given the strength of such an argument with respect to linguistic nativism, is with the poverty of stimulus argument. In contrast to the overwhelming empirical evidence about the poverty of stimulus in the realm of language, in the realm of reasoning the evidence mostly comes from armchair psychology. The thought is that children are able to apply principles of reasoning without having been explicitly taught them and without having had adequate experience from which they could infer them. For example, children seem to be able to reason from the statement

> Ernie has a red ball and a blue ball

to the statement

> Ernie has a red ball.

They can do this in novel situations and they are as confident about the truth of the conjunct as they are about the truth of the conjunction. This suggests that they have knowledge of the and-elimination principle.

They seem to have this knowledge even though they have not encountered enough instances of reasoning from particular instances of conjunctions to particular instances of one of the two conjuncts of particular conjunctions to deduce this abstract principle from what they have encountered (no finite number of instances of reasoning from particular sentences of the form *A* **and** *B* to sentences of the form *A* would justify the conclusion that the and-elimination principle is behind these instances of reasoning; no finite number of such instances would justify the confidence that subjects have in the truth of each conjunct). This line of argument suggests that, because children do not have the evidence to learn such rules, they must have some innate principles of reasoning.

The poverty of stimulus argument does not, however, entail that the and-elimination principle is innate. Rather, the argument is supposed to show that there are constraints on the principles of reasoning we can learn. This is parallel to what the poverty of stimulus argument shows about linguistics. In the realm of language, the poverty of stimulus argument does not show that the rules *of English* are innate; rather, it shows that the range of languages that we can learn are limited in particular ways by innate constraints on language learning. The same sort of conclusion is supposed to follow with respect to reasoning: there are innate constraints on the sorts of principles of reasoning we can learn, constraints that enable children to abstract from particular instances of reasoning to a certain range of general rules like the and-elimination principle. This leaves open that the and-elimination principle may be like a principle of English or a principle of our general knowledge of language.

Armchair psychology aside, what sort of experiments might be done to show that children know principles of reasoning before they could have been taught them?[34] Research on infants' ability to do arithmetic may be a good model. This research uses a well-established technique for studying infants. If one shows an infant a particular scene, for

---

[34] In the final stages of preparing this book, some experiments that provide evidence for the innateness of principles of reasoning were brought to my attention by Denise Cummins. See V. Girotto, P. Light, and C. J. Colbourn, 'Pragmatic Reasoning Schemas and Conditional Reasoning in Children', *Quarterly Journal of Experimental Psychology*, 40 (1988), 469–82; V. Girotto, M. Gilly, A. Blaye, and P. Light, 'Children's Performance in the Selection Task: Plausibility and Familiarity', *British Journal of Psychology*, 80 (1989), 79–95; P. Light, A. Blayne, M. Gilly, and V. Girotto, 'Pragmatic Schemas and Logical Reasoning in 6- to 8-year-old Children', *Cognitive Development*, 4 (1989), 49–64; and P. Light, V. Girotto, and P. Legrenzi, 'Children's Reasoning on Conditional Promises and Permissions', *Cognitive Development*, 5 (1990), 369–83.

example, a collection of objects, the infant will look at the scene for a while, become bored, and then look away. If the scene changes, the baby will look at the objects for a while longer than she would have if the scene had remained the same. This technique can be used to tell what sort of differences infants can perceive and, more generally, what sort of cognitive abilities infants have.[35] In some particularly interesting research on infant arithmetic, infants are shown a Mickey Mouse doll and then they are shown the doll being placed behind a screen, thereby making it invisible to them. The same process is repeated with a second Mickey Mouse doll. The screen is then removed. Some infants are shown two Mickey Mouse dolls behind the screen; they look only briefly at the two dolls. Other infants are shown one or three Mickey Mouse dolls behind the screen; they stare for a much longer period of time at what they see. The fact that infants look for a longer period of time at the arithmetically 'impossible' situation ('impossible' from the infant's point of view because one plus one equals two, not one or three)—along with similar experimental results involving subtraction—suggests that infants possess numerical concepts and can manipulate these concepts using basic tools of arithmetic.[36]

I want to glean two things from the research on infant arithmetic. First, such research might serve as a model for how research on nativism about reasoning might be done. Second, the results might be relevant to nativism about reasoning. Mathematics and logic are intimately related. It might be that the principles of reasoning that are based on rules of logic underlie the cognitive mechanism(s) involved in arithmetic. Further experiments are necessary to sort out these questions. The research on arithmetic principles is, however, suggestive.

Another source of evidence for nativism with respect to reasoning has to do with the universality of principles of reasoning. If the principles of reasoning that we follow in this culture are universally followed in all human cultures, this would suggest that the constraints on reasoning are quite tight. For example, if children in all cultures inferred the same particular rule of reasoning from the random and limited collection of instances of reasoning that they have encountered, this

[35] Elizabeth Spelke *et al.*, 'Origins of Knowledge', *Psychological Review*, 99 (1990), 605–32; Elizabeth Spelke, 'Where Perceiving Ends and Thinking Begins', in Albert Yonas (ed.), *Perceptual Development in Infancy* (Hillsdale, NJ: Erlbaum, 1988); and ead., 'Principles of Object Perception', *Cognitive Science*, 14 (1990), 29–56.

[36] Karen Wynn, 'Addition and Subtraction by Human Infants', *Nature*, 358 (1992), 749–50.

would suggest that the constraints on reasoning are so tight as to entail this particular rule. The evidence for such claims is, however, limited,[37] and is thus just suggestive of innateness. Again, more research seems required.

Additionally, there is possible neurological and genetic evidence for the innateness of our reasoning competence. Various neurological disorders such as Alzheimer's disease and cerebral infarction seem to cause people to lose specific cognitive or reasoning capacities while their other capacities remain intact.[38] Also, evidence about genetic disorders that lead to cognitive impairment might help reveal genetic structures that relate to reasoning;[39] in so far as genetic research can reveal that our genes code for domain-specific mechanisms of reasoning, such evidence counts for the innateness of our reasoning competence. Basically, little research has been done specifically on the innateness of our principles of reasoning; the research that I describe is just suggestive of what might be found.

In general, the sort of evidence that establishes linguistic nativism is, at best, suggestive of nativism with respect to reasoning. This difference may be due in part to the limited empirical evidence that we have about reasoning competence, but there are conceptual differences between the two realms that might lead to this disparity. To mention just two: first, some reasoning ability seems required for learning, but the same is not true for language, even if language is necessary for certain sorts of learning; second, there are some considerations (discussed below in Section 2.3) that suggest linguistic competence is modular, but it is not clear that they apply to reasoning competence. These two differences between language and reasoning give rise to considerations that could perhaps be brought to bear on the matter of the innateness of our reasoning competence. I will discuss two such considerations below: what I call the *bootstrap argument* and evidence from non-human animals.

---

[37] See Edwin Hutchins, *Culture and Inference* (Cambridge, Mass.: Harvard University Press, 1980), who argues that our inferential patterns are roughly universal. See also the discussion in Denise Cummins, 'Are Pragmatic Reasoning Schemas Innate?: Some Evidence', paper presented at the Conference on Epistemology and Evolutionary Psychology, Rutgers University, Apr. 1995.

[38] See e.g. Alfonso Caramazza *et al.*, 'Category-Specific Naming Deficit Following Cerebral Infarction', *Nature*, 316 (1985), 439–40.

[39] See also the discussion in Cummins, 'Are Pragmatic Reasoning Schemas Innate?', of U. Firth, J. Morton, and A. M. Leslie, 'The Cognitive Basis of a Biological Disorder: Autism', *Trends in Neuroscience*, 14 (1991), 433–8.

First, at least some part of the human reasoning system must be innate because some ability to draw inferences is required to learn *anything*, including principles of reasoning. Clearly some knowledge is not innate (for example, highly contingent knowledge, like my knowledge that Bill Clinton is President of the United States, cannot be innate). Still, one cannot learn anything new if one does not already have some capacity to make inferences on the basis of experience; this is almost true by definition—one cannot learn anything that is not innate without (at least implicitly) knowing the principles (or having the mechanisms) that enable one to learn. I call this the bootstrap argument for the innateness of reasoning competence. Even the most anti-nativist of thinkers would agree to this argument for the innateness of *some* principles of reasoning. This argument is, however, limited in scope for two reasons. First, it only gives us reason to believe that there is some very small set of principles of reasoning in our reasoning competence that are innate. Second, it is not clear that this argument shows that these bootstrapping principles are specific to reasoning. The bootstrapping argument shows that at least a few principles of reasoning are innate but it does not show that these principles apply to reasoning only; they may be more general principles, principles that constrain reasoning but also constrain other realms (below, I consider and reject an argument that the principles of reasoning are the most general principles). Further argument beyond the bootstrap argument is required to show that there are substantial innate principles specific to reasoning.

Second, there seems to be some evolutionary continuity with respect to human reasoning ability as compared to that of other species; other animals seem to behave in ways that accord with basic principles of reasoning.[40] Animals are relatively good at solving problems, even novel ones, yet it would be quite surprising if animals had any conscious understanding of the principles of reasoning (especially given that humans are not conscious of many of our principles of reasoning—as I will argue below). If these principles are innate in animals then, due to evolutionary continuity, it seems as if humans will have these basic

[40] C. R. Gallistel, *The Organization of Learning* (Cambridge, Mass.: MIT Press, 1990); Steven Walker, *Animal Thought* (Boston: Routledge, 1983); Susan Parker and Kathleen Gibson, *Language and Intelligence in Monkeys and Apes* (Cambridge: Cambridge University Press, 1990); Howard Rachlin *et al.*, 'Cognition and Behavior in Studies of Choice', *Psychological Review*, 93 (1986), 33–45; Richard Herrnstein, 'Level of Stimulus Control: A Functional Approach', *Cognition*, 37 (1990), 133–66; and Donald Griffin, *Animal Thinking* (Cambridge, Mass.: Harvard University Press, 1984). For a discussion of some ethological evidence, see Cummins, 'Are Pragmatic Reasoning Schemas Innate?'

principles of reasoning as well. There is little research, however, that proves animal reasoning ability is innate. For all we know, the general ability to learn principles of reasoning from observing one's environment might be relatively continuous between animals and humans, rather than there being significant continuity with respect to any innate principles of reasoning. In other words, animals might have quite basic innate principles that enable them to learn, but have nothing beyond this. If this is true, then the animal evidence would not count as evidence for the innateness of reasoning-specific rules. At best, animal evidence—because it might lend some support to genetic evidence of innateness—is of interest but it does not show anything conclusive.

Thus far, I have sketched several reasons for thinking that our reasoning competence is innate. These considerations do not constitute overwhelming evidence for nativism with respect to reasoning; further, they do not provide evidence that is as strong as the evidence for the innateness of linguistic knowledge, 'common-sense' (or 'folk') physics, common-sense (human) psychology, and knowledge of number and geometry.[41] Given this, are there any reasons for thinking that nativism about reasoning is wrong? One prima facie plausible idea (especially if one is not familiar with the arguments I discussed above in Section 1) is based on an analogy with language. We might notice that there is a great deal of variation among what particular language people speak—some speak Vietnamese, some speak Hebrew, and so on. As language and reasoning are both cognitive capacities, evidence of linguistic variation is suggestive of variation among other cognitive capacities including reasoning. This line of argument has been suggested by Stephen Stich: 'it may be the case that the strategies of reasoning a person employs, like the language he or she speaks, are determined in large measure by environmental variables and that variation in inferential strategies across persons or societies are largely independent of genetic factors'.[42] Whether this is a plausible claim depends on what exactly Stich means by 'may' here. Of course, there is a sense in which it *might* be the case that most (though not all, because of the bootstrap argument given above) of our inferential principles are learned, in the same way in which it *might* be

---

[41] Elizabeth Spelke, 'Initial Knowledge: Six Suggestions', *Cognition*, 50 (1994), 431–45, reviews the evidence concerning nativism in general and provides references for innateness concerning physics, psychology, and geometry. See also Pinker, *The Language Instinct*, ch. 13.

[42] Stephen Stich, *The Fragmentation of Reason* (Cambridge, Mass.: MIT Press, 1990), 69.

the case that (contrary to fact) people learn how to breathe or innately know how to drive a car with standard transmission. The more interesting question is whether we have any good reason for thinking that people *actually do* learn the inferential practices we use.

From the fact that the particular language a person speaks is not under genetic control but is rather due to a variety of social factors, the idea is to use the analogy with language as a way to argue that a person's reasoning competence may not be under genetic control either. I actually think that the analogy with language can be useful for thinking about reasoning, but I do not think that the argument under consideration draws the correct moral from this analogy. The argument concludes that just as there may be linguistic diversity that would show language is not primarily innate, there may be cognitive diversity that would show the principles of reasoning are not primarily innate.

A nice case for the appeal to linguistic diversity is that of two identical twins, one raised in a Korean-speaking environment and one raised in a Portuguese-speaking environment. The twins have the same genes but speak different languages. This shows that the language people speak is not genetically controlled and hence not innate. This is of course right, but the conclusion can be pushed too far. Consider the case of two twins, one brought up in an environment where she eats a balanced diet, gets lots of exercise, and does lots of other quite healthy things, and the other brought up in an environment where she eats poorly, gets no exercise, smokes cigarettes, and does lots of other *un*healthy things; the twins will end up with radically different body shapes and sizes, habits, personalities, and so forth. This would show, for example, that body size is not completely independent of environmental factors, but it does not show that body size is not *primarily* genetically controlled (it had better not show this, because body size *is* primarily genetic). The point that applies to body size applies to language as well: just because different people speak different languages does not mean that language is not *primarily* genetically controlled. Although there is linguistic diversity, it is the sort of diversity that is compatible with linguistic nativism. Ditto for reasoning: a diversity of reasoning capacities across people is compatible with nativism about reasoning competence.

I said that the analogy between language and reasoning with respect to the degree of innateness is a good one, but not in the way the argument for diversity of reasoning competence suggests. In Section 1, I argued that there are innate constraints on language learning behind all actual and possible (given our brains) human languages. This is consistent with the diversity of human languages and it also explains the similar abstract structure that all human languages have. Similarly, the view that our inferential principles are innate does not suffer from the vice of precluding *some* diversity with respect to reasoning competence; rather, it has the virtue of explaining why humans have structurally similar inferential principles.

A further point can be made: just because some trait is innate does not mean that it is universal. Nativism about reasoning competence is compatible with variation in reasoning ability; if there is such variation, it might be due to genetic differences.[43] Reasoning competence might be like eye colour: eye colour is genetic but there is variation among eye colour, that is, some people have blue eyes, some have brown eyes, and so on. There are, however, good reasons for thinking that there is little variation among our cognitive systems. First of all, even relatively simple cognitive programmes are genetically quite complex, that is, they involve many steps and probably are coded for on several different genes. As a result, they will evolve quite slowly, biologically speaking, and the odds that there would be much intra-species variation of cognitive programmes will be quite small. If we think of our reasoning capacities as constituting a mental organ (more on this issue in what follows) that is roughly analogous to a bodily organ, then, just as it is quite odd for a human to be born without a kidney or with a dramatically different organ in place of a kidney, it would be quite odd for a human to be born without a language organ or without the capacity for reasoning or with a dramatically different sort of capacity for language or reasoning. The point is that the amount of variation that is likely to occur in people's reasoning capacities as a result of genetic variation is going to be small. The reason for the small amount of genetic variation between people with respect to complex organs has to do with the details of sexual reproduction. In sexual reproduction, genetic material from an organism's two parents is combined in a novel way through the random shuffling of chromosomes. If there was a great deal of genetic variation among organisms of the same species, sexual reproduction between two dramatically different organisms would result in offspring that are unable to perform the crucial roles that our complex organs play. As Steve Pinker nicely puts it: 'If two people really had different designs, their offspring would inherit a mishmash of fragments from genetic

---

[43] Stich, ibid. 72–3, makes this point as well.

blueprints of each—as if the plans for two [quite different] cars were cut up with scissors and the pieces taped back together without our caring about which scrap originally came from which car.'[44] There is unlikely to be much genetic variation among humans with respect to the reasoning mechanism due to the details of sexual reproduction.[45]

One might reply by pointing out that human reproductive systems and organs are quite complex but there is rather significant variation between male and female reproductive systems. There might be similar sexual dimorphism with respect to reasoning competence.[46] This suggestion might seem particularly plausible because of apparent differences in reasoning between males and females[47] and evidence of other cognitive differences between males and females (for example, with respect to mating strategies[48]), and because of differential evolutionary pressures on males and females.[49] I am not convinced by this evidence for several reasons. First, the dimorphism that exists between male and female reproductive systems is what makes sexual reproduction possible. Once sexual reproduction is in place, the difference-minimizing effects of sexual reproduction described above occur. For this reason, the dimorphism of human reproductive systems is likely to be the major innate difference within (normal) humans; it is a mistake to infer that dimorphism is likely in other human systems on the basis of this one case. Second, the different reproductive systems and organs of males and females come from very similar genetic codes; most of the differences are the result of hormones. A chromosomal male that for some reason does not receive the appropriate doses of masculinizing hormones at critical periods will not develop a typical male reproductive system. Were it not for the influences of hormones, chromosomal males

---

[44] Pinker, *The Language Instinct*, 326.

[45] For a more extensive discussion of these points, see Leda Cosmides and John Tooby, 'From Evolution to Behavior: Evolutionary Psychology as the Missing Link', in John Dupré (ed.), *The Latest on the Best* (Cambridge, Mass.: MIT Press, 1987), esp. 304; and John Tooby and Leda Cosmides, 'On the Universality of Human Nature and the Uniqueness of the Individual: The Role of Genetics and Adaptation', *Journal of Personality*, 58 (1990), 17–67.

[46] Steve Stich made this suggestion to me in discussion.

[47] See e.g. Carol Gilligan, *In a Different Voice: Psychological Theory and Women's Development* (Cambridge, Mass.: Harvard University Press, 1982); and the writings of feminist epistemologists, for example, Sandra Harding, *The Science Question in Feminism* (Ithaca, NY: Cornell University Press, 1986); for a survey, see Mary Hawkesworth, 'Feminist Epistemology: A Survey of the Field', *Women and Philosophy*, 7 (1987), 112–24.

[48] Most recently, for example, David Buss, *The Evolution of Desire* (New York: Basic Books, 1994).   [49] See e.g. ibid.

and females would have similar reproductive systems. Although there is some evidence to suggest that hormones have an influence on the brain, there is no particular evidence these influences will affect reasoning competence.[50] Third, the apparent differences in reasoning competence between males and females may be primarily due to environmental factors rather than to biological ones. For example, there is considerable evidence to suggest that parents and schoolteachers treat young males and females differently. These environmental differences might be the source of what differences in reasoning there are between males and females. This is not to deny that there are differences, but rather to deny that they are genetic in nature. Fourth, the fact that males and females need to communicate and understand each other suggests that there will be evolutionary pressures for them to have the same or similar reasoning competence. If males and females employed different principles of reasoning, they would have a hard time understanding each other, making plans together, and so on.[51] These four considerations do not prove that there will be no sexual dimorphism with respect to reasoning competence, but they do provide strong reasons for thinking that all 'normal' humans have roughly the same reasoning competence.

This discussion gives rise to the question of whether human reasoning competence is a mental organ (like the eye or the language organ), that is, whether it is a cognitive system that constitutes a functional unit in roughly the way that a bodily organ does. Human reasoning is like the eye and the language faculty and *un*like the body parts involved in batting. Although there are various parts to the human reasoning system (particular parts of the system are involved in making particular inferences, probability judgements, and so on) and although these parts may result from different genes, they work together to perform an adaptive function (reasoning) and they are useful only in virtue of playing a role in the reasoning process. For example, the and-elimination principle on its own will not do much good. Its usefulness is dramatically increased in the presence of other principles of reasoning. This suggests that there is what might be called an inferential or reasoning organ.

Note, however, that none of what I have said establishes that the reasoning organ is a mental module, that is, a domain-specific, innately

---

[50] For a discussion relating to these two points, see Anne Fausto-Sterling, *Myths of Gender* (New York: Basic Books, 1985).

[51] This is a sketch of a detailed discussion in Roy Sorensen, 'Self-Strengthening Empathy', unpub. MS. Conversations with Sorensen on this matter as they relate to his article and his book 'I to I', in preparation, have influenced my thinking here.

specified, hardwired, autonomous, non-assembled mental organ. I want to consider briefly and reject an argument that our reasoning competence is not a module because it is not autonomous, that is, not insulated from other cognitive mechanisms. According to this argument, our principles of reasoning are quite general: they can be applied in a whole range of domains. We can have beliefs about anything and we may need to make inferences on the basis of any of these beliefs. The generality of the principles of reasoning suggests that they are not autonomous, which in turn suggests that they are not modular.[52]

This argument seems to confuse two different kinds of generality. Reasoning is only general in the sense that language is. We can reason about almost anything and we can talk about almost anything. This sort of generality—generality in terms of the content that a mental organ can range over—does not imply that a capacity is general in the sense that the principles that make it up are not domain-specific. The principles that constitute linguistic competence are not general in terms of their scope—the principles that characterize linguistic competence enable language use and comprehension, not vision or motor control. The same may well be true of reasoning competence. The principles that constitute reasoning competence might only be good for reasoning even though they are good for reasoning about almost any topic. The sense in which reasoning and language are both general does not entail that they are not insulated from other cognitive mechanisms; for all we know, our reasoning organ might be a reasoning module.[53]

The main purpose of this section has been to make somewhat plausible the view that human reasoning competence is based on reasoning-specific innate principles. Even if the evidence for the innateness of principles of reasoning is not as strong as that for the innateness of linguistic competence, there are some reasons for thinking that humans have a reasoning competence that is innate.

2.3. The Normative Component to Reasoning Competence

There is an important distinction between linguistic competence and reasoning competence that has to do with their relations to normative accounts of language and reasoning respectively. An account of a cognitive system is descriptive, that is, it says how the system in fact

---

[52] Fodor, *The Modularity of Mind, passim.*
[53] Paul Bloom helped me get clear on these issues.

TABLE 2.1. *The existence of norms and the relation between norms and competence in two realms*

Question about a realm	Language	Reasoning
Does it have a normative component?	yes	yes
Does giving an account of human competence have implications for what the norms are?	yes	no

behaves. Such an account may have a normative component as well, that is, it may implicitly say how the system *ought* to behave in order to best accomplish its function. Giving an account of linguistic competence has such normative implications. When a linguist offers an account of linguistic competence, she is giving a description of the capacity for language *and* she is articulating what the norms of human natural language are: a person should use a language that accords with the principles of linguistic competence, or else she might not be understood. In the realm of reasoning, as in the realm of language, there are straightforward normative principles. Giving an account of reasoning competence is, according to the standard picture of rationality, unlike giving an account of linguistic competence in that giving such an account does not have any normative implications. In Chapter 7, I will defend the naturalized picture of rationality, according to which giving an account of human reasoning competence does have implications for what the normative principles of reasoning are. For now, I assume the standard picture of rationality. See Table 2.1 for a summary of the view that results from such an assumption.

A disclaimer is needed here. Talk of the normative implications of an account of linguistic competence may cause some linguists to cringe. Linguists typically shun the notion that their discipline has a normative component. What they mean when they do so is that linguists should avoid the temptation to be *prescriptive*, for example, to say that English speakers should not use the word 'ain't'.[54] This does not mean that linguists think a person can use just any words to communicate a particular thought. Even the most virulent anti-prescriptivists use dictionaries and spell-checkers and correct other people's grammatical mistakes.

---

[54] For more on why linguistics should not be prescriptive, see Pinker, *The Language Instinct, passim*, esp. ch. 12.

Linguists agree that there are rules of English that we should follow if we want to communicate clearly. Anti-prescriptivists about language argue that languages should be allowed to evolve. For example, we should not say that it is wrong to occasionally split infinitives; this is acceptable because enough people no longer follow such a rule to create a social consensus against it. But even when linguists avoid being prescriptive in this sense, linguistics is still normative in the sense with which I am concerned—that is, it is normative in the sense in which an account of linguistic competence entails an account of the linguistic competence people *ought* to have.

To return to the difference between linguistic and reasoning competence, consider the following thought experiment. Suppose the human brain was constructed in such a way that linguistic competence was altered in a small but non-trivial way: some basic linguistic patterns that are in fact judged grammatical, would, if some part of the brain that deals with language were constructed differently, be judged ungrammatical (call these type A patterns) and some linguistic patterns that are in fact judged ungrammatical would, if the brain were constructed differently, be judged grammatical (call these type B patterns). In such a case, both linguistic competence and linguistic norms would change. If our brain were constructed differently, not only would type A patterns be *judged* ungrammatical and type B patterns be *judged* grammatical, but type A patterns would *be* ungrammatical and type B patterns would *be* grammatical. In other words, there is nothing grammatical about linguistic patterns that are in fact grammatical (for example, type A linguistic patterns) or ungrammatical about linguistic patterns that are in fact ungrammatical (for example, type B linguistic patterns) independent of the actual structure of the human brain. That human linguistic competence matches the normative principles of linguistics is true in the imagined case just as in the actual case because the normative principles of linguistics are read off linguistic competence.

Consider the same sort of case with respect to reasoning. Suppose that the rationality thesis is true and human reasoning competence matches the normative principles of reasoning. Now imagine the brain was constructed differently and certain principles humans in fact follow were, as a result of the different brain structure, not followed (call these type A principles). Further, imagine certain other principles that humans in fact do *not* follow were, as a result of the different brain structures, followed (call these type B principles). If this were the situation, someone who thinks that humans are *in fact* rational would have to say that humans, in this counterfactual situation, are *not* rational. This is because, by embracing the rationality thesis, one is accepting that the principles of reasoning that are in fact embodied in our reasoning competence are the right principles. This further commits one to the claim that any *other* principles (for example, type B princïples) are the *wrong* ones. This is different from language. The disanalogy is this: linguistic norms (principles of grammaticality) are *relative* to linguistic competence, while norms of reasoning (principles of rationality) do not seem to be relative to reasoning competence. Even if in fact human reasoning competence matches the norms of reasoning, it does not seem to do so because the norms are indexed to actual competence as they are in linguistics. This is the difference between linguistic competence and its relation to grammaticality on the one hand and reasoning competence and its relation to rationality on the other. The difference stems from the fact that giving an account of linguistic competence implies some norms while giving an account of reasoning competence does not. There are some arguments against our strong intuition that the normative principles of reasoning are not indexed to human reasoning competence. I will consider such arguments in future chapters (Chapters 5 and 7, primarily). Such arguments have their work cut out for them, because the difference between reasoning and language on the matter of the relationship between human competence and the normative principles in these realms seems basic to our understanding of rationality.

Matters are actually trickier than this discussion suggests because there is a normative part implicit in any descriptive account of a system, and I want to distinguish this normative part of simply giving a description of a component of a cognitive system from the normative implications that such an account can have, and, in particular, that it does have in the case of giving an account of linguistic competence. Any account of a competence involves some idealization and, as such, is normative—distinguishing between (actual) behaviour and (idealized) competence involves, at least implicitly, making normative claims. This is the normative part of the descriptive component, *not* the normative implications that giving an account of linguistic competence has: by giving an account of linguistic competence, one is (at least implicitly) saying what counts as correct human linguistic behaviour, that is, one is saying what the norms are.

The rationality thesis claims that the principles that characterize our reasoning competence match the normative principles of reasoning; the

norms are the same as the principles that describe the unfettered operation of the mechanism that underlies our reasoning capacity. It is tempting
for friends of the rationality thesis to draw on an analogy with language. In linguistics, as I have argued above, articulating an account of
linguistic competence implicitly articulates an account of the normative
principles of language (that is, the principles of grammaticality). If the
same was true in the realm of reasoning, the rationality thesis would
thereby be established. In other words, *if* articulating an account of
reasoning competence implicitly articulated an account of the normative principles of reasoning (which it does not)—that is, if the norms
of reasoning were indexed to actual reasoning competence—then the
rationality thesis would thereby be true. But reasoning is not like
language in the relevant way; the normative principles of reasoning are
not indexed to reasoning competence.

None of what I have said so far entails that the rationality thesis is
false. It is perfectly consistent with all of these considerations that the
normative principles of reasoning and the principles that characterize
reasoning competence match. My point is that it takes some argument
to show that they do; an analogy to linguistics is not enough to show
that they do.

Special care needs to be taken in the realm of reasoning not to
confuse giving a descriptive account of reasoning competence and giving a normative account of reasoning. Giving a descriptive account of
reasoning competence involves offering an empirically discoverable
set of principles that characterize our underlying capacity to reason. In
contrast, giving a normative account of reasoning involves offering a
set of principles that characterize how we ought to reason. While it
might be the case that these accounts would, as friends of the rationality
thesis argue, be the same (as their analogues are in linguistics), it begs
the question against the irrationality thesis to *assume* that a description
of what principles humans actually use matches the normative principles of reasoning. Making such an assumption would be tantamount to
using the competence–performance distinction as an immunization
strategy in reasoning. If it is *assumed* that the norms of reasoning are
indexed to reasoning competence, then any empirical evidence that
humans diverge from the norms of reasoning will a priori be explained
as performance errors. The results of the reasoning experiments, for
example, would a priori count as performance errors and hence as not
characteristic of human reasoning competence. As such, the competence–
performance distinction would be operating as an immunization strategy

within the realm of reasoning in the very way that I argued that it is not and must not be used in linguistics.

My argument here is important for future discussions in this book, so it is worth reviewing. Friends of the rationality thesis and of the irrationality thesis need to claim that humans have a reasoning competence; in this respect, the analogy with language and linguistic competence helps both of their cases. If friends of the rationality thesis try to use the existence of reasoning competence as itself constituting an argument for the rationality thesis, they are begging the question; they need an additional argument to establish their view. Seen another way, to use the competence–performance distinction as a way of showing that all errors of reasoning are performance errors—and thus that humans are rational—is to use this distinction as an immunization strategy, that is, to protect it from any possible falsification.

There is quite a lot, I think, to be learned by comparing reasoning to language. Throughout this book, I will often appeal to this analogy. The analogy can be pushed too far, and friends of the rationality thesis are particularly susceptible to doing this. In particular, the analogy between linguistics and reasoning is pushed too far when one *assumes* that the normative principles of reasoning are indexed to reasoning competence in the way that the principles of grammaticality are indexed to linguistic competence. I shall refer to this as assuming that a *strong analogy* holds between language and reasoning. There is a strong analogy between language and reasoning if the normative principles of reasoning match the rules that characterize reasoning competence in the way that the principles of grammaticality match the rules that characterize linguistic competence. While *some* analogy surely holds between linguistic competence and reasoning competence, it is a significant further step to show that a *strong* analogy holds between them—at least, prima facie, there may be a difference between the normative principles of reasoning and the competence that underlies human reasoning behaviour.

To clarify this notion of a strong analogy holding between language and some other realm, I offer an example. Consider how the competence–performance distinction might apply to ethics (assuming the truth of realism in ethics). Humans have an ability to make ethical judgements. No doubt, this ability may be interfered with in various ways—for example, excessive drug use—so it might be useful to talk of humans as having an ethical competence (even though this competence may well not be a mental module, a mental organ, and it may not be predominantly innate[55]). Further, we can imagine that this ethical competence is characterized by rules that match the normative principles of ethics (the principles of morality) or that it diverges from them, namely, someone could have an underlying ethical competence that, performance errors aside, sanctions only the morally right actions but also someone could have an ethical competence that often sanctions *immoral* actions. If our ethical competence matched the correct ethical theory, then a strong analogy would hold between ethics and language. But if this ethical competence diverges from the normative principles of morality, then only a weak analogy would apply. It is possible that a strong analogy might hold between ethics and language; our ethical competence could well be characterized by principles that match the norms of morality. To push the analogy too far would be to *assume*, in virtue of the applicability of the competence–performance distinction to ethics, that ethical competence matches the principles of morality. Whether or not ethical competence matches the principles of morality requires *further* argument than just applying the competence–performance distinction to the realm of ethics.

The main point that is relevant to the rationality thesis is that more of an argument than just establishing the existence of reasoning competence and the various similarities between linguistics and reasoning is required to show that humans are rational. It is a mistake to *assume* that rationality is entailed by reasoning competence.

[55] For arguments that there is an underlying ethical capacity that is innate, see e.g. Edward O. Wilson, *Sociobiology* (Cambridge, Mass.: Harvard University Press, 1975); id. and Charles Lumsden, *Genes, Minds and Culture* (Cambridge, Mass.: Harvard University Press, 1981); eid., *Promethean Fire* (Cambridge, Mass.: Harvard University Press, 1983); and Michael Ruse, *Taking Darwin Seriously* (Oxford: Blackwell, 1986).

3

Psychological Evidence

THE primary evidence for the irrationality thesis—the view that humans have an underlying ability to reason that is appropriately characterized by principles that diverge from the normative principles of reasoning—comes from psychological research concerning human reasoning. Such research is supposed to show that humans *systematically* violate basic principles of reasoning. In this chapter, I review two important psychological experiments. I choose them not just because they are paradigmatic of the reasoning experiments that are supposed to bear on the question of human rationality but because these particular experiments have been extensively discussed by philosophers and psychologists alike. The first experiment concerns whether we reason in accordance with principles of reasoning based on rules of logic and the second concerns whether we reason in accordance with principles of reasoning based on rules of probability theory. Both experiments seem prima facie to provide evidence that human reasoning competence diverges from the normative principles of reasoning.

As part of the discussion of each experiment, I will review particular instances of a general strategy to reconcile such experimental results with the rationality thesis. The strategy involves saying that subjects are in some way *misinterpreting* the experimental task before them; appropriately applied, this strategy is supposed to show that these experiments do not provide insight into human reasoning competence but instead uncover the variety of performance errors humans make. I do not attempt to discuss every possible way of interpreting the results of these reasoning experiments. Instead I try, first, to assess the plausibility of some obvious interpretations and, second, to assess the general strategy of favouring interpretations of the reasoning experiments that are compatible with the rationality thesis. Although much of this chapter focuses on the details of the two reasoning experiments and related research, in a way the particular details of the experiments are not crucial. What matters are the general features of these experiments that seem to support the irrationality thesis and the validity of the strategy that attempts to reconcile them with the rationality thesis.

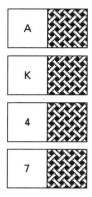

Fig. 3.1. *The basic selection task*

1. An Experiment Concerning Deductive Logic

1.2. The Basic Selection Task

In 1966 Peter Wason published the results of an experiment that tested human ability to apply principles of deductive logic.[1] This experiment involves a deck of cards with a number on one side and a letter on the other. Subjects are presented with four cards from this deck, each with one side covered and the other side visible. The four cards show a vowel, a consonant, an even number, and an odd number, respectively, say 'A', 'K', '4', and '7' (see Fig. 3.1). Subjects are then asked which cards they will need to see completely in order to test the truth of the rule

> If a card has a vowel on one side, then it has an even number on the other side.

Most of the subjects answered either that the covered sides of the cards showing 'A' and '4' need to be examined to test the rule or that just the card showing 'A' needs to be examined. The *correct* solution is

---

[1] The pilot study is Peter Wason, 'Reasoning', in Brian Foss (ed.), *New Horizons in Psychology* (Harmondsworth: Penguin, 1966). A more extensive experiment is reported in Wason, 'Reasoning about a Rule', *Quarterly Journal of Experimental Psychology*, 20 (1968), 273–81. For a detailed discussion, see Peter Wason and Philip Johnson-Laird, *Psychology of Reasoning* (Cambridge, Mass.: Harvard University Press, 1972), chs. 13–15. For a recent summary, see Keith Manktelow and D. E. Over, *Inference and Understanding* (New York: Routledge, 1990), ch. 6.

TABLE 3.1. *The truth table for* **if** p, **then** q

p	q	if p, then q
T	T	T
T	F	F
F	T	T
F	F	T

TABLE 3.2. *The truth table for the selection task*

Card showing	p	q	if p, then q
'A'	T	?	?
'K'	F	?	T
'4'	?	T	T
'7'	?	F	?

to look at the 'A' and the '7' cards; very few subjects said the '7' card should be one of the cards that is examined.

Which cards should be examined follows from a straightforward application of rules of logic. The rule subjects are asked to test ('If a card has a vowel on one side, then it has an even number on the other side') is a simple conditional statement of the form **if** p, **then** q. For a conditional to be true, it must be the case that when the antecedent (p, that is, 'the card has a vowel on one side') is true, the consequent (q, that is, 'the card has an even number on the other side') must be true (see Table 3.1 for a truth table of **if** p, **then** q). To test a conditional, one looks for cases in which the antecedent (p) is true but the consequent (q) is false. Subjects should follow the following principle:

CONDITIONAL-TESTING PRINCIPLE: To test the truth of a conditional, examine cases where the antecedent is true to make sure that the consequent is true and examine cases where the consequent is false to make sure the antecedent is false.

In the selection task as pictured in Fig. 3.1, the 'A' card needs to be checked because if it has an odd number on the other side, the antecedent will be true but the consequent false. Looking at the first row of Table 3.2, the truth-value of the conditional **if** p, **then** q can*not* be assessed without knowing whether the other side of the 'A' card has an odd or even number on it (that is, whether q is true or false). The 'K' card need not be checked because the antecedent is false—no matter what is on the other side (an odd or even number), the conditional will be true. Looking at Table 3.2, the truth-value of the conditional **if** p, **then** q in the 'K' card case *can* be known without looking at the unseen side of the card; if the antecedent is false, then the conditional is true no matter what the truth-value of the antecedent is. The '4' card, for similar reasons, need not be checked to test the truth of the conditional. Whether there is a vowel or consonant on the other side, the rule in question will not be violated. The conditional in the '4' card case will be true whether or not the antecedent is. Finally, the '7' card *does* need to be examined to see whether it has a vowel on the other side; if it does, then the conditional is false (because the antecedent would be true—the card has a vowel on it—and the consequent would be false—the card does not have an even number on it) and if it does not, then the conditional is true (because the antecedent would be false).

As this discussion has shown, subjects *should* examine the 'A' and '7' cards. Most subjects, however, fail to do so and thereby fail to follow the conditional-testing principle. In a typical version of this experiment, 33 per cent of the subjects said that just the 'A' card needs to be examined, 46 per cent said that both the 'A' and the 'K' cards need to be examined, and 17 per cent said that some other combination of the cards need to be examined; *less than 5 per cent* of the subjects said that both the 'A' and the '7' cards need to be examined, the correct selection.[2] Similar results have been found when the experiment is changed along various dimensions.

Not only is this mistake in reasoning common, it is also well entrenched. Some subjects continued to make the wrong selection in the selection task even after repeated trials. For example, a subject is shown the cards pictured above in Fig. 3.1. After she makes her selection, she is shown that the '7' card *could* falsify the rule and that the 'K' and the '4' card could *not*. This having been done, the subject is presented with another four cards. Many subjects continue to make mistaken predictions even after repeated trials.[3] Further, many subjects will stick to

[2] Wason and Johnson-Laird, *Psychology of Reasoning*, 182, table 14; I have converted the raw data into percentages.

[3] M. A. M. Hughes, 'The Use of Negative Information in Concept Attainment', Ph.D. thesis, University of London, 1966; see discussion in Wason and Johnson-Laird, *Psychology of Reasoning*, 178–9.

their erroneous selections even when they are made to realize that the general principles behind their choices are mistaken. For example, a subject who selects the '4' card would be confronted with the fact that the '4' card will *not* conflict with the rule 'If a card has a vowel on one side, then it has an even number on the other side' whether it has, for example, an 'I' or a 'R' on the back of it. Despite this, the subject might still insist that her choice of the '4' card was correct.[4]

1.2. The Concrete Selection Task

Studies have shown that in slightly different contexts, subjects do much better at applying the very same rules that they fail to apply properly in the standard selection task. Consider a *concrete* version of the selection task in which subjects are presented with a deck of cards each with the name of a city on one side of it and a mode of transportation on the other. Subjects are told to imagine each card as representing a trip made by the experimenter. They are asked to test whether a rule like

Every time I go to New York, I travel by train

is true of four cards respectively showing 'New York', 'Boston', 'train', and 'car' (see Fig. 3.2). Almost two-thirds of the subjects correctly selected the cards showing 'New York' and 'car' to examine; this is dramatically better than the less than 10 per cent who picked the correct cards in the standard selection task.[5]

The question that arises from the results of concrete versions of the selection task is why concreteness makes a difference in subjects' ability to apply principles based on rules of logic. In attempting to account for the different reasoning behaviours on the concrete versus the abstract selection task, psychologists have tended to prefer accounts that are most easily reconcilable with the rationality thesis. In particular, they have tended to prefer accounts of human reasoning ability on which

---

[4] See Wason, 'Reasoning about a Rule'; id., 'Regression in Reasoning?', *British Journal of Psychology*, 60 (1969), 471–80; id. and Philip Johnson-Laird, 'A Conflict between Selecting and Evaluating Information in an Inferential Task', *British Journal of Psychology*, 61 (1970), 509–15; and the discussion in eid., *Psychology of Reasoning*, ch. 15.

[5] This experiment is from Peter Wason and D. Shapiro, 'Natural and Contrived Experience in a Reasoning Problem', *Quarterly Journal of Experimental Psychology*, 23 (1971), 63–71. Philip Johnson-Laird *et al.*, 'Reasoning and a Sense of Reality', *British Journal of Psychology*, 63 (1972), 395–400, discuss another concrete version of the selection task. These experiments and related ones are discussed in Wason and Johnson-Laird, *Psychology of Reasoning*, chs. 14 and 15.

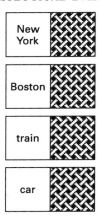

FIG. 3.2. *The concrete selection task*

human reasoning competence is characterizable as matching the normative principles of reasoning and to classify divergences from these norms as performance errors. When their experimental results suggest that humans are not rational, psychologists typically favour accounts of reasoning competence that involve content-*independent* rules, that is, accounts on which humans have principles of reasoning that are not' indexed to specific features of the content of the material that is the object of reasoning. These accounts can then be combined with some story involving performance errors in order to reconcile the rationality thesis with the experimental results that at first glance seem to favour the irrationality thesis. According to a content-independent account, the only effect that content can have is to facilitate (or interfere with) the application of the principles of reasoning that are in our reasoning competence. Note that the normative principles of reasoning are themselves content-independent; they apply to any domain. So, for example, the modus ponens principle that says if you believe two statements **if** *p*, **then** *q* and *p* then you should also believe *q*, applies both to abstract tasks and concrete tasks—it is a perfectly general principle that applies for any *p* or *q*. The same is true for the conditional-testing principle. A simple content-*dependent* principle of reasoning would say, for example, that if you believe the two statements **if** *p*, **then** *q* and *p* then you should only believe *q* if *p* and *q* are both statements about eating, transportation, or sexual activity. If we had this content-*dependent* rule in our reasoning competence, we would diverge from the normative principles when performing abstract tasks like the basic selection task but we would reason in accordance with them in certain concrete tasks like the city-transportation version of the selection task.

Psychologists have tried to develop content-independent rules to characterize our reasoning competence that would both explain our failure to follow the normative principles in the abstract task and, at the same time, explain our success at doing so in some concrete tasks. Among the virtues of doing this would be to preserve the rationality thesis. One general attempt to use content-independent rules of reasoning is called the *memory-cueing hypothesis*.[6] The idea is that if the content of the reasoning task is in some way familiar to the subject, then the appropriate principle of reasoning will be triggered and applied; if the content is *not* familiar, then the appropriate principle will not be triggered. Thus when I am asked to reason about familiar situations like taking a car to Boston, I am able to reason correctly, that is, I am able to apply principles like the modus ponens principle and the conditional-testing principle. When asked to reason about unfamiliar situations like abstract cases or cases involving unfamiliar concrete scenarios, I am, however, unable to apply the correct principle of reasoning because the unfamiliar situation fails to trigger the principle. According to the memory-cueing hypothesis, our reasoning competence is characterized by rules that are content-*independent* because the rules could apply to any situation regardless of its content so long as the situation is familiar to the subject; in time, almost any content could become familiar. To friends of the rationality thesis, the memory-cueing account has the virtue of seeing humans as having the right principles of reasoning in our reasoning competence. When we reason in ways that are not rational, according to this theory, it is not because of a problem with our reasoning competence but because of a failure to call up the right principle of reasoning.

The problem with the memory-cueing hypothesis is that it does not seem to characterize much of the relevant experimental data correctly: subjects make correct selections in some unfamiliar situations and they

[6] Richard Griggs, 'The Role of Problem Content in the Wason Selection Task and THOG Problem', in Jonathan Evans (ed.), *Thinking and Reasoning* (London: Routledge & Kegan Paul, 1983). The memory-cueing hypothesis comes in many flavours. See e.g. Johnson-Laird *et al.*, 'Reasoning and a Sense of Reality'; and the discussion in Jonathan Evans, *The Psychology of Deductive Reasoning* (London: Routledge & Kegan Paul, 1982), 180–8. For an early critique, see Keith Manktelow and Jonathan Evans, 'Facilitation of Reasoning by Realism: Effect or Non-effect', *British Journal of Psychology*, 70 (1979), 477–88.

make incorrect selections in some situations that are familiar. Perhaps the most interesting version of the selection task that shows the problem with the memory-cueing hypothesis is one designed by Leda Cosmides and replicated by Gerd Gigerenzer.[7] This experiment shows, among other things, that the memory-cueing hypothesis is mistaken. In this experiment, subjects are divided into two groups. One of the two groups is told the following story (called the *unfamiliar social contract story*):

You are a Kaluame, a member of a Polynesian culture found only on Maku Island in the Pacific. The Kaluame have many strict laws which must be followed, and the elders have entrusted you with enforcing them. Among the Kaluame, when a man marries, he gets a tattoo on his face: only married men have tattoos on their faces. . . . Cassava root is a powerful aphrodisiac—it makes the man who eats it irresistible to women. Moreover, it is delicious and nutritious—and very scarce. Unlike cassava root, molo nuts are very common, but they are poor eating—molo nuts taste bad, they are not very nutritious, and they have no interesting 'medicinal' properties. Although everyone craves cassava root, eating it is a privilege that your people closely ration. You are a very sensual people . . . but you have very strict sexual mores. The elders particularly disapprove of sexual relations between unmarried people, and particularly distrust the motives and intentions of bachelors. Therefore, the elders have made laws governing rationing privileges. The one you have been entrusted to enforce is as follows: 'If a man eats a cassava root, then he must have a tattoo on his face.' Cassava root is so powerful an aphrodisiac, that many men are tempted to cheat on this law whenever the elders are not looking. The cards below have information about four young men sitting in a temporary camp . . . A tray filled with cassava root and molo nuts has been left for them. Each card represents one man. One side of the card tells which food a man is eating, and the other side of the card tells whether or not the man has a tattoo on his face. Your job is to catch men whose sexual desires might tempt them to break the law—if any get past you, you and your family will be disgraced. Indicate only those card(s) you definitely need to turn over *to see if any of these Kaluame men are breaking the law*.[8]

The other group is told the following story (called the *unfamiliar descriptive story*):

You are an anthropologist studying Kaluame people, a Polynesian culture found only on Maku Island in the Pacific. Before leaving for Maku Island, you read

[7] Leda Cosmides, 'The Logic of Selection: Has Natural Selection Shaped how Humans Reason? Studies with the Wason Selection Task', *Cognition*, 31 (1989), 187–276; and Gerd Gigerenzer and Klaus Hug, 'Domain-Specific Reasoning: Social Contracts, Cheating and Perspective Change', *Cognition*, 43 (1992), 127–71.

[8] Cosmides, 'The Logic of Selection', 263–4.

a report that says some Kaluame men have tattoos on their faces, and that they either eat cassava root or molo nuts, but not both. The author of the report, who did not speak the language, said the following relation seemed to hold: 'If a man eats a cassava root, then he must have a tattoo on his face.' You decide to investigate your colleague's peculiar claim. When you arrive on Maku Island, you learn that cassava root is a starchy staple food found on the south end of the island. Molo nuts are very high in protein, and grow on molo trees, which are primarily found on the island's north shore. You also learn that bachelors live primarily on the north shore, but when men marry, they usually move to the south end of the island. When a Kaluame man marries, he gets a tattoo on his face; only married men have tattoos on their faces . . . Perhaps men are simply eating foods which are most available to them. The cards below have information about four Kaluame men sitting in a temporary camp at the center of the island. Each man is eating either cassava root or molo nuts which he has brought with him from home. Each card represents one man. One side of the card tells which food a man is eating and the other side of the card tells whether or not the man has a tattoo on his face. The rule laid out by your colleague may not be true; you want to see for yourself. Indicate only those card(s) you definitely need to turn over *to see if any of these Kaluame men are breaking the rule*.[9]

In both groups, subjects are presented with the rule

> If a man eats a cassava root, then he must have a tattoo on his face

and then they are presented with the four cards showing 'eats cassava root', 'has tattoo on face', 'eats molo nuts', and 'has no tattoo on face' (see Fig. 3.3).

If a version of the memory-cueing hypothesis is correct, then the responses on the two versions of the cassava root problem (a) should be the same since the rules subjects are asked to test are the same and (b) should diverge from the normative principles of reasoning since the rule they are asked to evaluate is quite unfamiliar. In fact, neither of these two outcomes holds: subjects perform very well on the social contract version of the task (over three-quarters of them correctly decided to examine the cassava root and the no tattoo cards) and rather poorly on the descriptive version of the task (about one-third or less of the subjects examined the correct cards in this task).[10]

The cassava root experiment shows that subjects can perform well on some unfamiliar rules. Other experiments have produced results that show subjects *fail* to perform well on some familiar ones. In one such

---

[9] Ibid. 265–6.   [10] Ibid., and Gigerenzer and Hug, 'Domain-Specific Reasoning'.

FIG. 3.3. *The unfamiliar selection task*

experiment, subjects were presented with a deck of cards that referred to what the experimenter ate and drank at a particular meal. Then they were presented with a rule like

If I eat pork, then I drink red wine

and with the four cards showing 'ate pork', 'ate shrimp', 'drank red wine', and 'drank beer' (see Fig. 3.4). Subjects performed roughly the same on the food and drink selection task as they did on the abstract selection task, suggesting that familiarity does not necessarily trigger the normative rules of reasoning.[11] Together with the cassava root version of the selection task, this version of the selection task suggests that the memory-cueing hypothesis is mistaken.

Results like these have lead some psychologists to consider whether we have content-*dependent* rules of reasoning in our reasoning competence. In particular, there are the accounts of Cosmides, on the one hand, and Cheng and Holyoak,[12] on the other. Cheng and Holyoak's account, called *pragmatic reasoning schema theory*, focuses on whether a particular version of the experimental task fits an abstract reasoning pattern that has been induced from experience. These induced patterns are abstract enough to be applied in different reasoning situations. Because they have been induced from a limited amount of experience

[11] Manktelow and Evans, 'Facilitation of Reasoning by Realism'.
[12] Patricia Cheng and Keith Holyoak, 'Pragmatic Reasoning Schemas', *Cognitive Psychology*, 17 (1985), 391–416.

FIG. 3.4. *The food and drink selection task*

(rather than deduced from an examination of principles of logic, probability, and the like), these principles will be pragmatic. An example of a pragmatic reasoning schema is one that involves the granting of permission. In abstract form, the permission granting schema would be:

If pre-conditions are met, then grant permission.

An example of a permission schema would be one followed by an usher at a theatre to decide whether to admit someone to the theatre. An instance of the permission schema that he might follow is:

If the person has a ticket, then let her into the theatre.

The idea is that through repeated experience with appropriately similar reasoning situations, we induce principles that guide our reasoning. These principles are content-*dependent* (the principles make reference to the particular details of the subject-matter that is being reasoned about rather than just to the formal structure of the subject-matter) but the induction process that produces them is content-*independent* (any situation that we are exposed to enough times in the right fashion would produce a pragmatic reasoning schema). This account has the virtue of explaining differential performance on the abstract version of the selection task and some concrete versions of it. For some concrete versions of the selection task, our experience has led to the development of principles of reasoning that enable us to reason correctly when faced with certain concrete situations—such as those involving the granting of permission[13]—but not in abstract cases. Further, although this account allows that our reasoning competence contains content-dependent rules, it gives a content-*independent* account of how these content-*dependent* rules are developed.

Cosmides' account, called *social contract theory*, involves whether the version of the task fits the pattern of social exchange situations (for example, 'If you help me plough my fields, then I will help you plough yours').[14] Briefly, Cosmides' idea is that people will do well on versions of the selection task that fit the form of social exchange situations and that involve the detection of *cheaters* with respect to the social contract (that is, those who try to get the benefit of the contractual arrangement without paying the cost for doing so; I, for example, would be a cheater if I did not help you plough your fields after you helped me plough mine). This explanation is supposed to account for the fact that subjects reason well on certain concrete tasks but not on others. Unlike pragmatic reasoning schema theory, according to social contract theory, the principles in our reasoning competence are content-*dependent* to the core. Situations that fit the social exchange template will evoke the correct response, while those that do not fit it may well not. Whether or not a situation fits this template is content-dependent. This is shown by contrasting the unfamiliar social contract story with the unfamiliar descriptive story. The rule that subjects are asked to test—'If a man eats cassava root, then he must have a tattoo on his face'—is the same in both cases, but the content in the social contract story fits the social contract template while the content in the descriptive case does not.[15]

The crucial point at the moment is that whatever the psychological explanation for the varied responses to the selection tasks, subjects seem, at least at first blush, to be violating the normative principles of reasoning in the abstract selection task as well as certain versions of the concrete selection task (for example, the unfamiliar descriptive story and the food and wine version). When it comes to inferences involving

---

[13] See Johnson-Laird *et al.*, 'Reasoning and a Sense of Reality', for an example involving a concrete version of the selection task that involves a permission schema; the rule subjects are testing in this case is 'If a letter is sealed, then it has a 50 lire stamp on it'.   [14] Cosmides, 'The Logic of Selection'.

[15] See ibid., and Gigerenzer and Hug, 'Domain-Specific Reasoning', for data that favours social contract theory over pragmatic reasoning schema theory. For criticisms of Cosmides' theory, see Patricia Cheng and Keith Holyoak, 'On the Natural Selection of Reasoning Theories', *Cognition*, 33 (1989), 285–333; and Paul Pollard, 'Natural Selection for the Selection Task: Limits to Social Exchange Theory', *Cognition*, 36 (1990), 195–204. For Cosmides' reply, see Leda Cosmides and John Tooby, 'Cognitive Adaptation for Social Exchange', in Jerome Barkow *et al.* (eds.), *The Adapted Mind* (New York: Oxford University Press, 1992).

deductive logic, people at least *seem* to diverge from the norms. If subjects reason according to pragmatic reasoning schemata or do especially well reasoning in situations involving social contracts, then it looks as if humans have some principles in our reasoning competence other than the normative principles of reasoning. The norms are content-*independent* but our reasoning competence seems to contain some content-*dependent* rules. This seems to provide good reason for thinking humans are irrational.

1.3. Misinterpretation Strategy

Whichever account of why subjects reason differently on logically similar reasoning tasks is right, there remains the question of whether subjects are rational in reasoning the way that they do. It is this question that is central to the truth of the rationality thesis. The data on the selection task remain robust: in some situations (abstract as well as some concrete), humans fail to reason in accordance with the normative principles of reasoning and their failure to do so is systematic and common. As such, the results of the selection task suggest that the irrationality thesis is true.

One strategy for reconciling the rationality thesis with the results of versions of the selection task that diverge from the normative principles of reasoning is to argue that all such divergences are performance errors. If this can be done successfully, then the results of the selection task are compatible with the rationality thesis, since this thesis is about our reasoning *competence*. L. J. Cohen makes just such an argument when he analyses the selection task:

[The] experimenters' power to generate an illusion here [namely, the illusion that the '7' card does not need to be examined to test the rule] depends on the relative unfamiliarity and artificiality of the experiment. . . . The findings about [the selection task] . . . may legitimately be said to support the view that most people manage to apply their logical competence without ever formulating it expressly at a level of generality sufficient for it to be readily applicable to wholly unfamiliar tasks. . . . *[S]ubjects who reason fallaciously about [the selection task] . . . need not be supposed to lack the correct deductive 'program'.* The subjects merely fail to recognize the similarity of their task to those familiar issues in which they have profited by using the [proper] deductive procedure . . . As a result, either that procedure received no input or its output is deleted and [subjects thus fail to follow the normative principles].[16]

---

[16] L. Jonathan Cohen, 'Can Human Irrationality be Experimentally Demonstrated?', *Behavioral and Brain Sciences*, 4 (1981), 324, emphasis added.

Cohen's suggestion is that in the abstract selection task, subjects, due to lack of recognition or a misinterpretation of the task, do not apply the appropriate principle of reasoning or ignore the results of applying it because they fail to realize that the task is similar to those they can and do solve correctly. Presumably, Cohen thinks that subjects (unconsciously) call up some *other* principle that generates an incorrect answer to the selection task (for example, following this principle might cause a subject to select the 'A' card but not the '7' card). If this is the case, then subjects may well have the right principle in their competence but fail to apply it. If this is true, then the fact that subjects make mistakes in the selection task does not show that their reasoning competence diverges from the norms of reasoning; it merely shows that subjects make performance errors—under certain circumstances, they misinterpret or fail to recognize the nature of their tasks and thereby fail to apply correctly a principle that is in fact part of their reasoning competence. Cohen goes on to cite those versions of the concrete selection task on which subjects reason in accordance with the norms as evidence for this analysis of the selection task. According to Cohen, subjects' performance on some versions of the concrete selection task show that subjects have the relevant principles in their reasoning competence—that they follow the norms *sometimes* is supposed to show that the norms must be in our reasoning competence. Whatever abstract considerations seem to support Cohen's proposal, Cosmides' results show that Cohen's particular interpretation of the selection task is mistaken.

The general conclusion that Cohen wants to draw from the various versions of the concrete selection task is that when subjects fail to apply the normative principles of reasoning in the abstract selection task they are making a performance error—they have a principle in their reasoning competence that would, if applied, produce the correct result, but this principle is not applied due to some sort of interference. A friend of the irrationality thesis would disagree with this step. She would argue that subjects' failure to apply the proper principle in the abstract selection task shows that they lack a *general* principle for performing selection tasks; subjects have some principle that they use for the selection task but it gives the correct results only on certain versions of the selection task, *not* on all versions. Cosmides' data support the view that people apply the cheater detection principle instead of the appropriate principle based on a rules of logic. Because humans are following the cheater detection principle rather than the normative principle of reasoning, in situations that fit the social exchange template we get the right answer and in situations that do not fit this template we get the wrong answer. Support for this reading of the selection task—which says the experiments show that humans violate logical principles—can be found in experiments performed to show that subjects do not seem to be misinterpreting the selection task and hence that their failure to apply the normative principle is not due to a performance error. Particularly convincing evidence for this is that even when subjects are shown (by actually revealing the other side of a card to them) that the '7' card might have (say) an 'E' on the other side, hence violating the rule 'If a card has a vowel on one side, then it will have an even number on the other' (and thus this card would be relevant to testing the rule), they insist that they were right not to select the '7' card as one that should be turned over. Even when subjects are given the correct interpretation of the task, they still seem to make the wrong inferences. This surprising neglect of the normative principle even in the face of a demonstration of it suggests that subjects truly lack the appropriate principle, *not* that they are misinterpreting the experimental task and thereby applying the wrong principle.

Everyone agrees that humans make systematic errors on the selection task; subjects clearly make mistakes on some versions of the task. This seems on the surface to count in favour of the irrationality thesis. The general strategy, however, of attributing divergence from the normative principles of reasoning to performance errors such as misinterpretation or misapplication has the potential to undermine the initial strength of the evidence in favour of the irrationality thesis. Evidence from Cosmides' social exchange version of the selection task seems, however, to tip the scales back in favour of the irrationality thesis and against the misinterpretation strategy. Before I attempt to evaluate the misinterpretation strategy as a general strategy towards the reasoning experiments, I turn to a discussion of another experiment.

2. An Experiment Concerning Probability Theory

2.1. The Basic Conjunction Experiment

The second experiment, published in 1983 by Amos Tversky and Daniel Kahneman, is supposed to show that humans, in making judgements about the likelihood of various events, systematically violate a basic and important principle of probability.[17] Subjects read a description of a person like the following:

> Linda is 31 years old, single, outspoken, and very bright. She majored in philosophy. As a student, she was deeply concerned with issues of discrimination and social justice, and also participated in anti-nuclear demonstrations.[18]

Subjects are then asked to rate the likelihood of various statements about this person, in this case, Linda's current profession and political affiliation. Among the options they are asked to rank are the following:

(1) Linda is active in the feminist movement.
(2) Linda is a bank teller.
(3) Linda is a bank teller and is active in the feminist movement.

Of the subjects 85 per cent—including both statistically naïve undergraduates and presumably *not* statistically naïve psychology graduate students—ranked (3) as being *more probable* than (2). In so doing, they made a serious mistake.

It is a basic rule of probability (called the conjunction rule) that the probability of two events occurring together must be less than or equal to the probability of either one of the two events occurring individually. This is the case because any instance of *both* of the events occurring is *necessarily* an instance of a particular *one* of them occurring, while every instance of a particular *one* of them occurring is *not* necessarily an instance of *both* events occurring. In other words, it is possible that one event might occur without both events occurring, but it is *not* possible that both events might occur without either one of them also occurring. In particular, Linda could be a bank teller but *not* a feminist bank teller (for instance, her career in banking might have turned her attention away from issues of social justice), but she could *not* (under *any* scenario) be a bank teller and a feminist yet *not* also a feminist. Subjects who say Linda is more likely to be a bank teller *and* a feminist than she is to be a bank teller violate the conjunction rule.

The conjunction rule gives rise to the conjunction principle, which says that you should not attach a lesser degree of probability to some event than you do to both that event and some distinct event occurring.

---

[17] Amos Tversky and Daniel Kahneman, 'Extensional versus Intuitive Reasoning: The Conjunction Fallacy in Probability Judgment', *Psychological Review*, 90 (1983), 293–315. My discussion in this section reviews some of the material in Chapter 1 but here I explore the issues in greater detail.   [18] Ibid. 297.

Violating the conjunction principle is a serious mistake. If a person consistently bet her money in violation of this principle, then she would lose all of her money. In more precise terms, a person who violates a rule of probability theory is susceptible to what is known as a Dutch book.[19] A person is *Dutch-bookable* if there is a series of bets she will accept such that she will lose all of her money no matter what the outcome of the relevant events.[20]

A further bit of terminology will be helpful. The *expected value* of a bet is the sum of the products of the pay-off of each result of the event bet on and the probability of that result occurring. If I make a straight (1-to-1 odds) $1 bet that a six will come up when a fair die is rolled, the expected value of the bet is the sum of (*a*) the pay-off if I win my bet—$1—multiplied by my chances of winning—$\frac{1}{6}$—and (*b*) the loss if I lose my bet—a loss of $1—multiplied by my chances of losing—$\frac{5}{6}$. This works out to be $\frac{1}{6}$ minus $\frac{5}{6}$, so the expected value of my bet comes out to be a loss of approximately 66 cents. A bet is *fair* if its expected value is equal to zero. My straight $1 bet that a six will come up is thus not fair. A fair bet would be if I was given 5-to-1 odds on this same bet (because $(($5 \times \frac{1}{6}) + (-$1 \times \frac{5}{6}))$ equals zero) or if I was given a straight (that is, 1-to-1 odds) bet than an even number would come up when a die is rolled (because $(($1 \times \frac{1}{2}) + (-$1 \times \frac{1}{2}))$ equals zero).[21]

With this background, consider the following example: suppose Henry is willing to bet in accordance with the likelihood judgements that subjects make about Linda, that is, he is more willing to bet that Linda is a bank teller *and* a feminist than he is willing to bet that she is a bank teller. If this is the case, Henry can be Dutch-booked. This is bad news for him because it means that he will accept sets of bets such that he will lose money no matter what happens. For example, suppose Henry

---

[19] I am not quite sure of the etymology of the phrase 'Dutch book', but it clearly is not saying anything nice about Dutch people. The phrase might suggest a series of bets that someone might agree to only if drunk (as in 'Dutch courage', which means courage inspired by having drunk too much alcohol), a series of bets that a greedy bookie might arrange (stereotypically, the Dutch are cheap, hence one uses the phrase 'Dutch treat' or 'going Dutch' when each person pays for her own meal), or it might suggest a series of bets that amount to 'financial suicide' (the expression 'to do a Dutch' or 'a Dutch act' refers to committing suicide). In any event, having spent a pleasant time in Amsterdam while writing a portion of this book, I do not want to suggest that I agree with any of the negative implications of the phrase 'Dutch book'.

[20] For a brief general discussion of Dutch books, see Brian Skyrms, *Choice and Chance* (Belmont, Calif.: Wadsworth, 1986), 185–9.

[21] For a discussion of fair bets and expected value, see ibid., chs. 5 and 6.

thinks the probability that Linda is a feminist is 0.5, the probability that she is a bank teller is 0.1, and the probability that she is a feminist *and* a bank teller is 0.25. These probabilities match with the responses the majority of subjects give in the conjunction experiment; Henry rates the probability that Linda is a bank teller *and* a feminist as greater than the probability that she is a bank teller. Suppose further that a bookie offers Henry the following three bets:

- (*a*) a $1 bet at 1-to-1 odds that Linda is *not* a feminist.
- (*b*) a $6 bet at 1-to-9 odds that Linda is *not* a bank teller.
- (*c*) a $2 bet at 3-to-1 odds that Linda is both a feminist and a bank teller.

For Henry, these are all fair bets, that is, they are bets that he should accept because he has a fair chance of winning them. Bet (*a*) is fair because the probability that Linda is not a feminist—0.5—multiplied by the pay-off—$1—minus the probability that Linda is a feminist—0.5—multiplied by the pay-off—the loss of $1—equals zero. Similarly, for bet (*b*), 0.9 multiplied by 11 cents (that is, $\frac{1}{9}$ of a dollar) minus 0.1 multiplied by the loss of $1 equals zero and, for bet (*c*), 0.25 multiplied by $3 minus 0.75 multiplied by the loss of $1 equals zero. Given his assessment of the particular probabilities that Linda occupies various occupational and political positions, Henry will judge all three bets offered by the bookie to be fair and thus will accept them. If he accepts all of these bets, *whatever turns out to be true of Linda*, Henry will lose money. If the bookie multiplies the dollar values of the three bets by 10,000 each, Henry will *still* think the bets are fair, and he will lose a *great deal* of money.

To show why this is true, four cases need to be examined, one for each of the following possible outcomes:

- (i) Linda is both a bank teller and a feminist.
- (ii) Linda is a bank teller but not a feminist.
- (iii) Linda is a feminist but not a bank teller.
- (iv) Linda is neither a feminist nor a bank teller.

I will examine these cases in turn. In case (i), Linda is both a bank teller and a feminist, so Henry will *win* $6 from bet (*c*) (since he bet $2 at 3-to-1 odds that Linda is both a feminist and a bank teller and she is) but *lose* $6 from bet (*b*) (since he bet $6 that Linda is *not* a bank teller and she is) and $1 from bet (*a*) (since he bet $1 that Linda is *not* a feminist and she is) for a total loss of $1. In case (ii), Linda is a bank teller but not a feminist, so Henry will win $1 from bet (*a*) but lose $6 from bet (*b*) and lose $2 from bet (*c*) for a total loss of $7. In case (iii), Linda is a feminist but not a bank teller, so Henry will win 66 cents from bet (*b*) but lose $1 from bet (*a*) and lose $2 from bet (*c*) for a total loss of $2.34. Finally, in case (iv), Linda is neither a bank teller nor a feminist, so Henry will win $1 from bet (*a*) and win 66 cents from bet (*b*) but lose $2 from bet (*c*) for a total loss of 34 cents. The following list reviews the results for each of the four cases:

(i) a loss of $1,
(ii) a loss of $7,
(iii) a loss of $2.34,
(iv) a loss of 34 cents.

No matter what happens, Henry will lose when he bets according to probability ratings that violate the conjunction principle. Betting money when there is no chance of winning—which is what people who violate the conjunction principle are committing themselves to doing—is irrational behaviour.

Violating the conjunction principle is thus irrational. Returning to the conjunction experiment, for this experiment to support the irrationality thesis, it must show that people do not have the conjunction principle in their reasoning competence. The phenomenon of subjects ignoring the conjunction principle seems common, systematic, and robust. Prima facie, this counts as evidence for the irrationality thesis.

A friend of the rationality thesis could rightly point out that the mere fact that subjects rate the probability that Linda is a feminist and a bank teller as being greater than that Linda is a bank teller may not establish that the relevant norm is being violated; perhaps subjects are misinterpreting the various choices they are given. If subjects are misinterpreting the options before them, then their failure to rank (2), 'Linda is a bank teller', as more probable than (3), 'Linda is a bank teller and is active in the feminist movement', might not shed light on human reasoning competence and thus would not count against the rationality thesis. Whether subjects are doing so can be determined by trying some variations on the conjunction experiment.

2.2. Variations on the Experiment

The irrationality thesis is a claim about human reasoning competence. If the results of the conjunction experiment are due to performance errors and not to a reasoning competence that diverges from the normative principles of reasoning, then the experiment does not bear on the irrationality thesis. In attempt to block this line of attack against the irrationality thesis, Kahneman and Tversky have tried a large number of variations on the conjunction experiment. One way that the experiment might not get at human reasoning competence is if subjects are misinterpreting the task at hand. One such possible misinterpretation is that subjects might be reading 'Linda is a bank teller' as meaning that Linda is a bank teller, *but not* a feminist. If subjects are reading 'Linda is a bank teller' in this way, it might explain why they think this statement is less likely to be true than 'Linda is a bank teller and a feminist'; 'Linda is a bank teller *but not* a feminist' would not be true in any of the same instances as 'Linda is a bank teller *and* a feminist' whereas 'Linda is a bank teller' would be true in some of the same instances as 'Linda is a bank teller and a feminist'. To test this possible explanation, subjects were presented with the following two statements about Linda and were asked to rate their probability:

(2′) Linda is a bank teller whether or not she is active in the feminist movement.

(3) Linda is a bank teller and is active in the feminist movement.

A majority of subjects rated (3) more probable than (2′). As before, subjects rated a conjunction as more probable than one of its conjuncts even though in this case it was made clear that (2′) is in fact logically equivalent to a conjunct of (3). This shows that subjects commit the conjunction fallacy even when they have been explicitly told that 'Linda is a bank teller' does *not* mean that Linda is a *non-feminist* bank teller.[22] This suggests that subjects are not misinterpreting the task before them, but that they *are* in fact systematically violating the conjunction principle and thus it seems that some other principle guides their reasoning.

Similar (though perhaps more troubling) results were achieved when a concrete version of the experiment was performed on a group of doctors. Subjects were given a description of a patient and asked to rate the probability of various symptoms including:

(4) The patient has hemiparesis.

(5) The patient has dyspnoea and hemiparesis.

Most of the doctors rated (5) more probable than (4) in violation of the conjunction principle. To test whether they might have been interpreting

---

[22] Tversky and Kahneman, 'Extensional versus Intuitive Reasoning', 299.

(4) as meaning that the patient has hemiparesis only (that is, the patient does *not* have dyspnoea), doctors were asked the following question:

> In assessing the probability that the patient described had a particular symptom X, did you assume that X is the *only* symptom experienced by the patient [or that] X is *among* the symptoms experienced by the patient?[23]

All but two of the sixty-two subjects said they assumed that X was *among* the symptoms rather than that X was the *only* symptom. Because doctors were not interpreting (4) to mean that the patient has only one of the symptoms, the results of this concrete version of the conjunction experiment suggest that they are following some principle other than the conjunction principle.

A thought that gives rise to a further variation on this experiment is that perhaps subjects have the conjunction principle in their reasoning competence and know that it is the right principle to apply in the Linda case, but somehow fail to make the correct probability judgement in spite of this. One way to flesh out this suggestion is that subjects correctly interpret the task and call up the right principle, but they somehow misapply it and thereby come up with the wrong result. This suggestion has also been tested by Kahneman and Tversky. After being presented with the description of Linda and alternatives (2) and (3)—that Linda is a bank teller and that she is a feminist bank teller, respectively—subjects were asked to indicate which of the two arguments for (2) and (3), respectively, they found the most convincing:

(A1) Linda is more likely to be a bank teller than she is to be a feminist bank teller because every feminist bank teller is a bank teller, but some women bank tellers are not feminists and Linda could be one of them.

(A2) Linda is more likely to be a feminist bank teller than she is likely to be a bank teller because she resembles an active feminist more than she resembles a bank teller.[24]

A majority of the subjects chose argument (A2), which advocates the violation of the conjunction principle. These results suggest that subjects *are* properly interpreting the task assigned to them but still violate the conjunction principle because they apply some other rule. This version of the conjunction experiment suggests that subjects are interpreting

---

[23] Ibid. 301.   [24] Ibid. 299.

the tasks in the way experimenters think they are; this counts against the attempt to reconcile the results of the conjunction experiment with the rationality thesis.

Gerd Gigerenzer discusses a variation of the conjunction experiment that he says undermines the results of the basic conjunction experiment.[25] Subjects are shown the Linda description and told that there are 100 people who fit it. They are then asked to indicate how many of these people are:

(a) bank tellers,
(b) bank tellers and feminists.

When the problem is phrased in such a way that subjects are being asked to indicate *frequency* rather than *probability*, their responses are in accord with the conjunction principle, that is, subjects' disregard for the conjunction principle largely evaporates.[26] The frequency version of the conjunction experiment is supposed to show that humans have the conjunction principle in their reasoning competence and that the experimental results that seem to show otherwise are in fact due to systematic performance errors. That subjects' seemingly irrational behaviour disappears when some details of the task are modified (that is, when they are asked to make frequency judgements rather than probability judgements) is supposed to show that the seemingly irrational behaviour is due to the details of the original experiment, *not* to any problems with human reasoning competence.

2.3. Interpreting the Results

Gigerenzer's experiment is supposed to prove that subjects have the conjunction principle in their reasoning competence because it shows that subjects are able to apply this principle in certain contexts (those involving frequencies rather than probabilities). This, however, is just one interpretation of the results of the conjunction experiment. Friends of the irrationality thesis could claim that Gigerenzer's results underscore the irrationality of subjects' responses to the original version of the conjunction experiment. They might point out that the frequency version of the experiment shows subjects can correctly interpret these

[25] Gerd Gigerenzer, 'How to Make Cognitive Illusions Disappear: Beyond "Heuristics and Biases"', *European Review of Social Psychology*, 2 (1991), 83–115.

[26] Klaus Fiedler, 'The Dependence of the Conjunction Fallacy on Subtle Linguistic Factors', *Psychological Research*, 50 (1988), 123–9.

types of experiment; thus, we have good reason to believe that subjects are correctly interpreting the *standard* conjunction experiment (that is, the version involving probability rather than frequency) and hence that they are not making performance errors, and that their reasoning about probability results from the application of principles that are in their reasoning competence. This would suggest, against the rationality thesis, that subjects do not have the conjunction principle in their reasoning competence. Gigerenzer's results are consistent with the view that we have the conjunction principle in our reasoning competence, but they are also consistent with the view that we have some context-*dependent* principle in our reasoning competence that results in reasoning in accordance with the conjunction principle in contexts involving frequency and violating the conjunction principle in contexts involving probability. For Gigerenzer's results to count in favour of the rationality thesis, a specific account of why subjects make performance errors in the standard conjunction task needs to be given. If friends of the rationality thesis want to embrace Gigerenzer's results, they need to explain why subjects fail to apply the conjunction principle when a problem is presented in terms of probability but not when it is presented in terms of frequency. More research seems needed to explain why subjects get the right results with frequency but not with probability.

Gigerenzer offers another—more radical—interpretation of the frequency version of the conjunction task: he says that Kahneman and Tversky, not their subjects, are making the mistake in the conjunction experiments.[27] According to this reading of the conjunction task, subjects are giving the correct answer to the question about Linda because the question is really asking about frequency, not probability. At least prima facie, this seems an odd move because the response subjects give to the Linda example makes them susceptible to a Dutch book and that hardly can be rational. Gigerenzer thinks, however, that he can handle this worry, but his way of doing so ultimately commits him to offering an alternative to probability theory. Exploring the details of his alternative is beyond the scope of this project.

Everyone agrees that humans make systematic errors when it comes to probability judgements. The disagreement is whether the errors are performance errors or whether they show that human reasoning competence diverges from the normative principles of reasoning. This parallels the point that I made at the end of the above discussion of the

---

[27] Gigerenzer, 'How to Make Cognitive Illusions Disappear'.

selection task. In the next section, I turn my attention to this general difficulty with interpreting experiments about human rationality.

3. Interpreting Reasoning Experiments

Towards the end of both Sections 1 and 2, I considered a strategy for reconciling the rationality thesis with the results of both the selection task and the conjunction experiment; I call this the *misinterpretation strategy*. The idea is to locate the source of the errors that subjects are making not in their reasoning competence but in their interpretations of the tasks. This would have the result of classifying their errors as *performance* errors. The misinterpretation strategy raises a general problem for friends of the irrationality thesis who want to use empirical evidence to make their case, namely it raises the question whether one can ever be sure that an experiment is actually getting at human reasoning competence. Any reasoning experiment is going to involve the *logical possibility* of misinterpretation or, more generally, of a performance error, so an experimenter can never be *sure* that her results demonstrate that humans have a reasoning competence that diverges from the norms. This much is true, but it does not entail that an experimenter can *never* be confident that she has isolated human reasoning competence.

3.1. Three Interpretative Strategies

Consider a reasoning experiment that tests subjects' ability to perform a certain task T. Call the normative principle of reasoning that should be involved in this task N. Suppose that subjects seem to reason in accordance with N only some of the time—in certain contexts, subjects diverge from N. The question is whether subjects have N in their reasoning competence and are just making performance errors in these contexts or whether subjects have some non-rational principle P that produces some of the same reasoning behaviour as N does but in some instances diverges from it. There are three general strategies for approaching this: what I call the *rational competence strategy*, the *no performance error strategy*, and the *neutral strategy*. I will consider these strategies in turn.

First, one might say that all divergences from N must be performance errors (the rational competence strategy).[28] One version of this strategy is to say that subjects must be misinterpreting the tasks in contexts in which they diverge from *N*. Another version is to say that although subjects correctly interpret the task and call up the right principle to handle it, they end up misapplying the principle in these contexts. This strategy is not in principle problematic but one needs to provide arguments for it. If every possible divergence from some normative principle of reasoning is unquestioningly rejected as a mere perform- ance error, then this is an immunization strategy, an *ad hoc* procedure that allows an advocate of a theory to discount any empirical evidence against her favoured theory (see my discussion of immunization strat- egies in Chapter 2, Section 1.5). Of course not every appeal to perform- ance errors is like this. Some such appeals are justified by an account of the performance mechanisms that lead to performance errors. Other such appeals are justified by well-articulated conceptual considerations. Attributing all divergences from the normative principles of reasoning to performance errors, as some friends of the rationality thesis would like to do, is not, however, justified given anything that has been said so far. This is not to say that there is no way to justify such a strategy. Perhaps there is a justification for classifying as performance errors all divergences from the norms, that is, for doing so in a way that is not *ad hoc*. In the three chapters that follow, I turn my attention to argu- ments that claim to do just this.

Second, at the other extreme, one might adopt the strategy of assum- ing that *none* of the divergences from *N* are due to performance errors but all are to be attributed to human reasoning competence (the no performance error strategy). This has got to be a mistaken strategy because there is always the possibility of performance errors *whatever* the principles embodied in our reasoning competence. Suppose that when subjects are performing task *T*, they are following rule *P*, which is not the normative principle of reasoning for *T*. In some contexts, even though subjects have *P* in their reasoning competence, they will diverge from it when, for example, they have had too much alcohol to drink or when memory limitations interfere with their ability to execute *P*. The

---

[28] In addition to the philosophical arguments to be discussed, see e.g. Mary Henle, 'On the Relation between Logic and Thinking', *Psychological Review*, 69 (1962), 376–82; and Foreword, in Russell Revlin and Richard Mayer (eds.), *Human Reasoning* (Wash- ington: Winston, 1978). Henle says that she has 'never found errors that could *unam- biguously* be attributed to faulty reasoning' (Foreword, p. xviii, emphasis added). See also Martin Braine *et al.* 'Some Empirical Justification for a Theory of Natural Propositional Logic', in Gordon Bower (ed.), *The Psychology of Learning and Motivation*, xviii (Orlando, Fla.: Academic Press, 1984).

point is that any plausible account of human reasoning competence (even one that seems to fit with the irrationality thesis) must allow for performance errors. This means that the strategy of attributing all divergences from the normative principles of reasoning to the proper operation of our reasoning competence is deeply problematic.

Third, one could adopt a middle position about the strategy for interpreting behaviour on reasoning tasks (the neutral strategy).[29] The middle position is to remain flexible about whether to call something a performance error and whether to let non-normative principles of reasoning into human reasoning competence. For example, one might start with a presumption in favour of N as an account of human reasoning competence and try to attribute divergences from N to performance errors. If plausible accounts of the mechanisms that cause performance errors can be developed, then it is reasonable to retain the assumption that N characterizes reasoning competence. If, for example, it turned out that subjects were interpreting 'Linda is a bank teller' as meaning Linda is a bank teller *but not* a feminist and that this misinterpretation accounted for their divergences from the conjunction principle, then it would be reasonable to say that, so far as this experiment is concerned, humans have the conjunction principle in their reasoning competence. As I discussed above, subjects do not, however, seem to be misinterpreting (2). In fact, violating the conjunction principle seems a robust reasoning phenomenon—even on reflection (and when possible misinterpretations seem blocked), subjects *still* seem to diverge from the conjunction principle. Thus it seems reasonable to infer that subjects do not have the conjunction principle in their reasoning competence. In more general terms, the presumption in favour of N is undermined in the absence of an account of how subjects are misinterpreting the task. This third position seems to me the most reasonable of the three; in fact, short of conceptual considerations in favour of the rational competence view, the neutral strategy seems the only plausible general strategy to adopt.

3.2. Drawing the Borders around Competence

In the previous chapter, I mentioned that there is a problem with trying to locate the borders around linguistic competence; it is quite hard to

---

[29] Tversky and Kahneman, 'Extensional versus Intuitive Reasoning', 304, defend this strategy: 'a psychological analysis should apply interpretive charity and should avoid treating genuine misunderstandings as if they were fallacies'.

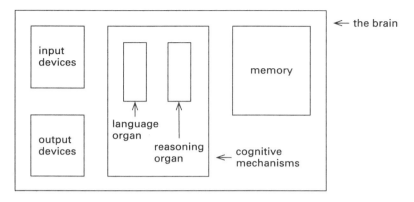

Fɪɢ. 3.5. *An incomplete, abstract, and overly simple picture of the brain*

say which cognitive mechanisms are part of linguistic competence and which are sources of performance errors. The problem with how to interpret the results of reasoning experiments parallels this problem. To see this, imagine a functional sketch of the brain (see Fig. 3.5). Inside the brain there are various mechanisms including input and output devices, a memory database of some sort, and various cognitive mechanisms, including the language organ and the reasoning organ (assuming, for simplicity, that these are organs rather than mere mechanisms). Consider what goes on in the brain when a person hears a question, understands it, and answers it (see Fig. 3.6). The sound-waves hit the ear-drum, which stimulates the auditory nerve, which is hooked up to (at least) one of the input devices in the brain. The resulting signal is processed in some fashion by some mechanism(s) in the brain (not pictured in Fig. 3.5) and is eventually passed into the language organ. In the language organ, the question is processed and converted to the form that the relevant portions of the brain—including the reasoning organ—can use to do whatever they do to figure out the answer to the question and send it back to the language organ, where it will be made into an intelligible sentence and sent back out through an output device. This is of course a very simplified story, but something roughly like it is probably true.[30]

---

[30] Another disclaimer is in order. The processing of a question is not necessarily a serial process; various steps in the process probably take place in parallel, that is, at the same time.

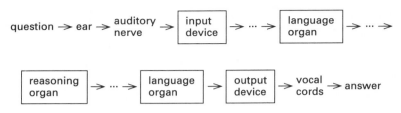

FIG. 3.6. *A simplified sketch of the processing of a question*

The problem about where to draw the borders around linguistic competence which I discussed at the end of the last chapter arises if we consider the uttering of an ungrammatical sentence. In some cases, ungrammatical utterances can be attributed to problems with the input or output device—caused perhaps if someone has taken a lot of LSD or has not had enough sleep—or by memory limitations. If the plausible sources of performance errors have been considered and found not to be responsible for the ungrammatical utterance, then it is difficult to know whether to adjust linguistic competence so that the ungrammatical utterance is part of competence or whether to posit some performance mechanism that causes it. I call incorporating such seemingly ungrammatical utterances into linguistic competence *drawing wide borders around linguistic competence* because this strategy is inclusive: it counts all sorts of mechanisms as part of linguistic competence. In contrast, I call positing a performance mechanism that causes such seemingly ungrammatical utterances *drawing narrow borders around linguistic competence* because according to this strategy one should be hesitant to let many mechanisms into linguistic competence and should go to great lengths in order to insulate the pre-existing view of linguistic competence (that is, to attribute divergences to as yet unidentified performance errors). Linguists typically draw *wide* borders around linguistic competence, namely, if they encounter linguistic behaviour that does not accord with their current theory of linguistic competence and they cannot identify any plausible sources of performance errors, they modify their theory of linguistic competence to include the linguistic behaviour that diverged from their initial theory. Drawing wide borders around linguistic competence seems appropriate since, as I argued in Chapter 2, linguistic norms are indexed to actual linguistic ability. If linguistic norms were not indexed to actual linguistic ability, then there might be reasons for not incorporating into linguistic competence the seeming divergences from our currently favoured theory of linguistic competence. Because linguistic norms are indexed to linguistic competence, linguists seem justified in drawing wide borders around linguistic competence.

The problem of how to interpret the reasoning experiments is connected to the question of how wide the borders of reasoning competence should be drawn, a question that is similar to the problem of where to draw the borders around linguistic competence, although perhaps the problem with respect to reasoning competence is harder. Take the conjunction experiment as an example. Consider someone faced with the task of ranking the likelihood of the various choices involving Linda's current profession and political interests. The task begins to be processed through some input device. Once it is processed by the language organ, other cognitive mechanisms are responsible for determining what ranking the person will select. Supposing this person, like most of the subjects in the conjunction experiment, says Linda is more likely to be a feminist and a bank teller than she is a bank teller, thereby violating the conjunction principle. Somewhere in the processing something went wrong. The question is whether to put the responsible mechanism into reasoning competence or not. On the one hand, we might be tempted to blame the violation of the conjunction principle on some as yet unidentified performance error. According to this strategy, the principles of probability are instantiated in human reasoning competence, and the mechanisms that cause subjects to reason in a manner that violates the principles of probability are outside reasoning competence. This would be drawing *narrow* borders around reasoning competence. On the other hand, in the face of these experimental results, we might be tempted to think that the principles of probability are not in our reasoning competence, but, instead, some other principles—principles that diverge from the principles of probability—are. For example, *plausibility heuristics*—principles that enable a person to choose the more plausible of some alternatives (plausibility is similar to but different from probability; the more plausible of two alternatives is usually, but not always, the more probable)—might be instantiated in our reasoning competence.[31] On this view, subjects say that Linda is more likely to be a bank teller and a feminist than a bank teller because they

---

[31] I am not here attempting to put forward the plausibility heuristic as a serious proposal of a principle that we in fact have in our reasoning competence that causes us to not follow the conjunction principle in certain contexts. See Tversky and Kahneman, 'Extensional versus Intuitive Reasoning', for a discussion of the heuristics that are likely to be the cause of our reasoning behaviour in contexts like the conjunction experiment.

are calling up plausibility heuristics and it is more plausible, given the description of Linda, that she is a bank teller and a feminist than it is that she is a bank teller. This would be drawing *wide* borders around reasoning competence. From the point of view of the rationality thesis, the strategy of drawing wide borders around reasoning competence is pessimistic because following this strategy is more likely to lead to non-rational principles of reasoning being incorporated into reasoning competence than drawing narrow borders around reasoning competence. The strategy of drawing narrow borders around reasoning competence is optimistic from the point of view of the rationality thesis because, on this strategy, reasoning competence is insulated against the possibility that non-rational principles of reasoning will be incorporated into it.

Recall that in the case of linguistics, there was some reason to draw wide borders around competence, namely, the fact that norms of grammaticality are indexed to linguistic competence. The same reason does not hold, however, for reasoning competence because the norms of rationality are not necessarily indexed to reasoning competence. Without this, there is no prima facie reason for favouring the drawing of wide borders around reasoning competence.

The issue of how the borders should be drawn around reasoning competence is similar to the issue between the rational competence strategy and the neutral strategy discussed in Section 3.1. If one adopts the rational competence strategy, one is drawing narrow borders around reasoning competence; if one adopts the neutral strategy, one is at least open to drawing wide borders around reasoning competence. This shows how the question of what sort of interpretative stance to adopt towards reasoning behaviour relates to the question of how to delimit cognitive mechanisms. In Section 3.1, I said that the neutral strategy seems prima facie more reasonable than the rational competence strategy, but I suggested that there were several arguments in favour of the rational competence strategy that are worthy of consideration. If what I have said in this section is right, the same arguments will count in favour of drawing narrow borders around reasoning competence; how we ought to delimit reasoning competence is thus also at stake in the chapters that follow.

3.3. Why Neuroscience does not Answer the Question

One might point out that something is strange about the above discussion of cognitive mechanisms because the issue seems much more concrete than I have characterized it: couldn't a neuroscientist just crack open a human brain and examine it to see what program is instantiated therein? On this picture, the issue between the rationality thesis and the irrationality thesis involves a clearly defined empirical question: if neurological examination results in the discovery of a program consisting of the normative principles of reasoning, then the rational competence strategy would be vindicated and the rationality thesis would be true. If a program diverging from the norms was discovered, then there would be good reason to give up the presumption in favour of a rational reasoning competence and embrace the irrationality thesis.

Although there is something right about this picture of what is at issue between the rational competence strategy and the neutral strategy and the rationality thesis and the irrationality thesis—there is, as I will argue towards the end of this book, a sense in which the issues are empirical—there is something misleading about this picture as well. Human reasoning competence does not consist of principles written in English or a programming language like LISP, which is used by artificial intelligence researchers. If the brain were cracked open, a description of reasoning competence would not simply leap out; there would remain the problem of interpreting the neurological structures that are discovered. If I knew that a specific part of the brain was responsible for reasoning competence, that would not settle what principles are embodied in our reasoning competence and whether these principles are rational or not.

This point can be made clearer by an example involving a computer. Imagine that you are assigned the task of figuring out the program a computer is running simply by observing its underlying physical states, that is, the states of its chips. No matter how long you observe the transition of the computer from one physical state to the next, there will still be a large number of possible interpretations of programs that these physical states could be instantiating. Instead, you have to know what the computer is doing. To know that you need to consult the manual; looking at the chips will not do the trick.

Trying to discover human reasoning competence is like trying to figure out what program a computer is running; the underlying physical structure alone will not provide an account of the program. We want to know what principles are embodied in human reasoning competence. Whatever principles are involved, they are going to be intentional, that is, they are going be about things, like about how beliefs ought to be moved around. You cannot figure out what a cognitive mechanism does or, more specifically, what principles of reasoning are in our reasoning competence, simply by looking at the neurophysiological constitution of the brain.[32]

4. Conclusion

The experiments reviewed in the first two sections of this chapter are concerned with human reasoning ability. These experiments seem, at first glance, to show that humans diverge from the normative principles of reasoning associated with the standard picture of rationality. Even within the standard picture, however, it is *possible* that subjects in these two reasoning experiments (as well as every other reasoning experiment that could be run) would make some misinterpretation that causes them to behave in a *seemingly* irrational manner. Even if this misinterpretation cannot be identified, a friend of the misinterpretation strategy can insist that there must still be some subtle, as yet undetected, misinterpretation occurring. For example, recall the modified version of the conjunction experiment in which subjects were asked to choose between two arguments—(A1), which advocates following the conjunction principle, and (A2), which advocates violating it. A friend of the rationality thesis could deny that subjects' selection of (A2) indicates that human reasoning competence lacks the general conjunction principle. Instead, she could argue, for example, that subjects misunderstand the choice between (A1) and (A2) or that the selection of (A2) is a performance error. In general, experimental evidence for the irrationality thesis can *always* be resisted in some such way. Prima facie, however, these resistance techniques offered by friends of the rationality thesis are *ad hoc* immunization strategies. Without some special theoretical considerations that suggest otherwise, it seems unlikely that interfering factors are always behind all divergences from the norms. In particular, defenders of the rationality thesis need to offer theoretical considerations that would justify the misinterpretation strategy or other strategies that reconcile the rationality thesis with the results of the reasoning experiments. In the next three chapters, I turn to just such arguments.

[32] Daniel Dennett, *The Intentional Stance* (Cambridge, Mass.: MIT Press, 1987), esp. 'Evolution, Error and Intentionality', for reasons similar to those I mention here, is sceptical about the very possibility of knowing what a cognitive state means. I do not attempt to deal with this sceptical position in the present book. My position in this brief section is not sceptical like Dennett's; I just say that neuroscience alone cannot determine what principles of reasoning are embodied in human reasoning competence.

4

Charity

IN the previous chapter, I considered a general strategy for interpreting
the results of the reasoning experiments whereby all reasoning behaviours
that diverged from the normative principles of reasoning are interpreted
as performance errors. I argued that, unless special considerations could
be offered in favour of it, this strategy amounts to an immunization
strategy for the rationality thesis. In this chapter, I focus on one type
of consideration in favour of interpreting all divergences from the normative principles as performance errors, namely *charity*. W. V. O. Quine
developed this principle as a guide for language translation. The idea
under discussion in this chapter is to extend this principle as a guide for
interpreting human reasoning competence. In Section 1, I discuss the
principle of charity and arguments for it. I then turn to how this principle
might be extended to reasoning competence. If charity should be applied
to the interpretation of human reasoning ability, then the errors that
subjects make in the reasoning experiments should be interpreted as
performance errors, thereby making the case for the rationality thesis. I
examine this possibility in Section 2. In Section 3, I consider an alternative to the principle of charity known as the principle of humanity.
If the principle of humanity is preferable to the principle of charity,
perhaps the charity argument for the rationality thesis is undermined. In
Section 4, I consider an elaboration of the principle of charity that is
supposed to answer the worries that give rise to the principle of humanity
and revitalize the charity argument for the rationality thesis. In Section
5, I consider further objections to the charity argument. In Section 6,
I conclude.

1. The Principle of Charity

Quine, in his seminal work *Word and Object*,[1] sketches what he calls
the principle of charity,[2] a principle for guiding language translation in

---

[1] W. V. O. Quine, *Word and Object* (Cambridge, Mass.: MIT Press, 1960).

[2] Ibid. 59, where Quine credits N. L. Wilson, 'Substances without Substrata', *Review
of Metaphysics*, 12 (1959), 521–39, with coining the term 'principle of charity'.

cases of 'radical interpretation' which involves the 'recovery of a man's current language from his currently observed responses . . . [by someone] who, unaided by an interpreter, is out to penetrate and translate a language hitherto unknown'.[3] To quote his section 'Translating Logical Connectives' at length, Quine writes:

let us suppose that certain natives are said to accept as true certain sentences translatable in the form *p* **and not-***p*. Now this claim is absurd under our semantic criteria. And, not to be dogmatic about them, what criteria might one prefer? Wanton translation can make natives sound as queer as one pleases. Better translation imposes our logic upon them . . .[4]

That fair translation presumes logical laws is implicit in practice even where, to speak paradoxically, no foreign language is involved. Thus when to our querying of an English sentence an English speaker answers 'Yes and no,' we assume that the queried sentence is meant differently in the affirmation and the negation; this rather than that he would be so silly as to affirm and deny the same thing. . . . The maxim of translation underlying all this is that assertions startlingly false on the face of them are likely to turn on hidden differences in language. This maxim is strong enough in all of us to swerve us even from the homophonic method [of translation, i.e. translating a speaker's utterance as the phonetically equivalent sentence in the language that is being translated into] . . . The common sense behind the maxim is that one's interlocutor's silliness, beyond a certain point, is less likely than bad translation or . . . linguistic divergence.[5]

The idea is that if I translate someone speaking an unknown language as saying something absurd, I should scrutinize my translation, not the rationality of the person. Of course, it is *sometimes* appropriate to translate someone as saying something absurd. For example, when Woody Allen says that his one regret in life is that he is not someone else,[6] he *intends* to be saying something absurd (namely, that he could be someone other than himself)—the absurdity of the comment is what makes it funny. Certainly, there are ways to construe Allen's comment so it does not violate the law of non-contradiction; for example, one could translate him as saying that he wishes he had gone into some other line of work rather than being a film director. Such a translation, however, is not appropriate; given the context (namely, a line delivered in a stand-up routine), it makes sense to interpret Allen's utterance as

---

[3] Quine, *Word and Object*, 28.   [4] Ibid. 58.   [5] Ibid. 59.
[6] Woody Allen, *Side Effects* (New York: Random House, 1975), 151.

silly and absurd. Quine need not be read as saying otherwise; Quine should be (charitably) read as focusing on 'sincere assertion'.[7]

To understand better the motivation for this view, consider the following example: suppose a computer is running a program and you are assigned the task of figuring out what program it is running on the basis of its output. Attempting to do so requires assuming the computer is, for the most part, working properly. To see this, consider how difficult the task would be if you did not assume that at least *some* of the computer's output was the right output. If you took every behaviour of the computer as a mistake, you would have no clue at all as to the proper function of the computer; without assuming that the computer behaves properly *some* of the time, your task would be impossible. In order to offer an interpretation of the computer's behaviour, you have to assume that the computer does what it should at least some of the time. This is basically the motivation behind the principle of charity: in order to interpret a person's utterances, you have to assume that her sincere utterances are rational much of the time.

Quine's injunction about translation is, however, ambiguous. Sometimes he seems to be suggesting that a person's utterances should be interpreted charitably *unless* there is strong empirical evidence to the contrary (for example, when he says that 'silliness, beyond a certain point, is *less likely* than bad translation'[8]) while at other times he seems to be suggesting that people should *never* be interpreted uncharitably (for example, when he says that our logic should be *imposed* on the people we translate[9]). Rather than engaging in Quine exegesis with the aim of determining which version of the principle of charity he holds, I will simply distinguish between a *strong* and a *weak* version of the principle of charity. On the weak version, a person's (sincere) assertions should not be judged irrational *unless* there is strong evidence for doing so; on the strong version, a person's assertions should *never* be interpreted as irrational.[10]

---

[7] The phrase is from Stephen Stich, *The Fragmentation of Reason* (Cambridge, Mass.: MIT Press, 1990), 30–2.

[8] Quine, *Word and Object*, 58, emphasis added.   [9] Ibid.

[10] Paul Thagard and Richard Nisbett, 'Rationality and Charity', *Philosophy of Science*, 50 (1983), 252, distinguish between five 'levels of stringency' that might be applied to the principle of charity:

(1) Do not assume *a priori* that people are irrational.
(2) Do not give any special prior favor to the interpretation that people are irrational.
(3) Do not judge people to be irrational unless you have an empirically justified account of what they are doing when they violate normative standards.

Quine is also not clear whether the claim that the principle of charity is useful should be interpreted as an empirical or a conceptual claim. I shall argue below that the principle of charity cannot be successfully defended if its usefulness is meant to be an empirical matter. I will thus turn my attention to assessing arguments that it is a conceptual truth that the principle of charity should be applied when interpreting a person's utterances.

Just as it is an empirical fact that knowledge of Latin is useful in trying to translate a hitherto unknown Romance language, it might be an empirical fact that the principle of charity would be usefully applied in situations requiring radical interpretation. An empirical argument for using the principle of charity would go something like this:

(1) Up to now, all the people we understand rarely make irrational (sincere) assertions.

(2) Therefore, all people rarely make irrational (sincere) assertions.

(3) Therefore, people should not be interpreted as making irrational assertions (the principle of charity).

It is not at all clear that we are justified in making the initial observation about the people we understand if the appropriateness of the principle of charity is in question. Even assuming the validity of inductive arguments, (1) seems to assume (3). In order for me to translate (homophonically) my neighbour's sincere English assertions, I need to invoke the principle of charity because the epistemological situation in the case of radical translation is the same as that encountered when trying to translate homophonically the utterance of someone who speaks a seemingly phonetically identical language.[11] Other empirical arguments in favour of the principle of charity will suffer from the same problem: any attempt to ground the general application of the principle of charity will have to appeal to its success in some particular interpretation. If the value of the principle of charity is really in question, we cannot assume that it is usefully applied to any particular interpretative

(4) Interpret people as irrational only given overwhelming evidence.
(5) Never interpret people as irrational.

My weak version of the principle of charity is more or less their (3) and my strong version is more or less their (5).

[11] According to Quine, *Word and Object*, 78, 'we could scorn that hypothesis [that homophonic translation provides the right translation] and devise other analytic hypotheses that would attribute unimagined views to our compatriot, while conforming to all his dispositions to verbal response to all possible stimulations'.

task. Attempting to justify the use of the principle of charity empirically by appealing to the seeming rationality of those people we think we understand thus begs the question.[12] The usefulness of the principle of charity is, thus, a conceptual matter.

Having settled the nature of the question as to whether the principle of charity should be used as a guide for interpretation, I now turn to the question itself. The argument in favour of the principle of charity, simply put, is that we should interpret people's assertions as being rational because their assertions reflect their beliefs and it is constitutive of what a belief is that the holder of a belief is rational. It follows from our thinking other people have beliefs that we think their assertions are rational and that we must interpret them according to the principle of charity because instances of irrationality cannot be described in our everyday vocabulary of beliefs, desires, and the like. This is not supposed to be an empirical fact; it is supposed to be true in virtue of what beliefs are, what intentional interpretation is, and so on. Daniel Dennett writes:

An intentional interpretation of an agent is an exercise that attempts to make sense of the agent's acts, and when acts occur that make no sense, they cannot be straightforwardly interpreted in sense-making terms. Something must give: we allow that the agent either sort of believes this or that 'for all practical purposes', or believes some falsehood which creates a context in which what had appeared to be irrational turns out to be rational after all.[13]

When we cannot make sense of a person's utterances through straightforward interpretation, we adopt an interpretative stance that makes sense of her utterances. For example, suppose that I interpret Juanita as saying something that means 'It is raining and it is not raining'. The principle of charity says I should question the accuracy of my interpretation of her utterance rather than decide that she believes a blatant contradiction. The argument for this principle that I am sketching is roughly as follows: a person's utterances (typically) reflect her beliefs; beliefs, by their nature, cannot be contradictory; therefore, a person should not (typically) be interpreted as uttering contradictions. With this argument in hand, I turn to the question of whether the principle of charity should be a guide to interpreting human reasoning competence.

[12] For a somewhat similar argument, see Stich, *The Fragmentation of Reason*, 35–6.
[13] Daniel Dennett, 'Making Sense of Ourselves', in *The Intentional Stance* (Cambridge, Mass.: MIT Press, 1987), 87.

2. Charity Extended to Reasoning Competence

Various philosophers have argued for applying the principle of charity to the interpretation of the principles of reasoning embodied in our reasoning competence.[14] The idea is to think of interpreting a principle in our reasoning competence as analogous to translating an utterance. Proper interpretation of a person's behaviour in general (and her reasoning behaviour in particular), like proper interpretation of a person's utterances, requires the rationality of that person; if a person is not rational, it is impossible to attribute beliefs, thoughts, and judgements to her. This is true because the principle of charity applies in so far as the person (or system) has beliefs; if a system has beliefs, then it must be rational.[15] In other words, in order to characterize a person's reasoning competence, you have to assume that the principles she uses are basically rational. If it is appropriate to apply the principle of charity to human reasoning competence, then the rationality thesis seems to follow.

Just as there are weak and strong versions of the principle of charity as applied to interpreting utterances, there are weak and strong versions of the principle of charity as applied to interpreting human reasoning ability. The strong version of the principle of charity is that people should *never* be interpreted as irrational. If it is appropriate to apply the principle of charity to human reasoning competence, then the principle would justify the adoption of the rational competence strategy for interpreting human reasoning. According to this interpretative strategy, all divergences from the normative principles of reasoning should be classified as performance errors. The truth of the rationality thesis follows from adopting this strategy. The weak version of the principle of charity applied to reasoning is that *unless* there is strong empirical evidence to the contrary, people should be interpreted as rational. The weak version would justify some version of the rational competence strategy in the absence of strong empirical evidence against the rationality of human reasoning competence.

The argument for the principle of charity applied to interpreting reasoning competence is similar to, but even simpler than, the argument

---

[14] e.g. Donald Davidson, 'Incoherence and Irrationality', *Dialectica*, 39 (1985), 345–54; Davidson, 'On the Very Idea of a Conceptual Scheme', *Proceedings and Addresses of the American Philosophical Association*, 47 (1974), 5–20; repr. in *Inquiries into Truth and Interpretation* (Oxford: Oxford University Press, 1984); and Daniel Dennett, *Brainstorms* (Cambridge, Mass.: MIT Press, 1978); and *The Intentional Stance*.

[15] See Dennett, *The Intentional Stance*, esp. 'Making Sense of Ourselves'.

for the principle of charity applied to interpreting utterances. Recall that the argument supporting the principle of charity applied to interpreting utterances pointed out that utterances reflect beliefs and that rationality is a necessary pre-condition for a person to have beliefs. The argument for the principle of charity applied to interpreting reasoning competence requires only the second part of the argument for charity applied to utterances. Simply put, the argument says that if an agent has beliefs, then she must be interpreted as being rational. The clearest formulation of an argument for it comes from Stephen Stich, who ultimately disagrees with the argument. He writes:

It is part of what it is to be a belief with a given intentional characterization, part of the concept of such a belief, if you will, to interact with other beliefs in a rational way—a way which more or less mirrors the laws of logic. This sort of interaction with other beliefs is a conceptually necessary condition for being the belief that **not-p** or for being the belief that **if p, then** q. Thus if a belief fails to manifest the requisite interactions with other beliefs, it just does not count as the belief that **not-p** or the belief that **if p, then** q.[16]

The point is that what makes a mental state count as a belief is the appropriateness of its interaction with other mental states, especially other beliefs. For example, a mental state M would not count as a belief that p if M is believed at the same time as **not-p** is. Similarly, a mental state S would not count as the belief that **if p, then** q if S is believed at the same time as both p and **not-q**. If this argument is valid, then one need only argue that humans have beliefs to support the strong principle of charity. The strong principle of charity would, in turn, justify adopting the rational competence strategy for characterizing human reasoning competence, which interprets all divergences from the normative principles of reasoning as performance errors, and thereby establishes the rationality thesis.

As an example of how the principle of charity would help to reconcile the rationality thesis with the results of the reasoning experiments, consider the conjunction experiment. The prima facie plausible interpretation of the results of this experiment is that humans should be characterized as having a reasoning competence that leads them to violate the conjunction principle systematically. This, in turn, suggests that human reasoning competence should be characterized as lacking the conjunction principle and, hence, that humans are irrational. The natural interpretation of these results is not, in this case, a charitable

---

[16] Stich, *The Fragmentation of Reason*, 37.

one because a charitable interpretation would interpret people as rational. Adopting an interpretation strategy that reconciles the reasoning experiments with the rationality thesis would be justified by the principle of charity applied to human reasoning competence because such a strategy does not interpret the experiments as showing that humans are irrational. Simply put, charity suggests that all errors are performance errors. This underscores the fact that even the strong principle of charity is compatible with attributing mistakes to people—but only if the mistakes are due to performance errors. The strong principle of charity is *not* compatible with seeing humans as having a reasoning competence that diverges from the normative principles of reasoning.

The principle of charity applied to human reasoning competence supports interpreting the results of the reasoning experiments as compatible with the rationality thesis by saying that all divergences from the normative principles of reasoning are due to performance errors. In Chapter 3, I said that adopting the rational competence strategy without a general argument for doing so is an immunization strategy, an *ad hoc* procedure that discounts all empirical evidence against a theory. Note that the rational competence strategy does not function as an immunization strategy in the argument for the rationality thesis currently under consideration, because the principle of charity, if it is appropriate to apply to human reasoning competence, provides the very sort of general argument for the rational competence strategy that was missing in the argument under consideration in the previous chapter.

I want to step back and lay out the argument under discussion. The argument from the principle of charity to the conclusion that the results of the conjunction experiment are compatible with the rationality thesis can be spelled out as follows:

(C4) Humans should not be interpreted as diverging from the normative principles of reasoning (the principle of charity).

(C5) On the natural interpretation of the conjunction experiment, people violate the conjunction principle (a normative principle of reasoning).

(C6) The natural interpretation of the conjunction experiment is mistaken; a proper interpretation of the conjunction experiment would be one that does not interpret people as irrational.

The argument from (C4) and (C5) justifies the application of strategies that reconcile the results of the conjunction experiment with the rationality thesis. This argument can easily be generalized to an argument for the conclusion that the reasoning experiments do not count for the irrationality thesis (and hence are compatible with the rationality thesis) as follows:

(4) Humans should not be interpreted as diverging from the normative principles of reasoning (the principle of charity).

(5) On the natural interpretation of the reasoning experiments, people violate a normative principle of reasoning.

(6) The natural interpretation of the reasoning experiments is mistaken; a proper interpretation of these experiments would be one that does not interpret people as irrational.

The argument from (4) and (5) justifies interpreting the reasoning experiments as uncovering performance errors but not competence errors.

Are the arguments for (C6) and (6) valid? This depends on whether the principle of charity invoked in the first premise of each argument is the strong or the weak version. Friends of the irrationality thesis can (and some do) embrace something like the weak version of the principle of charity; they claim, however, to have strong evidence for interpreting the reasoning experiments as providing support for the irrationality thesis.[17] The weak version of premise (4) would be:

(4′) Unless there is strong evidence otherwise, humans should not be interpreted as diverging from the normative principles of reasoning (the weak principle of charity).

Since friends of the irrationality thesis claim that there *is* strong evidence for interpreting the reasoning experiments as showing humans to be irrational, they would accept (4′) but not (4); (6) does not, however, follow from (4′) and (5). If only the weak version of charity is invoked, the argument is not valid; only the strong version of the principle of charity can provide a good argument for the rationality thesis. But is the strong version of the principle of charity true? If not, then the principle of charity, regardless of whether the weak version of the principle of charity is true, would be of no help to the rationality thesis. In the sections that follow, I will set aside the weak version of the principle of charity in order to turn my attention to whether the strong version is true.

---

[17] See e.g. Amos Tversky and Daniel Kahneman, 'Extensional versus Intuitive Reasoning: The Conjunction Fallacy in Probability Judgment', *Psychology Review*, 90 (1983), 304, where a *weak* version of the principle of charity is endorsed. In the same article, evidence for the view that humans violate the conjunction rule is cited.

3. The Principle of Humanity

Consider the following example, which is sometimes taken to count against the principle of charity.

> Suppose Paul has just arrived at a party and asserts 'The man with a martini is a philosopher.' And suppose that the facts are that there is a man in plain view who is drinking water from a martini glass and that he is not a philosopher [call him Biff]. Suppose also that in fact there is only one man at the party drinking a martini, that he is a philosopher, and that he is out of sight [call him Ludwig] . . .[18]

According to the principle of charity, one should interpret Paul as asserting that Ludwig, the man out of sight, is a philosopher, because this interpretation 'is simple and makes his remark true'[19] and hence interprets Paul as rational. But what one really would do, and what one ought to do, is interpret Paul as asserting that *Biff*, the man drinking water from the Martini glass, is a philosopher. Although this interpretation of Paul's utterance sees him as saying something *false* (since Biff is not a philosopher), it is explicable by putting ourselves in Paul's place. I can easily imagine myself both inferring that someone drinking a clear liquid out of a Martini glass is drinking a Martini and mistaking a non-philosopher for a philosopher (particularly, for example, if the non-philosopher is talking about philosophy or if he looks like someone I know who is a philosopher). I can thus imagine myself in Paul's situation saying 'The man with the Martini is a philosopher' and, by this, intending to refer to Biff. In contrast, I cannot imagine a plausible story of how I could be in Paul's situation and mean to refer to Ludwig when saying 'The man with the Martini is a philosopher'.[20]

The moral of the story is that sometimes we should interpret people as saying things that are false if doing so is the more plausible thing to do when we put ourselves in their point of view; with respect to interpretation, preserving *empathy* is more important than preserving truth.

---

[18] Richard Grandy, 'Reference, Meaning and Belief', *Journal of Philosophy*, 70 (1973), 445.   [19] Ibid.

[20] Actually, this is a bit fast. I can imagine lots of such stories. For example, perhaps Paul was told in advance that the only philosopher at the party will be drinking lots of Martinis, or perhaps, just outside the party, Paul ran into a friend of his who told him that Ludwig the philosopher was in the back yard drinking a Martini. We can take the above example, however, to exclude these possibilities; given that Paul has no more information about philosophers and Martini-drinkers at the party than what he can see when he arrives, the interpretation I describe above that interprets Paul as referring to Biff, and thus asserting a falsehood, is the *natural* interpretation even if it is not the charitable one.

The empathic interpretation of Paul's comment is sanctioned by an alternative to the principle of charity known as the *principle of humanity*. Richard Grandy, who coined the phrase, describes the principle of humanity as a constraint on the translation of a person's utterances and the interpretation of a person's reasoning practice in such a way that 'the imputed pattern of relations among beliefs, desires, and the world be *as similar to our own as possible*'.[21] Simply put, whereas the principle of charity constrains translation so as to maximize the rationality of the translatee, the principle of humanity constrains translation so as to maximize agreement between the translatee and the translator.[22]

Just as the principle of charity can be extended to reasoning, so too can the principle of humanity. The principle of charity says that we should always interpret another as following normative principles of reasoning, while the principle of humanity says that we should always interpret another as following principles of reasoning that we would use in the same situation. Often, these two strategies result in the same interpretation because often the principle we would expect ourselves to use would be the normative one and vice versa. Sometimes, however, as in the Martini example, the two strategies diverge. As another example, consider charity-type and humanity-type principles applied to the realm of vision. If I interpreted another using a charity-type principle, I would expect that she would never succumb to optical illusions, whereas, if I used a humanity-type principle, I would expect that she would succumb to the sort of optical illusions that I succumb to in roughly similar situations to those in which I succumb to them.

The same reasons that prove that the usefulness of the principle of charity cannot be an empirical truth also prove that the usefulness of the principle of humanity cannot not be an empirical truth. An empirical justification of the principle of humanity might go as follows:

(H1) People we understand rarely reason in ways unlike the ways we reason.

[21] Grandy, 'Reference, Meaning and Belief', 443, emphasis added.

[22] Instead of seeing the principle of humanity as an alternative to the principle of charity, one can see it as a *version* of the principle of charity. Quine in some places can be read as suggesting this. In *Word and Object*, 219, he says that when translating, 'we project ourselves into what, from his remarks and other indications, we imagine the speaker's state of mind to have been, and then we say what, in our language, is natural and relevant for us in the state just feigned'. Whether the principle of humanity is a version or an alternative to charity does not matter much beyond the fact that the principle of humanity seems plausible for many of the same reasons that the principle of charity does.

(H2) Therefore, all people reason like we do.

(H3) Therefore, we should interpret people as reasoning the way we do (the principle of humanity).

But unless we have already applied the principle of humanity, we have no good reason for thinking that the people we think we understand reason like we do. (H1) assumes (H3), hence this argument begs the question. Other empirical arguments for the usefulness of the principle of humanity suffer from the same problem. Without assuming the principle of humanity, an empirical justification of this principle cannot get off the ground.

The principle of humanity diverges from the principle of charity in some of the interpretations it will sanction. Given this, someone who wants to use either of these principles to support the rationality thesis has two alternatives: she could show that the principle of humanity can be used in place of the principle of charity to defend the rationality thesis or she could argue that the principle of charity is justified while the principle of humanity is not. I will consider these alternatives in turn.

First, suppose for the sake of argument that the Martini-type example shows that the principle of humanity is right. The question then becomes whether the principle of humanity is strong enough to support the rationality thesis. Recall the charity argument for the rationality thesis:

(4) Humans should not be interpreted as diverging from the normative principles of reasoning (the principle of charity).

(5) On the natural interpretation of the reasoning experiments, people violate some normative principles of reasoning.

(6) The natural interpretation of the reasoning experiments is mistaken; a proper interpretation of these experiments would be one that does not show people are irrational.

On the humanity reading of the principle of charity, (4) would be modified as follows:

(4″) Humans should not be interpreted as diverging from the principles of reasoning that I (the person doing the interpreting) would follow.

But (4′) and (5) do not entail (6). To get (6), (5) needs to be modified as follows:

(5′) On the natural interpretation of the reasoning experiments, people diverge from the principles of reasoning that I would follow.

But $(5')$ is just false. Consider the selection task. I might well select the wrong cards to examine if I am asked to turn over only those cards necessary to test the rule 'If a card has a vowel on one side, then it has an even number on the other side'. Even if I do not think that I would make such a mistake given my actual experiences (for example, given that I have read dozens of articles about the selection task), if my experiences had been different (that is, if I had not read these articles), I could easily make such a mistake as selecting the vowel card and the even-number card rather than the vowel card and the odd-number card. In general, the principle of humanity does not guarantee that the results of the reasoning experiments ought to be read as consistent with the rationality thesis because, for all the principle of humanity says, the person doing the interpreting might well be irrational. This shows that, for the purposes of finding an argument for the rationality thesis, the principle of humanity will not work; if anything will provide the basis for an argument for the rationality thesis, it will be the strong version of the principle of charity.

That the principle of humanity will not suffice as the basis for an argument for the rationality thesis (of the form of the argument from (4) and (5) to (6)) should not be a surprise since the principle of humanity can be seen as a particular instance of the weak version of the principle of charity and the weak version of the principle of charity also fails as the basis for an argument for the rationality thesis. Recall that the weak version of the principle of charity says that unless there is strong evidence otherwise, humans should not be interpreted as diverging from the normative principles of reasoning. One kind of evidence that suggests humans should be interpreted as diverging from the norms might be that I do in fact diverge from the norms or that I might do so. If this sort of evidence is considered, the weak version of the principle of charity encompasses the principle of humanity. But, as I argued above in Section 2, the weak version of the principle of charity will not suffice as a basis for an argument for the rationality thesis. Thus, it should be no surprise that the principle of humanity will also not suffice in this capacity.

The first alternative available to those friends of the rationality thesis who want to use the principle of charity to make their case thus fails. I turn, therefore, to the second alternative, namely to arguments that say the principle of humanity should not be preferred to the principle of charity. I began this section by noting that the Martini example is often taken to count against the strong principle of charity. According to the strong principle of charity applied to translation of utterances, we ought to interpret Paul's assertion that 'The man with the Martini is a philosopher' as meaning that *Ludwig*, the philosopher who is out of sight, is drinking a Martini because, on this interpretation, what Paul says is true. But this is not how we naturally do (or should) interpret Paul. Instead, we interpret (as we ought to) Paul as meaning that Biff, the man Paul can see, who is drinking water out of a Martini glass, is a philosopher. But if this is right, then the strong principle of charity is mistaken—sometimes we ought to interpret people as saying things that are false. This, in turn, does not bode well for either the strong principle of charity applied to reasoning or its use in an argument for the rationality thesis. Friends of the principle of charity do not, however, take this argument to be a strong one. Some of them argue that the principle of charity is immune to such objections because it is supposed to be applied *holistically*, that is, because the principle of charity applies not to isolated utterances or individual principles of reasoning, but to whole sets of utterances or principles. This response holds some promise for answering the challenge of the principle of humanity and thereby saving the principle of charity argument for the rationality thesis. I turn to this response in the next section.

4. Holism

The principle of charity applied to language is more complex than my initial exposition of it suggested. I implicitly suggested that interpreting an utterance is a piecemeal procedure. This is an over-simplification of the principle of charity. The interpretation of an utterance is a *holistic* process; 'only in the context of a language does a sentence have meaning'.[23] One cannot interpret the single utterance of a person without having an interpretation (at least an implicit one) of her language in general. The same sort of point is relevant to the application of the principle of charity to reasoning and reasoning competence. A particular inferential behaviour or a particular principle in reasoning competence that causes such behaviour cannot be interpreted on its own but rather must be interpreted holistically, that is, as part of a collection of behaviours and/or principles.

The holistic version of the principle of charity provides its defenders

---

[23] Donald Davidson, 'Truth and Meaning', in *Inquiries into Truth and Interpretation*, 22.

with a powerful resource for dealing with cases like the Martini example in which it is tempting to see people as making mistakes. The Martini example was a problem for the principle of charity because the natural interpretation of Paul's beliefs attributed a false (and, hence, uncharitable) belief to him (namely, it attributed to him the belief that Biff is a philosopher drinking a Martini when in fact Biff is neither a philosopher nor, at present, a Martini-drinker), while the principle of charity interprets Paul charitably, that is, as having true beliefs. The friend of the principle of charity can say that this was just an overly simple picture of the principle of charity. On the holistic version of charity, one does not offer interpretations in isolation; one does so only in the context of a *complete* interpretation of a person's beliefs, reasoning competence, and so on. According to the holistic version of the principle of charity, what matters is not only whether Paul's beliefs about Biff's profession and his drinking habits are true, but whether Paul's principles of reasoning are rational and whether his *whole system* of beliefs are for the most part true. Seen in this way, the principle of charity does not entail a counter-intuitive interpretation of Paul's belief in the Martini example, but is compatible with interpreting his belief in the more natural way (that is, Paul believes that Biff, not Ludwig, is the Martini-drinker and the philosopher); this is because the natural interpretation of Paul's belief about the Martini-drinking philosopher arguably fits with the most charitable interpretation of Paul's entire belief set and cognitive faculties. In general, the holistic version of the principle of charity is compatible with attributing false beliefs or faulty faculties in the context of a charitable interpretation of a person's entire network of beliefs and cognitive mechanisms.

Having elaborated the holistic version of the principle of charity, I now turn to whether it can be used to support the charity argument for the rationality thesis. Recall that this argument is as follows:

(4) Humans should not be interpreted as diverging from the normative principles of reasoning (the principle of charity).

(5) On the natural interpretation of the reasoning experiments, people violate some normative principles of reasoning.

(6) The natural interpretation of the reasoning experiments is mistaken; a proper interpretation of these experiments would be one that does not show people are irrational.

The question is whether this argument is valid when (4) is construed as the holistic version of the principle of charity. Whether it is depends on whether the holistic version of the principle of charity is compatible with seeing human reasoning competence as containing principles that diverge from the normative principles of reasoning.

The holistic reading of the principle of charity deals with examples like the one involving the Martini example by allowing for local error in the quest for an overall interpretation that is preferable to the one sanctioned by the non-holistic version of the principle of charity. In virtue of allowing for local error, the holistic version seems to allow non-normative principles of reasoning into human reasoning competence as part of an overall charitable interpretation. The potential problem with this is that by letting in error, the holistic principle also lets in irrationality; doing so has the effect of making the holistic version of the principle of charity an inappropriate premiss in an argument for the rationality thesis.

Take, for example, the abstract selection task in which subjects' behaviour violates the rules of logic. The misinterpretation strategy or some other version of the rational competence strategy would attribute this divergence from the normative principles of reasoning to performance errors rather than to humans having a reasoning competence that diverges from principles based on rules of logic. For the principle of charity to justify the misinterpretation strategy, it must require that people always be interpreted as rational, in particular, as having only rational principles in their reasoning competence. The holistic version of the principle of charity does not make this requirement. The holistic version of charity is compatible with the fact that subjects in the abstract selection task do not follow principles based on the rules of logic because they do not have these principles in their reasoning competence, as long as this divergence from the normative principles of reasoning is offered in the context of an account that sees humans as for the most part rational. For example, the holistic version of charity would allow that humans might have some short-cut heuristics in their reasoning competence responsible for logical reasoning that approximate the rules of logic in some instances (as in the concrete selection task). The problem with this is that, if, for the sake of overall charity, the principle of charity permits interpreting people as making some errors, it is in danger of permitting, also for the sake of overall charity, the interpretation of people as being irrational. Once such irrationality is allowed, the principle of charity no longer provides an adequate premiss for use in an argument for the rationality thesis.

A friend of both the charity argument for the rationality thesis and the holistic version of the principle of charity might try to come up with an argument that the holistic version of the principle of charity will not permit *any* irrationality. The idea is to develop a defence of the strong reading of the principle of charity—that is, the principle that humans should *never* be interpreted as irrational—that in some way encompasses holism. If this could be done, then a holistic version of the principle of charity could make an adequate premiss in a charity argument for the rationality thesis. I am not at all clear that this can be done. Doing so would require two steps: first, defend the strong reading of the principle of charity and, second, argue that this reading is compatible with a holistic reading of the principle of charity. In the next section, I will turn my attention to the first step: defending the strong version of the principle of charity. I will argue that the strong reading of the principle is too strong to be defensible. Because the charity argument for the rationality thesis requires the strong principle of charity, it fails to establish the rationality thesis.

5. The Strong Principle of Charity

Recall the argument for the rationality thesis that is based on the principle of charity:

(4) Humans should not be interpreted as diverging from the normative principles of reasoning (the principle of charity).

(5) On the natural interpretation of the reasoning experiments, people violate some normative principles of reasoning.

(6) The natural interpretation of the reasoning experiments is mistaken; a proper interpretation of these experiments would be one that does not show people are irrational.

I have thus far argued that for this argument to work, (4) should be read as saying that people should *never* be interpreted as being irrational and as advocating a non-holistic version of charity; failure to read (4) according to both of these constraints may allow principles that diverge from the normative principles of reasoning into reasoning competence. The upshot is that a *strong* version of the principle of charity is required for this argument to be relevant to the rationality thesis. There is a problem: examples like the one involving the Martini-drinking philosopher give rise to the worry that the strong principle of charity is mistaken because the strong principle of charity recommends a counter-intuitive

reading of Paul's assertion and his corresponding belief. Further examination of the soundness of the principle of charity is needed to address
this worry. I turn now to such an examination.

5.1. *Extending the Argument for the Principle of Charity*

Recall (from Section 2) how the principle of charity is supposed to be
applied to reasoning competence. The basic idea is that rationality is a
necessary pre-condition for ascribing beliefs to people; in so far as we
attribute beliefs to people, we must assume that they are rational. This
sort of argument seems to work for logical consistency. A mental state
does not seem to count as a belief that p if this state is believed at the
same time as **not-**p. What would it mean to say that Helen believes that
the moon is made of green cheese if she also believes that the moon is
not made of green cheese? Ascribing beliefs to a person seems to
require that she is rational in the sense of having principles in her
reasoning competence that preserve logical consistency.

This argument seems to justify using the principle of charity to support application of the misinterpretation strategy (or some other strategy for interpreting the reasoning experiments as compatible with the
rationality thesis) to the selection task because subjects, in selecting the
wrong cards, are violating principles that stem from rules of logic.
The principle of charity so justified would not, however, work to support
the application of the misinterpretation strategy to the conjunction experiment. In the conjunction experiment, subjects violate the conjunction
principle, which says that the probability of p occurring should be greater
than the probability of p **and** q occurring. It is, however, possible to fail
to follow this principle without violating the rules of logic. The argument that principles stemming from the rules of logic are required for
having beliefs is that the rules of logic are constitutive of having beliefs: a belief that p would not count as a belief that p if it did not interact
with beliefs like **not-**p, **if** p, **then** q, and so on, in the appropriate ways.
The question is whether the principles of probability are similarly constitutive of having beliefs. If not, then the sense of rationality involved
in the principle of charity is not broad enough to establish that the
rationality thesis is compatible with the results of all the reasoning
experiments, in particular, with those of the conjunction experiment.
Friends of the rationality thesis who want to use the principle of charity
argument to undermine the empirical support that the reasoning experiments give the irrationality thesis thus need to argue that having beliefs

requires not just the principles that stem from the rules of logic but also the principles that stem from probability theory. In particular, what the friend of the rationality thesis needs to show is that a belief that p would not count as a belief that p if the believer of p holds that the probability of p is *less* than the probability of p **and** q.

I am not convinced that such an argument can be made. If it cannot be made, then the principle of charity argument ultimately fails to be of help to the rationality thesis. If it *can* be made, the argument would have to focus on the connection between violating the conjunction principle and being susceptible to a Dutch book. Recall from Chapter 1 that if someone violates the conjunction principle, she is vulnerable to a Dutch book, that is, if she violates the conjunction principle, there is a set of bets that she will accept as fair such that she will lose money no matter what the outcome of the events on which she is betting. Just as it seems reasonable to say that a person does not really believe p if her belief that p contradicts her other beliefs, it might be reasonable to say that a person does not really believe p if her belief that p interacts with her other beliefs in such a way that she is susceptible to a Dutch book. If such an argument could be made, it would show that following the principles of probability is constitutive of beliefs; this would make the principle of charity broad enough so as to support the application of the misinterpretation strategy (or a similar strategy) to the conjunction experiment and other reasoning experiments relating to ascriptions of probability.

5.2. *The Finitary Predicament*

Assuming that such an argument could be successfully made for the principles of probability and the other normative principles of reasoning (this may be quite difficult in the case of some normative principles of reasoning besides those stemming from the rules of logic and probability), there is still another problem facing the argument in favour of the principle of charity. In Chapter 1, Section 3.3, I discussed the consequences of the human finitary predicament, namely that we have a limited amount of time, memory, computational resources, and the like to devote to the project of reasoning.[24] One consequence of this predicament is that a person does not have enough time to check a candidate new belief for logical compatibility with every other new belief

---

[24] Christopher Cherniak, *Minimal Rationality* (Cambridge, Mass.: MIT Press, 1986). I discuss additional implications of the human finitary predicament in Ch. 7, Sects. 2–4.

she holds; for every new belief p that she acquires, she does not have time to check all her old beliefs to see if any of them are logically equivalent to **not-p**. Given the human finitary predicament, it is quite possible that she will sometimes come to believe both p and **not-p**. Yet, if someone sometimes believes both p and **not-p**, it is sometimes reasonable to interpret her as believing p **and not-p**. The principle of charity is not compatible with this interpretation. Because the principle of charity conflicts with the human finitary predicament, the principle of charity seems in trouble.

Note that the finitary predicament is only a worry for friends of the strong principle of charity, that is, a version of the principle of charity incompatible with the attribution of *any* irrationality. A friend of a weak version of the principle of charity or a friend of a holistic account of charity that allows for the attribution of *some* irrationality for the sake of overall charitability could embrace the finitary predicament and in fact use it as an argument for the weaker version of the principle of charity. The idea would be that humans are *usually* rational but, due to the finitary predicament, our reasoning competence must diverge from the norms in some instances. The details of this are not important at the moment; the present question is whether the strong principle of charity is compatible with the human finitary predicament.

The argument for the strong principle of charity can be laid out as follows:

(7) If an agent has beliefs, the agent must be interpreted as always being rational.

(8) Humans have beliefs.

(9) Humans should be interpreted as being rational (the principle of charity).

One possible (though quite radical) reaction to the combination of the human finitary predicament and the argument for the principle of charity that involves (7) is to accept *eliminativism* about beliefs, namely, accept the view that humans have no beliefs because the word 'belief' is merely a term of common-sense psychology that does not actually refer to any of our mental states. The argument for eliminativism is as follows:

(7) If an agent has beliefs, the agent must be interpreted as always being rational (that is, the agent must be interpreted using the strong principle of charity).

(10) Because of our finitary predicament, humans are not rational
     (for example, we cannot maintain logical consistency among
     our own beliefs).

(11) Therefore, humans have no beliefs (eliminativism about
     beliefs).

Some people are willing to embrace (11); others are willing to embrace
a limited version of this conclusion—for example, in the case of insane
people[25]—while resisting it in general.[26] If you are a friend of the
rationality thesis and if you want to use the principle of charity in
defence of your view, you should avoid eliminativism about beliefs for
the following reasons. The principle of charity might support the rationality thesis by suggesting that our principles of reasoning should—
perhaps using the misinterpretation strategy or a similar strategy—be
interpreted as being compatible with the rationality thesis. The principle of charity can only do this work in so far as it is applied to beliefs,
principles of reasoning, cognitive mechanisms, and the standard entities
of psychological explanation. If humans have no beliefs and our mental
states are properly characterized in some other way, there is no telling
what mental-state attributions would count as charitable. The principle
of charity, if it works at all, only works in the familiar territory of
psychological explanation; without beliefs to interpret charitably, the
principle can provide no interpretative guidance and can be of no help
to the rationality thesis. This is not to say that eliminativism about
beliefs is incompatible with the rationality thesis. However, the argument for the rationality thesis based on the principle of charity will not
succeed if eliminativism is true.

Another possible response to the argument that the human finitary
predicament counts against using the principle of charity as a guide for
interpreting the reasoning experiments involves the competence–
performance distinction. According to this response, the limitations
resulting from the human finitary predicament affect *performance* not
competence. The fact that humans do not check candidate new beliefs
against all currently held beliefs to make sure they are compatible
would not, on this response, be due to the fact that human reasoning

---

[25] Dennett, *Brainstorms*, 10. Dennett thinks that our common-sense notion of what a
belief is requires scrutiny and alteration. See esp. 'Beyond Belief', in *The Intentional Stance*.

[26] For discussion of eliminativism about beliefs, see Dennett, 'Beyond Belief'; Paul
Churchland, *Scientific Realism and the Plasticity of Mind* (Cambridge: Cambridge Uni-
versity Press, 1979); and Stephen Stich, *From Folk Psychology to Cognitive Science*
(Cambridge, Mass.: MIT Press, 1983).

competence lacks the normative principles of reasoning but would rather be due to performance errors, in particular, they would be performance errors due to *psychological factors*, that is, errors due to basic facts about the human condition.

As an analogy, consider the following example from linguistics. Imagine a sentence so long that no human could have enough time in her life to read it completely. Such a sentence, despite its length, could well be grammatical. That humans cannot make this determination is not a limit on human linguistic *competence*—we may have the proper principles in our linguistic competence to make correct judgements about grammaticality—rather, it is a limit on the amount of time that humans live, which is clearly a performance factor. This is like a computer that is programmed to generate prime numbers: no matter how long the computer runs, there will always be more prime numbers that it will not have had time to generate. This does not reflect poorly on the quality of the algorithm the computer is running—the computer's prime-number-calculating competence—rather it reflects the time limitations facing the computer.

With respect to reasoning, the suggestion is that the human finitary predicament constrains reasoning performance but not reasoning competence; even given the human finitary predicament, it is possible that we have the normative principles of reasoning in our reasoning competence. The problem with using this move as a response to the finitary predicament objection to the principle of charity is that either this move is unsupported or it begs the question. The principle of charity is being invoked as a reason for *not* interpreting the results of the reasoning experiments as providing support for the irrationality thesis; in other words, the principle is being invoked to provide support for the view that humans make certain sorts of performance error but not errors due to our competence. The finitary predicament is a challenge to the invocation of this principle. Without any independent reason for believing in the rationality thesis, there is no justification for responding to this challenge with the claim that all errors due to the finitary predicament are performance errors. To cite (whether implicitly or explicitly) the principle of charity as a reason for thinking that the finitary predicament is not relevant to reasoning competence but is only relevant to performance begs the question. The point is that, without particular support for doing so, friends of the rationality thesis cannot just claim that the limitations due to the finitary predicament do not apply to reasoning competence for the same reason that they cannot, without particular support, claim that the reasoning experiments do not provide any evidence about reasoning competence. The principle of charity is supposed to provide support for interpreting the reasoning experiments as pointing merely to performance errors. Friends of the rationality thesis must find another way to defend this application of the principle of charity because invoking the competence–performance distinction in the manner suggested above simply fails.

5.3. Minimal Rationality

Another possible response to the finitary predicament objection to the strong principle of charity involves weakening (7)—the claim that for an agent to have beliefs, she must be rational—to get the claim that for an agent to have a belief, she only needs to be rational enough.[27] Christopher Cherniak tries to flesh out just how rational humans need to be to have beliefs. His answer is that for a mental state to count as a belief, it must interact in some *significant subset* of the ways that such a belief would interact if it were held by an agent who was fully rational. For example, rather than *always* eliminating inconsistencies among her beliefs, according to Cherniak, to count as rational enough, an agent need only reason in accordance with the following:

> MINIMAL CONSISTENCY PRINCIPLE: If inconsistencies arise in your belief set, you should *sometimes* eliminate *some* of them.[28]

Cherniak argues that *minimal rationality*—sometimes the agent reasons in accordance with some of the norms of reasoning—is a sufficient condition for the attribution of beliefs to an agent and for an agent to qualify for psychological explanations.

The argument for the principle of charity currently under consideration is:

(7) If an agent has beliefs, the agent must be interpreted as always being rational.

(8) Humans have beliefs.

(9) Humans should be interpreted as being rational (the principle of charity).

If (7) is rejected because of the finitary predicament of humans, this argument fails. (7) might, however, be modified to take the human

---

[27] See Cherniak, *Minimal Rationality*; and Stich, *The Fragmentation of Reason*, 39– 43.   [28] This principle is adapted from Cherniak, *Minimal Rationality*, 16.

finitary predicament into account by applying the notion of minimal rationality. This would result in an argument that humans should be interpreted as minimally rational, that is, as sometimes following the norms of reasoning. The recast argument would go as follows:

(7′) If an agent has beliefs, the agent must be interpreted as being *minimally* rational.

(8) Humans have beliefs.

(9′) Humans should be interpreted as being *minimally* rational (call this the *minimal principle of charity*).

The question is whether the minimal principle of charity is strong enough to undercut the irrationality thesis in the way the principle of charity is supposed to. Recall that if the strong principle of charity is justified, it can support the application of the misinterpretation strategy (or other similar strategy) to all of the reasoning experiments; so interpreted, the reasoning experiments do not count in favour of the irrationality thesis and are compatible with the rationality thesis. The human finitary predicament, however, counts against the strong principle of charity. The minimal principle of charity takes this predicament into account. Can, then, the minimal principle of charity take the place of the principle of charity in an argument for the rationality thesis, namely, the argument from (4) and (5) to (6)?

Consider again the selection task. Subjects in this experiment seem, at first glance, to be violating a principle that stems from the rules of logic. The principle of charity justifies interpreting the results of the selection task as compatible with the rationality thesis. It does so because interpreting someone as violating a principle based on a rule of logic is interpreting her as irrational and it is uncharitable to interpret someone as irrational. In contrast, it seems consistent with the minimal principle of charity to interpret someone as making such a violation. An agent is minimally rational if she makes *some* but not necessarily all of the inferences a perfectly rational agent would make. Thus, reasoning as a subject does in the selection task is consistent with an agent's being minimally rational; the selection task could be one of those rational inferences she does not make.

The same is true for any reasoning experiment. The strong principle of charity is of use to friends of the rationality thesis because it counts against *any* interpretation of an agent as irrational. The minimal principle of charity, because it allows for some irrationality, fails to fulfil this function. The results of any reasoning experiment are consistent with minimal rationality so long as there are some occasions in which humans reason in accordance with the norms of reasoning (and no friend of the irrationality thesis would deny that there are some such occasions). Thus, the minimal principle of charity does not support the application of the misinterpretation strategy or any similar strategy that interprets the results of the reasoning experiments as compatible with the rationality thesis.

I began this section with an eye towards defending the strong principle of charity as a guide to interpreting the reasoning experiments. If this principle could be defensibly applied to these experiments, then the natural interpretation of them—that they show humans are irrational—could be rejected in favour of some interpretation on which humans are rational. Having shown that the argument for using this principle cannot be an empirical argument, I turned my attention to a conceptual argument. The conceptual argument was that charitable interpretation is required for anything to count as a belief because, for a mental state to be a belief requires that it interact with other mental states according to principles that are based on rules of logic. The first problem for this argument is that, even if it works to show that humans need to be interpreted as following principles based on rules of logic, such an argument does not suffice to establish enough charity to require that humans must be interpreted as rational; for example, it does not show that humans ought to be interpreted as following principles based on probability theory. The second problem for the conceptual argument for the principle of charity has to do with the human finitary predicament; there is not enough time in a human life or enough space in a human brain for humans to be completely rational and hence to justify using the strong principle of charity to interpret the reasoning experiments. One might attempt to save this conceptual argument by saying that all of the errors of reasoning that we make are performance errors due to limitations on human reasoning that follow from the finitary predicament. This move cannot be supported; the attempt to support it by appeal to the principle of charity begs the question. The upshot of this section is that there is no satisfactory support for using the strong principle of charity as an argument for the rationality thesis.

6. Conclusion

This chapter considered a set of arguments designed to undercut the support that the reasoning experiments seem to provide for the irrationality thesis. Even if one of these arguments had been successful, it is not clear that this would provide a strong *positive* argument for the rationality thesis. It would, however, provide a good negative argument against the irrationality thesis because it would undercut all of its empirical support. In Chapter 3, Section 3, I sketched some plausible interpretations of the results of the reasoning experiments according to which these results should *not* be interpreted as evidence for the irrationality thesis. These interpretations were shown to be empirically problematic. I argued that conceptual considerations favouring interpretations that fit with the rationality thesis are needed. In this chapter, I explored some such conceptual considerations.

In Section 2, I asked whether the principle of charity could be successfully imported from the realm of language translation to the interpretation of principles of reasoning. The idea was to underwrite interpreting the results of the reasoning experiments as compatible with the rationality thesis. I argued that only the strong version of the principle of charity could underwrite this interpretative stance. In Section 3, I considered an objection to the principle of charity and a modification to it, known as the principle of humanity, that takes this objection into consideration. I argued that the principle of humanity is not strong enough to provide support for the rationality thesis. In Section 4, I considered the implications of coupling charity with interpretive holism. While a holistic version of charity is more plausible than the principle of charity applied in a piecemeal fashion, to the extent that holism allows for interpreting people as making some errors, it also allows for interpreting people as being irrational. As such, the holistic version of the principle of charity is not strong enough to support an argument for the rationality thesis. In Section 5, I considered and rejected an argument in favour of the strong principle of charity. This, together with the conclusions of the previous sections, leads to the conclusion that considerations of charity will not suffice to support an interpretation of the reasoning experiments as compatible with the rationality thesis. Nothing I have said in this chapter counts against any version of the principle of charity except the strong version. Weaker versions of this principle may well be appropriate guides for interpreting people's utterances and their principles of reasoning; however, such weaker versions will not suffice to support the rationality thesis.

5

Reflective Equilibrium

THE argument for the rationality thesis that I focus on in this chapter begins by saying that human reasoning competence cannot diverge from the normative principles of reasoning because both the normative principles and competence are intimately connected with our intuitions about what constitutes good reasoning. As such, the conclusion of the argument requires interpreting the reasoning experiments as not in fact providing evidence for the irrationality thesis. I will be concerned with both the general version of this argument and a particular version of it that draws on the epistemological theory of reflective equilibrium. In Section 1, I will sketch the general argument, examine why it might initially seem plausible, and argue that this initial plausibility is deceptive. In Section 2, I spell out the reflective equilibrium version of the argument for the rationality thesis. In the next three sections, I discuss this argument in detail. In Section 3, I discuss the reflective equilibrium account of how we justify our normative principles of reasoning. In Section 4, I discuss the reflective equilibrium account of reasoning competence. In Section 5, I attempt to modify the reflective equilibrium argument to take into consideration some objections raised in the previous section. In Section 6, I conclude.

1. The Basic Argument

The idea of the reflective equilibrium argument is that human reasoning competence cannot diverge from the normative principles of reasoning because both are intimately connected with our intuitions about what constitutes good reasoning; they cannot diverge because they both come from the same source. In its simplest form, the argument is as follows:

(1) The normative principles of reasoning come from our intuitions about what constitutes good reasoning.

(2) Our intuitions about what constitutes good reasoning come from our reasoning competence.

(3) Therefore, the normative principles of reasoning come from our reasoning competence.

(4) Therefore, reasoning competence must match the normative principles of reasoning.

Versions of this argument have been defended by philosophers and psychologists alike.[1] I will consider briefly what makes this argument seem plausible.

Consider first the question of where our normative principles of reasoning come from. It seems that the only place to start an inquiry into what the normative principles are is with our own intuitions about what counts as good reasoning. Of course, such intuitions are fallible, as the reasoning experiments show, but our reflection on these experiments indicates that our intuitions can be used to help us realize that our reasoning behaviour is in some cases mistaken. In the conjunction experiment, the probability that Linda is a bank teller *and* a feminist might seem greater than the probability that she is a bank teller (whether or not she is a feminist), but, on reflection, we realize that this cannot be the case. It is our intuitions that tell us, on reflection, that Linda cannot be more likely to be a bank teller and a feminist than she is to be a bank teller. This fits nicely with (1), the view that our normative principles of reasoning come from our intuitions.

The next premiss is that our considered intuitions are derived from our reasoning competence (2). Roughly, the idea is that when we are careful and reflect on our intuitions, we ensure that we are blocking out the effects of interfering factors, lack of concentration, and so on. Our considered intuitions provide us access to our reasoning competence by ensuring that we are not committing any performance errors. It basically follows from the definition of competence that considered intuitions provide a window on to human reasoning competence.

Finally, the argument from (1) and (2) to (3) looks valid because (3) follows from these two premisses by the principle of transitivity—if the normative principles come from our intuitions and our intuitions come from our reasoning competence, then the norms come from our competence. If our normative principles come from our reasoning competence, then our reasoning competence and the norms must match.

---

[1] L. Jonathan Cohen, 'Can Human Irrationality be Experimentally Demonstrated?', *Behavioral and Brain Sciences*, 4 (1981), 317–31; John Macnamara, *A Border Dispute* (Cambridge, Mass.: MIT Press, 1986); and Elliott Sober, 'Psychologism', *Journal of Social Behavior*, 8 (1978), 165–91.

Consider some principle P which, by stipulation, is in our reasoning competence. When we reflect on our intuitions about reasoning, we would say that P is an intuitively plausible principle of reasoning. Since the normative principles of reasoning are based on our intuitions, we will judge P to be a normative principle. This is the idea behind (4), the claim that our reasoning competence matches the normative principles of reasoning, which is equivalent to the rationality thesis.

The initial plausibility of its premises aside, perhaps the primary reason why this argument for the rationality thesis seems so convincing is because of the apparent strength of the oft-stated analogy between reasoning and language.[2] We determine what linguistic competence is by studying our linguistic intuitions and we determine what the normative principles of linguistics are in the same way—there is no higher court of appeal as to what the principles of grammar are than our linguistic intuitions. The justification for this idea parallels the argument for the rationality thesis given above.

(L1) The normative principles of grammaticality come from our intuitions about what constitutes grammaticality.

(L2) Our intuitions about what constitutes grammaticality come from our linguistic competence.

(L3) Therefore, the normative principles of grammaticality come from our linguistic competence.

(L4) Therefore, linguistic competence must match the normative principles of grammaticality.

(L1) and (L2) are true and (L4) seems to follow directly from their truth. It is the obvious strength of this argument that, by analogy, seems to lend support to the parallel argument for the rationality thesis. If the analogy between reasoning and language is a strong one, then the argument for the rationality thesis is in good shape.

I argued in Chapter 2 that this feature of the analogy between language and reasoning is not strong: norms of reasoning are not necessarily linked to reasoning competence in the way that norms of grammaticality are linked to linguistic competence. This undermines the strength of the analogy between linguistics and reasoning which makes the argument from (1) and (2) to (3) and (4) plausible. This does not, so far as what I have said, blame the weakness of the argument for

[2] Cohen, 'Can Human Irrationality be Experimentally Demonstrated?'; Macnamara, *A Border Dispute*; and Sober, 'Psychologism'.

(4) either on the logical structure of the argument or on one or both of the premisses, but it does undermine the plausibility of the argument none the less. Although the normative principles match human competence in the realm of language, further argument is required to show that they do so in the realm of reasoning. Fortunately, the general argument for the rationality thesis need not rely on the analogy with linguistics; one can try to make premisses (1) and (2) and the form of the argument plausible independent of the analogy with linguistics. In the next section, I turn to just such an attempt.

2. *The Reflective Equilibrium Argument*

If some version of premisses (1) and (2) can be defended independent of the analogy to linguistics, then the argument for the rationality thesis would be on strong footing. L. J. Cohen attempts to defend the rationality thesis by an argument of similar structure to the one discussed above but that makes use of the theory of reflective equilibrium.[3] The theory of reflective equilibrium is an account of justification that says a set of principles is justified in some domain if the principles provide a coherent and explicit characterization of our judgements about that domain. On the reflective equilibrium account of justification, to justify a set of principles that characterize judgements in a given domain, one generates principles that conform to commonly accepted judgements. If one such principle sanctions judgements that do not conform to general practice, the principle is modified; if, however, such a modification would produce a principle that is intuitively unacceptable, then the judgement is rejected. This process may be circular, but, according to Nelson Goodman, it is a 'virtuous' circle—principles and inferences are justified together by being brought into agreement. He writes:

Principles of deductive inference are justified by their conformity with accepted deductive practice. Their validity depends upon accordance with the particular deductive inferences we actually make and sanction. If a rule yields inacceptable inferences, we drop it as invalid. Justification of general rules thus derives from judgments rejecting or accepting particular deductive inferences.

This looks flagrantly circular. I have said that deductive inferences are justified by their conformity to valid general rules, and that general rules are

---

[3] Cohen, 'Can Human Irrationality be Experimentally Demonstrated?'; 'On the Psychology of Prediction: Whose is the Fallacy?', *Cognition*, 7 (1979), 385–407; and *The Dialogue of Reason* (Oxford: Oxford University Press, 1986), 149–92.

justified by their conformity to valid inferences. But this circle is a virtuous one. The point is that rules and particular inferences alike are justified by being brought into agreement with each other. A rule is amended if it yields an inference we are unwilling to accept; an inference is rejected if it violates a rule we are unwilling to amend. The process of justification is the delicate one of making mutual adjustments between rules and accepted inferences; and in the agreement achieved lies the only justification needed for either.

All this applies equally well to induction. An inductive inference, too, is justified by conformity to general rules, and a general rule by conformity to accepted inductive practice. Predictions are justified if they conform to the valid canons of induction; and the canons are valid if they accurately codify accepted inductive practice.[4]

Since the time of Goodman's formulation of reflective equilibrium, this method has been used to justify principles in other realms besides deduction and induction. Most notably, perhaps, is John Rawls's application of reflective equilibrium to moral theory.[5] According to Rawls, to develop a theory of ethics, we begin with a set of moral judgements— for example, judgements like 'It is wrong to torture babies'. These judgements are collected with an eye towards producing a set of principles—for example, principles like 'Always do whatever will minimize the total amount of pain and suffering and maximize the total amount of happiness'—that not only underlie these judgements but also extend and systematize them. We begin by articulating our strongly held considered judgements and a set of principles that would fit with these convictions. Presumably, there will be discrepancies that arise: some judgements that follow from the principles will not be among our considered judgements and some of our considered judgements will not fit with the principles. We will then endeavour to eliminate these discrepancies by modifying some principles and retracting some judgements. Eventually, Rawls says, we will come upon 'principles which match our considered judgments duly pruned and adjusted'.[6] He calls this *reflective* because 'we know to what principles our judgments conform and the premises of their derivation'[7] and *equilibrium* 'because our principles and judgments coincide'.[8] The justification of moral principles cannot, according to Rawls, 'be deduced from self-evident premises

[4] Nelson Goodman, *Fact, Fiction and Forecast*, 4th edn. (Cambridge, Mass.: Harvard University Press, 1983), 63–4.

[5] In the remaining part of this paragraph, I paraphrase John Rawls, *A Theory of Justice* (Cambridge: Harvard University Press, 1971), 20, but omit reference to his so-called 'original position'.

[6] Ibid. [7] Ibid. [8] Ibid.

or conditions on principles; instead, its justification is a matter of the mutual support of many considerations, of everything fitting together into one coherent view'.[9]

The reflective equilibrium argument has a similar structure to the argument from premises (1) and (2). The two parts of the reflective equilibrium argument for the rationality thesis are, first, to show that the normative principles of reasoning, like the principles of morality, come from a reflective equilibrium process with our intuitions as input and, second, to show that we develop our account of our underlying reasoning ability from a process of reflective equilibrium with our intuitions about what counts as good reasoning as input. Specifically, the reflective equilibrium version of the argument for the rationality thesis is as follows:

(RE1) The normative principles of reasoning come from a process of reflective equilibrium with our intuitions about what constitutes good reasoning as input.

(RE2) A descriptive theory of reasoning competence comes from a process of reflective equilibrium with our intuitions about what constitutes good reasoning as input.

(RE3) Therefore, since both come from the same process with the same inputs, reasoning competence must match the normative principles of reasoning.

The similar form of the argument for the rationality thesis to the one discussed in Section 1 is apparent. Both arguments see the normative principles of reasoning and the proper account of reasoning competence as coming from intuitions about what counts as good reasoning and both conclude that the norms and reasoning competence must match. The reflective equilibrium argument for the rationality thesis is, however, plausible independently of the analogy to linguistics discussed above. In particular, the argument is plausible because it is based on a respectable epistemological theory, reflective equilibrium.

The strategy of the reflective equilibrium argument for the rationality thesis involves applying the reflective equilibrium account of how norms are justified to the realm of reasoning (RE1). This seems a reasonable starting-place for an account of how the normative principles of reasoning are justified. The next step of the argument is to defend a reflective equilibrium account of reasoning competence (RE2). Combined with

---

[9] Ibid. 21.

the reflective equilibrium account of norms, the reflective equilibrium account of competence seems to provide a strong defence of the rationality thesis.

3. Reflective Equilibrium and Normative Principles

Recall the first premiss in the reflective equilibrium argument for the rationality thesis:

(RE1) The normative principles of reasoning come from a process of reflective equilibrium with our intuitions about what constitutes good reasoning as input.

There is a general objection to this premiss: the process of reflective equilibrium will count some principles of reasoning as normative that are not in fact the right principles. There is evidence to suggest that included among the inferential principles that will be in reflective equilibrium for people are principles we have good reason to think are *not* rational. This is exactly the sort of evidence provided by the reasoning experiments, experiments that suggest, even in the face of evidence and extensive briefing to the contrary, that subjects continue to violate principles that stem from rules of logic and probability theory.

Another example of a principle that is likely to be in reflective equilibrium but that is not rational is the gambler's fallacy, a particular instance of which would be the belief that a long stretch of coin-flips that come up as heads increases the probability that the next coin-flip will be a tail. Following this fallacy and failing to apply the principles of logic and probability properly as subjects in the reasoning experiments do are practices that would be in reflective equilibrium for lots of people. According to (RE1), if a principle is in reflective equilibrium, then it is justified, but it is absurd, for example, to think people are justified in reasoning in accordance with the gambler's fallacy. The general point is that the reasoning experiments count against the reflective equilibrium account of the justification of principles of reasoning because they suggest that there are some principles that are *not* normative principles but *are* in reflective equilibrium. In the remainder of this section, I will examine the resources that friends of the reflective equilibrium account of norms have to avoid the objection that some of the principles that are in reflective equilibrium are not rational.

3.1. Bite the Bullet

One possible reply open to friends of the reflective equilibrium model is to bite the bullet, that is, to say that what it means to be justified just *is* to be in reflective equilibrium.[10] For example, if ignoring the conjunction principle is in reflective equilibrium for someone, then she is justified in reasoning in a way that violates the conjunction principle. This seems a doomed strategy since this fails to do justice to what justification is. If violating a principle like the conjunction principle could be justified, then being justified seems a vacuous notion. An advocate of the bite-the-bullet strategy might try to defend this strategy by comparing reasoning to linguistics. Such an advocate might point out that, in linguistics, if a principle is the result of balancing judgements about what particular utterances are grammatical with judgements about what in general is grammatical (that is, if a linguistic principle is in reflective equilibrium), then the principle is part of linguistic competence. Even if this was the right picture of how linguistics works, it would not help support the bite-the-bullet strategy because, as I have pointed out in Chapter 2, linguistic norms are indexed to actual linguistic competence but norms of reasoning are not obviously indexed to actual reasoning competence. The analogy to linguistics will not help the bite-the-bullet strategy; without some such help, this strategy is a non-starter.

3.2. Considered Intuitions

Another possible response to the general objection to the reflective equilibrium model of the justification of the norms of rationality is to argue that only *considered* intuitions are involved in the reflective equilibrium process. The implication of this move is that the intuitions of the sort which support non-normative principles of reasoning are not considered intuitions but *naïve* ones. The idea is to modify (RE1) in the following manner:

(RE1′) The normative principles of reasoning come from a process of reflective equilibrium with our *considered* intuitions about what constitutes good reasoning as input.

---

[10] Stephen Stich and Richard Nisbett, 'Justification and the Psychology of Human Reasoning', *Philosophy of Science*, 47 (1980), 197–8, refer to this response as 'digging in'.

By preventing unconsidered intuitions from entering the reflective equilibrium process, the hope is that no non-normative principles of reasoning would end up being in reflective equilibrium. The idea of modifying the reflective equilibrium process to prevent non-rational principles from being in reflective equilibrium is promising; there are, however, several points to make about this suggested modification.

This suggested modification to (RE1) is not open to Cohen. By 'intuition', he means 'an immediate and untutored inclination, without evidence or inference',[11] to make a particular judgement. It is these immediate and untutored inclinations that Cohen sees as being the input to the reflective equilibrium process. His main reason for focusing on naïve intuitions is connected to what he thinks is the right picture of linguistics and linguistic intuitions. Cohen's insistence that naïve intuitions are the ones relevant to developing a theory of reasoning competence seems a mistake. If this is right then Cohen's hesitance to embrace (RE1′) as an attempt to save the reflective equilibrium account of norms from the objection at hand seems unwarranted.

Cohen bases his focus on naïve intuitions on an analogy with linguistics. This analogy will not do the work he wants it to since linguists in fact focus on *considered* intuitions. Consider the sentence

The girl the cat the dog the farmer owned chased scratched fled.

Our naïve intuition is that this sentence is ungrammatical. If, however, you sit down and carefully consider the sentence, you will see that it *is* grammatical. Note that the core of the sentence is:

The girl fled.

'Which girl fled?' The answer is: 'The girl the cat scratched'. So, we now have:

The girl the cat scratched fled.

'But which cat scratched the girl?' The answer is: 'The cat the dog chased'. We now have:

The girl the cat the dog chased scratched fled.

Finally, 'Which dog chased the cat?' The answer is: 'The dog the farmer owned'. We can now see the grammaticality of the sentence, but note that the sentence seems grammatical only on reflection. Further,

---

[11] Cohen, 'Can Human Irrationality be Experimentally Demonstrated?', 318.

despite the fact that I know that the sentence is grammatical, each time I look at it, I require a few moments to reconvince myself of its grammaticality. *Considered* linguistic intuitions are thus relevant to developing an account of linguistic competence.[12] The analogy Cohen tries to make to justify his emphasis on naïve intuitions is that reasoning competence is like linguistic competence, but linguistic competence is accessible only through considered (linguistic) intuitions.

Cohen's insistence that the reflective equilibrium account of the norms of reasoning involves only naïve intuitions is unsupported because the picture of linguistics as only involving naïve intuitions is mistaken. Thus, the suggestion that considered intuitions are involved in this reflective equilibrium process (RE1′) seems motivated. The idea behind (RE1′) is that the focus on considered intuitions will ensure that only rational principles will be in reflective equilibrium. For example, while the gambler's fallacy might be in reflective equilibrium with naïve intuitions as input to the balancing process, the gambler's fallacy might not be in reflective equilibrium with only considered intuitions as input.

The problem with this suggestion is that there is no particular reason to think that restricting the intuitions involved in reflective equilibrium just to considered intuitions will block gambler's-fallacy-type objections to the reflective equilibrium model. Lots of people who fall prey to the gambler's fallacy will presumably accept the fallacy even under careful consideration. The same is true for the results of the reasoning experiments; not only do subjects in the experiments make systematic errors of reasoning, they sometimes stubbornly insist, even in the face of evidence to the contrary, that they are right to reason as they do.

Part of the reason why narrowing the input to the reflective equilibrium process to just considered intuitions is unhelpful as a way to address the objection that non-normative principles will be in reflective equilibrium is that it is unclear what is involved in the process of considering intuitions. The suggestions that follow attempt to take what seems right about modifying (RE1) to produce (RE1′)—namely, that the reflective equilibrium process of justifying norms of reasoning needs to be narrowed in response to the objection that involves the gambler's fallacy

---

[12] L. Jonathan Cohen, 'A Reply to Stein', *Synthese*, 99 (1994), 173–6, replies to this argument by saying that considered linguistic intuitions are only relevant to reflective equilibrium because they rest on naïve intuitions (like the intuition that 'The girl the cat scratched fled' is an answer to the question 'Which girl fled?'). He does not, however, explain why such naïve intuitions trump intuitions like the intuition that 'The girl the cat the dog the farmer owned chased scratched fled' is ungrammatical. The natural answer, which he does not avail himself of—because he cannot consistently do so—is that the former intuition is also a considered intuition while the latter one is not.

and the results of the reasoning experiments—while putting forward a more specific proposal for what sort of modification ought to take place. I consider three such replies to the general argument against the reflective equilibrium view. First, one could narrow the range of people whose intuitions count in the reflective equilibrium process. A set of inferential principles would be justified, on this view, if they were in equilibrium for some class of experts. Second, one could widen the scope of reflective equilibrium by considering a broader set of principles and judgements, namely, besides our inferential principles and judgements, we could include principles and intuitions from epistemological, metaphysical, and other philosophical theories. Third, the wide reflective equilibrium view could be combined with the expert view, resulting in the view that a set of inferential principles are justified if they are in wide reflective equilibrium for some class of experts.[13] I will consider each possibility in turn.

3.3. Experts

The first suggested modification to the reflective equilibrium view of the justification of principles of reasoning, known as the *expert version* of reflective equilibrium, is to say that a principle is established as a normative principle of reasoning if it is in reflective equilibrium for those people in a position to assess the relevant considerations. Drawing on Hilary Putnam's theory of the division of linguistic labour,[14] the expert reflective equilibrium view says that a principle is justified if it is the result of reflective equilibrium performed by society's experts.[15] Putnam's theory says that, in every speech community, there are terms 'whose associated "criteria" are known only to a subset of the speakers who acquire the terms, and whose use by the other speakers depends upon a structured cooperation between them and the speakers in the relevant subsets'.[16] In the realm of reasoning, the idea is that some of the principles of reasoning (that apply for all humans) are not the result of reflective equilibrium applied to everyone's judgements about what counts as good reasoning but rather are the result of reflective equilibrium applied by a certain subset of people, namely the set of people

---

[13] Stephen Stich, *The Fragmentation of Reason* (Cambridge, Mass.: MIT Press, 1990), 83–6, discusses and rejects the first two views; presumably, he thinks that what he says against the first two views counts against the third.

[14] Hilary Putnam, 'The Meaning of "Meaning"', in *Mind, Language and Reality: Philosophical Papers*, ii (Cambridge: Cambridge University Press, 1975).

[15] Stich and Nisbett, 'Justification and the Psychology of Human Reasoning', 198–202.   [16] Putnam, 'The Meaning of "Meaning"', 228.

who are the experts, to their own judgements. This would avoid the problem of the gambler's fallacy and similar principles being in reflective equilibrium and hence being deemed justified because the experts —for example, probability theorists—would not accept the gambler's fallacy in reflective equilibrium. The expert reflective equilibrium view seems to work well in deeming as justified the inferences we think (on reflection) are justified.

A response to this modification to the reflective equilibrium account is to say that the modification only works to avoid cases like the gambler's fallacy because the experts we consult are already known for their reliability when it comes to following principles we think are justified. But this, so the response goes, is a question-begging way to justify our inferential practice.[17] The challenge is to develop a *general* account of justification; appealing to those experts who follow principles that are justified without a general account of how to figure out who the experts are simply begs the question.

An attempt to give a non-question-begging account of who the experts are might say that the people who count as experts in the justification of some particular inference are those who the person making the inference thinks are the experts.[18] So modified, the expert reflective equilibrium view is again open to the gambler's fallacy counter-example. Suppose, when it comes to gambling, I think the average Las Vegas compulsive gambler is the expert (after all, such people have a great deal of practice at gambling); such a person, however, may well believe that the gambler's fallacy is justified. The gambler's fallacy would, in turn, be justified for me. It is not just that I would *believe* it is justified—I may or I may not—but that, on the interpretation of the expert reflective equilibrium view under consideration, I *would* be justified. The problem is that often the people who are deferred to are no more justified in their beliefs than those who defer to them.[19] In a nutshell, the complaint against the expert modification to the reflective equilibrium account of how our principles of reasoning are justified is that there is no non-question-begging way to pick out the experts.

Friends of the reflective equilibrium account might plead guilty to this charge. It is circular to appeal to experts, but the reflective

---

[17]   Stich, *The Fragmentation of Reason*, 86.

[18]   Stich and Nisbett, 'Justification and the Psychology of Human Reasoning', 201.

[19]   For further criticism of this modification to the expert view, see Earl Conee and Richard Feldman, 'Stich and Nisbett on Justifying Inference Rules', *Philosophy of Science*, 50 (1983), 326–31; see also Stich, *The Fragmentation of Reason*, 164 n. 16.

equilibrium account is unashamedly circular. Who counts as an expert is just another part of what is figured into the reflective equilibrium process. Just as some intuitions about which particular inferences count as good reasoning might be rejected in reflective equilibrium, some intuitions about which particular people count as experts might be rejected. Just as originally counter-intuitive principles of reasoning might be accepted in reflective equilibrium, some people who originally seemed non-experts might be counted as experts in reflective equilibrium. This is circular, friends of reflective equilibrium would admit, but they would say that it is a 'virtuous' circle.

Although friends of the expert version of reflective equilibrium have resources to respond to the charge of circularity, it is not clear that they have adequate resources to respond to the original objection to the reflective equilibrium account of the norms of reasoning. This original objection is that reflective equilibrium will count some principles that are not in fact rational as normative principles of reasoning. This objection can rear its head again with respect to the expert modification in one of two ways depending on who counts as an expert. If an expert is someone for whom the principles that are in reflective equilibrium are always rational, then the objection to the expert view is that reflective equilibrium may deem as an expert someone who is not in fact an expert. If an expert is *not* someone who is always right about the normative principles of reasoning, that is, if an expert might accept a non-normative principle in reflective equilibrium, then the objection to the expert view is that those people who are deemed experts might endorse principles that are in fact *not* rational. The choice between these two different accounts is a forced option—either an expert is always right in reflective equilibrium or not—and either way, the expert view is open to the same objection that counted against the unmodified reflective equilibrium account.

3.4. Wide Reflective Equilibrium

The second suggested modification to the reflective equilibrium view of the justification of principles of reasoning is to say that a principle is established as a normative principle of reasoning if it is in *wide* reflective equilibrium.[20] Rawls makes a distinction between wide and narrow

---

[20] Cohen, 'Can Human Irrationality be Experimentally Demonstrated?', 320, explicitly rejects this suggestion, saying that the norms of reasoning 'require a *narrow*, not a *wide*, reflective equilibrium' (emphasis added); see also 323.

reflective equilibrium.[21] *Narrow* reflective equilibrium is achieved when a set of judgements is coherently systematized by (that is, brought into balance with) a set of general principles. This would be accomplished in ethics, for example, if we produced a set of principles from which all and only our somewhat altered and refined first-order moral judgements followed. The result of narrow reflective equilibrium is a coherent systematization of our moral judgements. *Wide* reflective equilibrium is achieved when a set of judgements, a set of principles, *and* a set of general philosophical theories (theories of personal identity, metaphysics, the social role of moral and political theory, and the like) are brought into agreement. The search for wide reflective equilibrium begins as does the search for narrow reflective equilibrium, but once our judgements and a set of general principles are brought into basic agreement, various alternative sets of balanced judgements and general principles are considered and these alternatives are then brought into balance with philosophical theories through the same sort of balancing process. This process, rather than producing a systematization of our judgements, is more revisionary; the set of principles that results from wide reflective equilibrium has a broader network of support and a reflective philosophical backing. As a result, there is a greater likelihood that wide reflective equilibrium will produce a theory that diverges from intuitions.[22]

As an example of wide reflective equilibrium, consider Derek Parfit's argument for *utilitarianism*.[23] Utilitarianism is the view that one ought to do whatever will cause the greatest amount of happiness and the least amount of unhappiness. A standard objection to utilitarianism is that it is not acceptable to balance losses and gains between people (what I call *interpersonal balancing*). To the extent that we have intuitions in favour of utilitarianism, these intuitions should be outweighed by our strong intuitions against interpersonal balancing. One set of intuitions that counts against interpersonal balancing is the *separateness of persons*, the claim that people are separate beings, each

[21] John Rawls, 'The Independence of Moral Theory', *Proceedings and Addresses of the American Philosophical Association*, 48 (1974–5), 8. The distinction is implicit in Rawls, *A Theory of Justice*, 49.

[22] For discussion of the distinction between wide and narrow reflective equilibrium, see Norman Daniels, 'Wide Reflective Equilibrium and Theory Acceptance in Ethics', *Journal of Philosophy*, 76 (1979), 256–82; 'Wide Reflective Equilibrium and Archimedean Points', *Canadian Journal of Philosophy*, 10 (1980), 83–103; and 'On Some Methods of Ethics and Linguistics', *Philosophical Studies*, 37 (1980), 21–36.

[23] Derek Parfit, *Reasons and Persons* (Oxford: Oxford University Press, 1984).

with his or her own life to lead, and, as such, people are the relevant units for moral theory. This is an objection to utilitarian theory because utilitarianism sees an important role for such interpersonal balancing. Intuitions about the separateness of persons suggest that utilitarianism will not be in narrow reflective equilibrium.

Parfit's response to these objections can be seen as fitting the wide reflective equilibrium model. Parfit can grant that the separateness of persons is an objection to utilitarianism in *narrow* reflective equilibrium. However, he produces arguments from metaphysics to the effect that persons are not the relevant units for moral theory. Identity of persons, he argues, is not what matters to moral theory; rather, psychological continuity and connectedness are what matters. But, since I may be psychologically connected to other people besides myself, benefits and harms, pleasures and pains can, contrary to the separateness of persons objection to utilitarianism, be balanced among various people. If benefits and harms can be balanced in this fashion, our original intuitions against utilitarianism should be revised in the face of Parfit's arguments about metaphysics to the effect that persons are not the relevant units for moral theory. Utilitarianism is, according to Parfit, the result of wide reflective equilibrium applied to ethical theory.

I do not mean to endorse Parfit's conclusion in favour of utilitarianism; I just cite it as an example of wide reflective equilibrium. In fact, following Rawls's discussion of the relationship of moral theory to philosophy of mind and metaphysics,[24] I am not clear whether the metaphysical conclusions that Parfit defends ought to count against the *narrow* reflective equilibrium conclusions in moral theory (namely, that utilitarianism is wrong) or whether the strength of our intuitions against utilitarianism (stemming, for example, from the strength of our intuitions in favour of the separateness of persons) ought to count against Parfit's metaphysical view in *wide* reflective equilibrium. This is obviously not the place to settle this issue; the relevant point is that settling it would be part of the wide reflective equilibrium process of bringing our moral intuitions, the moral principles that match these intuitions, and various philosophical arguments into agreement.

Returning to reasoning, the idea of appealing to the notion of wide reflective equilibrium is to argue that ·the gambler's fallacy and the (non-normative) principles suggested by the results of the reasoning experiments would not be in *wide* reflective equilibrium even if they

---

[24] Rawls, 'The Independence of Moral Theory', sect. IV.

are in narrow reflective equilibrium; such principles, says the defender of the wide reflective equilibrium view, would be rejected as a result of the process of balancing general principles of reasoning with philosophical and other theoretical considerations. For example, if people were to be persuaded by theoretical arguments in favour of probability theory, they would see that the gambler's fallacy is in fact a fallacy. This line of thought can be seen as suggesting the following modification to (RE1):

(RE1″) The normative principles of reasoning come from a process of *wide* reflective equilibrium with our intuitions about what constitutes good reasoning as input.

Like the other two modifications to the reflective equilibrium account of norms—the expert view and the considered intuitions view—the wide reflective equilibrium account attempts to prevent non-rational principles of reasoning from being deemed rational by the reflective equilibrium account.

A virtue of the wide reflective equilibrium account is that it makes clear why the normative principles of reasoning are not indexed to reasoning competence. Recall from Chapter 2, Section 2.3 that there is an important disanalogy between linguistics and reasoning—linguistic norms are indexed to linguistic competence while norms of reasoning do not seem to be indexed to reasoning competence. If the wide reflective equilibrium account of the norms of reasoning is right, this disanalogy is explained. According to the wide reflective equilibrium account, the norms of reasoning are the result of bringing into balance our inferential practices, our intuitions about what counts as good reasoning, and—this is the crucial part of the picture—general philosophical and theoretical considerations. Because theoretical considerations are included, a wide reflective equilibrium account can be highly revisionary with respect to our original intuitions and practices; the result is that our intuitions and naïve practices can be dispensed with in wide reflective equilibrium. Normative principles of reasoning are thus not indexed to reasoning competence. This is in contrast to linguistics. In linguistics, general philosophical considerations do not get brought into the process of determining the linguistic norms;[25] the process of developing linguistic

---

[25] This does not mean, however, that there are no interesting (philosophical) debates about the nature of linguistic rules.

norms is *not* highly revisionary and thus *is* indexed to linguistic competence. (RE1″) thus has the virtue of fitting with an important fact about the justification of norms of reasoning.

Against (RE1″), Stephen Stich has pointed out that it is difficult to assess whether, for example, a person who actually accepts and follows the gambler's fallacy will give up this principle in the face of theoretical considerations against it (after all, a gambler is likely to give much less weight to some 'bookish' principle of probability than to a principle he has 'learned to trust' after years of experience in casinos).[26] Stich goes on to argue that it is possible for a person to settle on a wide reflective equilibrium that includes 'some quite daffy' principles of reasoning.[27]

3.5. Expert Wide Reflective Equilibrium

One possible reply to this argument (the third modification to the reflective equilibrium view) is the *expert wide reflective equilibrium view* that combines the first two modifications. On this view, a principle is justified if it is the result of experts engaging in the process of wide reflective equilibrium. This view might be seen as an improvement to the wide reflective equilibrium view because it might seem to reduce the likelihood that an unjustified principle will be in wide reflective equilibrium. The same problem, however, remains for the expert wide view; even if the chances are reduced that an unjustified principle will be deemed justified, it remains *possible* for this to happen.

There are some interesting and potentially strong defences of the wide reflective equilibrium account (in both its expert and its non-expert versions) against Stich's objection that even in wide reflective equilibrium, a person (even an expert) might embrace a 'daffy' principle of reasoning. The problem is that it is not clear what Stich means by the word 'daffy' in this argument. If by a daffy principle, he means a principle that we would currently judge not to be justified, then surely it is true that a daffy principle might turn out to be justified on the wide reflective equilibrium view. But this is not an objection to wide reflective equilibrium. Widening the scope of reflective equilibrium allows for the possibility that certain principles that naïvely seem unjustified (that is, daffy) will, when various philosophical considerations are presented, be seen to be justified after all (that is, *not* daffy). While it

---

[26] Stich, *The Fragmentation of Reason*, 85.   [27] Ibid. 86.

is a result of the wide reflective equilibrium picture that principles we currently think of as daffy will be justified, this fact is not an objection at all to the view. No doubt, some of the principles we currently think of as daffy *are* justified; whatever method actually justifies principles of reasoning, *some* of the principles of reasoning that we currently reject ought to be accepted on the right account of justification.

On the other hand, by a daffy principle, Stich might mean an *objectively* daffy principle, that is, a principle that is not in fact a normative principle of reasoning (regardless of whether we *think* it is a norm). On this reading of the term, a principle that is (objectively) daffy could be the result of wide reflective equilibrium. Simply put, this objection against wide reflective equilibrium is that the principles that wide reflective equilibrium deems rational might not, in fact, be rational; as such, wide reflective equilibrium is not an adequate account of how normative principles of reasoning are justified.

I will briefly sketch two possible replies to this objection. The first—and perhaps the most radical—reply is to embrace a coherence account of truth, that is, an account on which the true complete theory of the world is the most coherent collection of beliefs about the world.[28] On this account of what it means to be true, a particular belief is true if and only if it fits with the maximally coherent theory of the world. Similarly, on this theory, a principle would be rational if and only if it is among the maximally coherent set of principles. The process of wide reflective equilibrium arguably produces a maximally coherent set of principles; therefore the principles justified by wide reflective equilibrium would be guaranteed to be the most rational. This is not the place to spell out all the problems and disadvantages of this view, but I will just mention that perhaps its most serious consequence is its rejection of the most prima facie plausible metaphysical theory, namely, realism. This consequence alone may involve too high a price to pay for defending a wide reflective equilibrium account of justification.

Another reply to the argument that wide reflective equilibrium will deem justified some principles that in fact are *not* rational would be to grant that it is possible for the principles justified by wide reflective equilibrium to diverge from the normative principles of reasoning while

---

[28] Nicholas Rescher, *The Coherence Theory of Truth* (Oxford: Oxford University Press, 1973); Laurence Bonjour, *The Structure of Empirical Knowledge* (Cambridge, Mass.: Harvard University Press, 1985); Keith Lehrer, *Theory of Knowledge* (Boulder, Colo.: Westview, 1990); for a short summary discussion, see Lehrer, 'Coherentism', in Jonathan Dancy and Ernest Sosa (eds.), *A Companion to Epistemology* (Oxford: Blackwell, 1992).

denying that this is a serious criticism of wide reflective equilibrium. This strategy might be motivated by pragmatic considerations; namely by denying that there is any strategy for justifying principles of reasoning that could do better than wide reflective equilibrium. On this view, wide reflective equilibrium tells us what people in the human episte-mological position are justified in believing and what principles people in the human epistemological position are justified in following. Per-haps what humans are justified in believing is not in fact true and perhaps the principles humans are justified in following are not in fact justified, but there is no particular reason to think that they are not and no better way of figuring what beliefs are true and what principles are justified other than wide reflective equilibrium. In other words, this reply embraces a coherence theory of justification without embracing a coherence theory of truth.[29]

This is not the place to mount a complete defence of a reflective equilibrium account of the normative principles of reasoning. Suffice to say that, in so far as reflective equilibrium is an interesting epistemo-logical theory, it seems a good place to look for a theory of the jus-tification of the normative principles of reasoning, particularly since there do not seem to be any serious competitors. Friends of the reflective equilibrium account have ample resources to employ in answering the primary objection to their favoured account. Narrowing the range of people whose balancing of judgements is relevant to justification (the expert modification), expanding the inputs to the balancing process to include broader theoretical consideration (the wide modification (RE1″)), and embracing some version of coherentism (especially about justifica-tion) seem promising strategies to prevent non-rational principles from being counted as rational ones. For my purpose of assessing the reflec-tive equilibrium argument for the rationality thesis, some version of (RE1) is plausible enough both to make the reflective equilibrium argu-ment interesting and to turn my attention to other parts of the argument. In the next section, I evaluate (RE2).[30]

---

[29] For discussion of coherence theories of justification, see Laurence Bonjour, 'Holistic Coherentism', *Philosophical Studies*, 30 (1976), 281–312; id., *The Structure of Empirical Knowledge*; and Lehrer, *Theory of Knowledge*.

[30] Stich, *The Fragmentation of Reason*, ch. 4, calls the project of attempting to salvage using something like reflective equilibrium to justify norms of reasoning the 'neo-Goodmanian project'. He argues that this project is doomed to failure. My general criti-cism of his arguments, based on my discussion so far, is that he underestimates the resources available to friends of reflective equilibrium.

4. Reflective Equilibrium and Reasoning Competence

4.1. Developing an Account of Reasoning Competence

How can an account of human reasoning competence be developed? According to one plausible account, psychologists start their investigation of reasoning competence by looking at the reasoning behaviour of particular individuals. From this behaviour, researchers attempt to develop a general characterization of human reasoning ability, namely, a set of rules that approximately fit actual inferential behaviour. These rules would not perfectly characterize the observed behaviour because some of this behaviour would be the result of interference with the operation of reasoning competence, that is, performance errors. Researchers then ask individuals whether they think they are following these rules of inference. If the individual identifies a rule as one she uses and given that it accords with her behaviour, the rule is accepted as part of competence; otherwise, if the rule is not accepted by an individual reasoner, it is rejected as a rule of competence unless it is strongly supported by her behaviour.

To see the plausibility of this, imagine trying to learn the rules of chess just by watching people play chess. You would just watch the moves that people make and then try to abstract the rules of the game from these moves. These rules would then be used to make predictions about what people will do in various situations, predictions that you can test by further observing chess games. Because you do not know the rules of chess when you start, you will not initially be able to determine if someone has made an illegal move; you will simply note the moves without being able to distinguish between the legal and illegal ones. When you try to abstract from the behaviour of players, you may find it difficult to generate any rules that fit with *all* of the observations except those that are very complex. For example, suppose you note that a certain-shaped chess piece (what those of us in the know call a rook) always gets moved horizontally or vertically except on one occasion when someone moves a rook diagonally. The rule 'Rooks can move vertically, horizontally, and diagonally' would fit with all the observations you have made, but it might seem odd, if this is one of the actual rules, that only one person in all the games you have watched has taken advantage of the rook's ability to move diagonally. Further, the part of the rule that sanctions diagonal moves would not help you to make any additional correct predictions (unless, of course, someone made the same sort of (illegal) move again). The rule 'Rooks can move vertically and horizontally unless it is 3 September 1990 [the day you observed the rook being moved diagonally], in which case it can also move diagonally' would also fit with all the data. None of the other rules of the game seem, however, to be indexed to a particular date. Instead, a sensible strategy would be to throw out the aberrant rook move as some sort of performance error and opt for the rule 'Rooks can move vertically or horizontally'. This would be a rule of competence.[31]

According to the account under discussion, the study of human reasoning competence involves a similar process. The principles that characterize reasoning competence are not directly accessible to cognitive scientists in the same ways that the rules of chess are not directly accessible to a naïve observer of chess. In both cases, the observers must start by looking at behaviour (chess-playing behaviour on the one hand and reasoning behaviour on the other). In the chess example, however, it may be more difficult to generate idealized, abstract rules through observation alone than it is to discover a person's reasoning competence. The strategy of observe, abstract, idealize can be supplemented in the case of human reasoning by asking the subject whether she thinks a specifically chosen inference is valid or whether a particular principle fits with her intuitions. From just observing behaviour, we might develop a principle that says to infer q from **if** p, **then** q and p except when very drunk or very tired. A person would not agree to this rule because she believes that **if** p, **then** q and p together entail q regardless of the amount of alcohol or sleep any person has had; instead, she would accept the idealized version of the principle (that is, infer q from **if** p, **then** q and p) as a rule of competence. The strategy for developing principles that characterize reasoning competence is thus observe, abstract, idealize, test, revise, test, revise, and so on. This account is behind the second premiss in the reflective equilibrium argument for the rationality thesis, namely:

(RE2) A descriptive theory of reasoning competence comes from a process of reflective equilibrium with our intuitions about what constitutes good reasoning as input.

---

[31] This is roughly how José R. Capablanca, the great chess master, *allegedly* learned how to play chess. According to his book *My Chess Career* (New York: Dover, 1965), when he was 5 years old, Capablanca watched his father and a friend, both chess novices, play the game several nights in a row. After his father won a game by making an illegal move, the young Capablanca pointed out his father's error and proceeded to demonstrate his secretly learned ability to play chess.

In the remainder of this section, I shall argue that the reflective equilibrium account of reasoning competence is false. (RE2) offers this as an account of how cognitive science ought to be done, in particular, as a theory of how human reasoning competence ought to be researched and characterized. There are two general reasons why this account is wrong: first, the account gives too much weight to either naïve intuitions or introspection and, second, it ignores other .sorts of data relevant to developing a theory of reasoning competence.

4.2. *The Role of Intuition*

My first objection to (RE2) is that people's intuitions about their own reasoning competence should not be given the central role the reflective equilibrium account gives them. By 'intuition', Cohen means 'an immediate and untutored inclination, without evidence of inference',[32] to make a particular judgement. He thinks that intuitions, so defined, are central to a theory of reasoning competence. In Section 3, I argued that this emphasis on naïve rather than considered intuitions is a mistake because it is based on an analogy with an erroneous picture of linguistics; Cohen mistakenly assumes that linguistic competence is based on naïve intuitions, but it is really based on considered ones. Cohen's insistence that naïve intuitions are the ones relevant to developing a theory of reasoning competence is problematic for another reason as well. Focusing on naïve intuitions will include as part of reasoning competence just the sorts of mistake friends of the reflective equilibrium argument for the rationality thesis want to count as performance errors, namely those mistakes that are uncovered by the reasoning experiments. For example, if psychologists observe people's reasoning behaviour, they will see that, in cases like the Linda example, people violate the conjunction principle. People's naïve intuitions will tend to agree that it is reasonable to violate the conjunction principle. Violating the conjunction principle is thus likely to be included in an account of reasoning competence that results from bringing into reflective equilibrium a person's naïve intuitions about what principles she is following. This is because people admit they are violating the conjunction principle, but they often do not admit that in doing so, they are reasoning fallaciously.

These two considerations suggest that, to be successful, the reflective equilibrium account of reasoning competence ought to focus on

---

[32] Cohen, 'Can Human Irrationality be Experimentally Demonstrated?', 318.

considered intuitions.[33] The suggestion is that our considered intuitions about what counts as good reasoning are to be taken into consideration in the development of an account of actual human reasoning competence, namely:

(RE2′)   A descriptive theory of reasoning competence comes from a process of reflective equilibrium with our *considered* intuitions about what constitutes good reasoning as input.

This modification moves the reflective equilibrium argument towards considering reflection on a person's own cognitive processes as a source of data for reasoning competence. Cognitive scientists should not observe behaviour and then compare the principles they abstract from this behaviour to people's naïve intuitions about what principles they are following. Instead, they should compare the principles that characterize observed reasoning behaviour with people's carefully considered intuitions as to what principles they are following. This sort of careful self-examination of what principles one is following is called introspection. Introspection is a method of research with a long tradition in psychology. I shall argue, however, that the move to introspection will not save the second premiss of the reflective equilibrium argument.[34]

In 1879, when Wilhelm Wundt set up the first psychology laboratory, introspection was *the* method of research. Subjects in Wundt's laboratory were trained to report their own cognitive processes under experimental conditions. One reason why introspection is not the research method of choice in cognitive science is that dozens of psychological experiments have shown that introspective reports about human psychology are wrong.[35] One classic experiment of this sort, performed by Saul Sternberg, involves giving subjects a list of randomly chosen single-digit numbers to memorize and then timing them to see how long they take to indicate whether a particular number is on the memorized list.[36] For example, a subject might be shown the list '4 2 7 9 6' and asked

---

[33] The emphasis on considered intuitions is present in Macnamara, *A Border Dispute*, 22–42, but without any talk of reflective equilibrium.

[34] Cohen, 'Can Human Irrationality be Experimentally Demonstrated?', 318, rejects the method of introspection, but for reasons different from those I give here.

[35] For a discussion of introspection in the history and pre-history of cognitive science, see Owen Flanagan, *The Science of the Mind* (Cambridge, Mass.: MIT Press, 1984). For a detailed philosophical discussion of introspection in psychology, see William Lyons, *The Disappearance of Introspection* (Cambridge, Mass.: MIT Press, 1986).

[36] Saul Sternberg, 'High-Speed Scanning in Human Memory', *Science*, 153 (1966), 652–4.

whether the number nine is on the list. Sternberg found that subjects' reaction times (the amount of time it takes a subject to determine whether a number is on the list) vary with the length of the list but do *not* vary with a number's position on the list. This suggests that subjects are searching the list number by number and that searching through the list continues even after the number has been found earlier in the search. For example, if the subject has been shown the list '4 2 7 9 6' and is asked whether the number two is on the list, she might (subconsciously) first look at the four and ask 'Is this a two?' and so on. Further, she might continue searching through the list until the end, examining seven, nine, and six, asking if each is a two, even though the number two has already been found to be on the list.[37] That this is the procedure we use to determine if a number is on a list is highly counter-intuitive. It is much more intuitive that we stop looking through the list once we find the number we are looking for. It seems highly unlikely that an observe, abstract, idealize, etc. process using our considered intuitions as data would produce Sternberg's description of our reasoning competence; even careful introspection would be unable to discover that this procedure governs our list-searching behaviour. The reflective equilibrium account of reasoning competence, as characterized thus far, does not fit with the facts of what we actually know about human cognitive processes.

Further reason that our cognitive mechanisms may be inaccessible to introspection (not to mention to untutored intuitions) can be shown by examining linguistics. Although humans can utter and comprehend highly structured, complex linguistic sentences, most non-linguists have little understanding of how we perform the linguistic feats we do. Most of us have almost no intuitive sense of underlying linguistic structure and how it works. For example, consider the sentence 'John saw Bill's father shoot himself'. All native English speakers are able to interpret this sentence unambiguously as meaning that Bill's father was the one who got shot, not John or Bill, but complex linguistic theories need to be brought in to explain how we do this. We all have (implicit) knowledge of abstract linguistic principles but few people (if any) have any *conscious* knowledge (or even introspectively accessible knowledge) of

---

[37] Sternberg's results do not in fact indicate whether subjects look through the lists from left to right, from right to left, or, as implausible as it may seem, in some other (perhaps random) order; all his data show is that subjects take the same amount of time to identify a number as being on the list if the number is at or near the beginning of the list as they do if the number is at or near the end.

these underlying linguistic principles; further, those who do understand them get their knowledge from years of research, not simply from introspection. The upshot of this discussion is that a reflective equilibrium account of reasoning competence that only or primarily takes intuitions as input, (RE2), or even that takes only or primarily considered intuitions as input, (RE2′), does not do justice to the way cognitive scientists actually study human reasoning competence.[38]

4.3. The Data Relevant to Reasoning Competence

The second, and more serious, problem with the reflective equilibrium account of reasoning competence is that there are several *other* sources of data besides behaviour, intuitions (naïve or considered), and introspection that cognitive scientists can and do make use of including, for example, neurophysiology, theory of computation, and evolutionary theory. To see this, suppose neuroscientific research advances in such a fashion that neuroscientists can isolate cognitive mechanisms in the brain. Although such research may be quite far from the current state of neuroscience, it is possible for such discoveries to be made. If they were, these results would surely be relevant to a theory of reasoning competence. In the realm of the technologically more realistic, basic neuroscientific facts like the size of the brain and the speed at which neurons operate are important considerations for the development of a theory of reasoning competence.[39] Given the size of the brain, the number of neurons in it, the speed at which neurons operate, and the time it takes a human to make a calculation, there are many seemingly plausible principles of reasoning that are *not* realizable in the human brain. Neuroscientific data is thus relevant to cognitive science and the development of a theory of reasoning competence; it is not, however, the sort of data that is deemed relevant by the (RE2) and (RE2′) account of how reasoning competence is researched. Note that this does not conflict with the fact (discussed in Chapter 3, Section 3.3) that we cannot read particular principles of reasoning competence directly off groups of

[38] Leda Cosmides and John Tooby, 'Beyond Intuition and Instinct Blindness: Toward an Evolutionarily Rigorous Cognitive Science', *Cognition*, 50 (1994), 66, say that there are evolutionary and design reasons why the principles of reasoning are inaccessible to introspection.

[39] Christopher Cherniak, 'Undebuggability and Cognitive Science', *Communications of the Association for Computing Machinery*, 31 (1988), 402–12. See also Cherniak, 'The Bounded Brain: Toward Quantitative Neuroanatomy', *Journal of Cognitive Neuroscience*, 2 (1990), 58–68.

neurons. Neuroscientific evidence may not be able to tell us whether we in fact have a particular principle of reasoning in our reasoning competence, but such evidence can still be relevant to developing such an account.

In addition to neuroscience, evolutionary theory is relevant to the study of reasoning competence. Leda Cosmides, in her paper 'The Logic of Selection', offers an account of deductive reasoning that is influenced by the constraints that evolution and natural selection place on psychological mechanisms.[40] Cosmides writes:

> Natural selection, in a particular ecological setting, constrains which kinds of traits can evolve. For many domains of human activity, evolutionary biology can be used to determine what kind of psychological mechanisms would have been quickly selected out, and what kind were likely to have become universal and species-typical. Natural selection therefore constitutes 'valid constraints on the way the world is structured'; hence, knowledge of natural selection can be used to create computational theories of adaptive information-processing problems. Natural selection theory allows one to pinpoint adaptive problems that the human mind must be able to solve with special efficiency, and it suggests design features that any mechanism capable of solving these problems must have.[41]

The point is that, because certain adaptive problems are likely to be important for survival and, hence, to be selectively advantageous, certain cognitive mechanisms will be more likely to have evolved given the evolutionary history of human beings. Evolutionary considerations can therefore inform research into reasoning competence by suggesting which mechanisms are evolutionarily feasible and probable. The reflective equilibrium account of the study of reasoning competence has no room for such considerations.

Finally, computational theory is relevant to developing a theory of reasoning competence.[42] Principles that might seem plausible candidates for being part of human reasoning competence cannot be implemented in the amount of time that humans in fact take to make certain inferences. For example, Cherniak criticizes Quine's 'web of belief' model of human memory[43] as requiring particular principles—

---

[40] Leda Cosmides, 'The Logic of Selection: Has Natural Selection Shaped how Humans Reason? Studies with the Wason Selection Task', *Cognition*, 31 (1989), 187–276.

[41] Ibid. 189.

[42] Christopher Cherniak, *Minimal Rationality* (Cambridge, Mass.: MIT Press, 1986).

[43] Willard V. O. Quine, 'Two Dogmas of Empiricism', in *From a Logical Point of View* (Cambridge, Mass.: Harvard University Press, 1961); and id. and J. S. Ulian, *The Web of Belief* (New York: Random House, 1970).

that is, principles of belief modification, principles for testing consistency, and so on—that are too computationally demanding for the human brain to handle in a reasonable amount of time.[44] Computational considerations thus provide constraints on developing an account of reasoning competence, but such considerations are not available to the reflective equilibrium account.

Cohen insists that no scientific data could count against the view that the normative principles of reasoning are in our reasoning competence. Any such data would be relevant to developing an account of our reasoning *performance* but not our reasoning competence.[45] Cohen says that if, for example, a neurophysiological account suggests that our reasoning competence is characterized by principles that diverge from the normative principles, then this is reason to reject the neurophysiological account. Against Cohen, I think that such empirical evidence can give us good reason to think that our reasoning competence does not match the norms. Here is the sort of case I have in mind. Suppose we have the intuition that before a person commits herself to some belief *p*, she should check to make sure that *p* is logically compatible with all her other beliefs (call this the *consistency preservation principle*). Suppose, as seems plausible, that the consistency preservation principle is judged to be a normative principle of reasoning through the process of reflective equilibrium. The question is whether we actually have this principle of reasoning in our reasoning competence. One set of reasons for thinking that we do *not* is that, given the size of our brains, the number of neurons in them, and the amount of time it takes us to acquire new beliefs, it is impossible for us to check to make sure that *p* is logically compatible with all our beliefs. Cohen would see our failure to do this as a *performance* error, not a flaw in our underlying competence. To support this view, Cohen might reasonably point to an example from linguistics. There are grammatical sentences too long for us to parse that we consistently judge to be ungrammatical. Despite this, linguists still say that the ability to parse such sentences is part of our linguistic competence; limitations on performance (for example, lack of sufficient memory space) prevent us from exhibiting this underlying ability. The analogous point is that we have the consistency preservation principle in our reasoning competence but we do not exhibit it because of limitations on performance (e.g. time and/or memory limitations). I agree

---

[44] Cherniak, *Minimal Rationality*, 47–54. Cherniak's critique specifically applies to Quine's account of the principles needed to maintain the web of belief, not necessarily to other similar 'network' theories of belief.   [45] See Cohen, 'A Reply to Stein'.

this is *possible*. Where Cohen and I disagree is that I think it is possible that our failure to behave in accordance with this principle might be due to the fact that the principle is not in our reasoning competence. It seems to me a possibility that we can recognize consistency preservation as a normative principle of reasoning even if it is not part of our reasoning competence.

Some think there is a tension here:[46] how can I recognize that a rule is a norm without having it in my reasoning competence? I agree with Cohen that the normative principles of reasoning are the result of a process of reflective equilibrium with our intuitions about what counts as good reasoning as input. A principle can, however, be the result of such a process without being a principle that characterizes my underlying ability to reason. The considerations that are brought to bear as part of the reflective equilibrium process may move us away from some of our original intuitions and the reasoning competence on which these original intuitions are based.

An example from another realm may help make this clear. Suppose that the principle 'You can never make a compound word that contains a regular plural noun' (an example of such a compound word that would be prohibited would be 'fingersprint') is a principle that applies to all possible human languages, that is, it is a principle of human linguistic competence. Still, there are possible *non*-human languages (e.g. Martian) in which you *can* make a compound word that contains a regular plural noun. It is perfectly consistent with my having a linguistic competence that lacks this Martian principle that I could consider this principle, understand it, and even eventually learn to follow it (presumably, using my general learning capacities rather than my linguistic ones) and, thereby, to speak Martian (although I would not be able to learn Martian as fast as children can learn human languages and I would probably make mistakes in applying this principle). The general point is that with respect to language it seems I can consider, understand, and learn principles not in my linguistic competence. The same seems true of reasoning competence: I can consider, understand, and possibly even learn principles of reasoning not in my reasoning competence. Take consistency preservation as an example. When I consider a candidate belief, I do not in fact check for compatibility with all my other beliefs. It is possible that I fail to do this because I lack the principle of consistency preservation in my reasoning competence. This

---

[46] e.g. Macnamara, *A Border Dispute*.

is consistent with my understanding what consistency preservation is and being able to say it is right to preserve consistency. Cohen's attempt to insulate our reasoning competence from non-normative principles fails.

That neurophysiological, computational, and evolutionary data are relevant to the study of reasoning competence counts against (RE2) and (RE2′). This conclusion should be of no surprise because (RE2) gets its initial plausibility from an analogy with linguistics, a research programme that in fact includes the study of more types of data than just actual linguistic behaviour and linguistic intuitions; neuroscience,[47] theory of computation,[48] and, perhaps, evolutionary theory[49] are relevant to linguistics as well. This is not to say that linguistic behaviour and linguistic intuitions are not relevant to the study of linguistic competence. Nor is it to say that reasoning behaviour and intuitions about what counts as good reasoning are not relevant to the study of reasoning competence. It is, however, to say that these considerations are not the only evidence relevant to the study of reasoning competence.

These two objections to the reflective equilibrium account of reasoning competence—that the account cannot explain actual advances in the understanding of reasoning competence and that other considerations besides behaviour and intuitions are relevant to reasoning competence—are connected. The reason why the reflective equilibrium account of reasoning competence is impoverished is because it does not include the variety of other considerations that are relevant to reasoning competence. The reflective equilibrium account of reasoning competence is mistaken; (RE2) and (RE2′) are thus both false.

[47] See e.g. David Caplan and Nancy Hildebrandt, *Disorders of Syntactic Comprehension* (Cambridge, Mass.: MIT Press, 1988).

[48] See e.g. Ken Wexler and Peter Culicover, *Formal Principles of Language Acquisition* (Cambridge, Mass.: MIT Press, 1980); and Robert Berwick and Amy Weinberg, *The Grammatical Basis of Linguistic Performance* (Cambridge, Mass.: MIT Press, 1980).

[49] Steven Pinker and Paul Bloom, 'Natural Language and Natural Selection', *Behavioral and Brain Sciences*, 13 (1990), 707–84, argue that our innate linguistic capacity is the result of natural selection. If they are right, as I think they are, then perhaps evolutionary theory might be used to inform linguistic theory in the way that evolutionary theory can inform cognitive science. Pinker and Bloom's thesis is, however, highly contentious. For opposing views, see the commentaries on Pinker and Bloom, *Behavioral and Brain Sciences*, 13 (1990), 727–65; also see Noam Chomsky, *Language and Problems of Knowledge* (Cambridge, Mass.: MIT Press, 1980); Richard Lewontin, 'The Evolution of Cognition', in Daniel Osherson and Edward E. Smith (eds.), *Thinking: An Invitation to Cognitive Science*, iii (Cambridge, Mass.: MIT Press, 1990); and Massimo Piattelli-Palmarini, 'Evolution, Selection and Cognition', *Cognition*, 31 (1989), 1–44.

5. Revisions

Recall the reflective equilibrium argument for the rationality thesis:

(RE1) The normative principles of reasoning come from a process of reflective equilibrium with our intuitions about what constitutes good reasoning as input.

(RE2) A descriptive theory of reasoning competence comes from a process of reflective equilibrium with our intuitions about what constitutes good reasoning as input.

(RE3) Therefore, since both come from the same process with the same inputs, reasoning competence must match the normative principles of reasoning.

In Section 3, I defended the plausibility of (RE1) appropriately modified; some version of the wide reflective equilibrium account of the norms of reasoning is at least plausible. If the balancing process is broadened to consider general theoretical considerations, if the class of people whose balancing processes are relevant is narrowed, and so on, then it seems the objection that the reflective equilibrium process endorses some non-normative principles may be answered or at least the objection may be shown to be irrelevant. In Section 4, I argued that (RE2) was not at all so plausible. The reflective equilibrium account of reasoning competence is mistaken. Both our *considered* intuitions and evidence from various scientific disciplines are relevant to reasoning competence.

A friend of the reflective equilibrium argument for the rationality thesis might attempt to modify (RE2). The aim of such a modification would be twofold. First, this modification would be designed to defend a reflective equilibrium account of reasoning competence that is true, in particular that takes the objections of Section 4 into account. Second, this modification would be designed to defend a reflective equilibrium account of reasoning competence according to which the inputs to the reflective equilibrium process and the reflective equilibrium process itself were the same as the inputs to the reflective equilibrium process involved in determining the normative principles of reasoning. In this section, I will sketch a modification to the reflective equilibrium account of reasoning competence (RE2) that avoids the objections of Section 4 and that matches the reflective equilibrium account of the normative principles of reasoning. I will argue that even this attempt to save the reflective equilibrium argument for the rationality thesis fails.

My candidate modification is to see the study of reasoning competence as a process of bringing our considered intuitions about reasoning
into reflective equilibrium with our advanced scientific theories. On this
picture, our considered intuitions about reasoning would be brought
into balance with the relevant scientific theories—for example, neuroscientific, psychological, evolutionary, and computational theories. This
picture of how a descriptive theory of reasoning competence is studied
is similar to the picture I painted at the end of Section 4 of how linguistic
competence is properly studied. Linguists do make use of (considered)
linguistic intuitions, but scientific data (for example, neurophysiology,
computational theory, and perhaps evolutionary theory) are relevant as
well. Further, the relationship between our linguistic intuitions and the
scientific data relevant to linguistics does seem to fit the sort of balancing involved in reflective equilibrium. While this picture diverges from
Cohen's picture of reasoning competence, it does fit with the reflective
equilibrium account. Further, it explicitly answers the objections I raised
in the previous section. The suggestion is that (RE2) be modified as
follows:

(RE2″) A descriptive theory of reasoning competence comes from
a process of reflective equilibrium with both our intuitions
about what constitutes good reasoning and scientific evidence
relevant to what constitutes good reasoning as input.

The crucial question for the reflective equilibrium argument for the
rationality thesis is whether this account of reasoning competence is
parallel to the reflective equilibrium account of the norms in such a way
that the reflective equilibrium argument for the rationality thesis will go
through.

For the reflective equilibrium argument for the rationality thesis to
work, the reflective equilibrium process involved in developing an
account of reasoning competence must have the same data as input as
does the reflective equilibrium account of how the norms are justified.
For the reflective equilibrium account to apply to reasoning competence, it must include scientific evidence as input. It seems, however,
that for reflective equilibrium to apply to the justification of normative
principles of reasoning, it must *not* include scientific evidence as input.
Determining what the normative principles of reasoning are, according to
the standard picture of rationality, is a conceptual question—empirical
considerations are, thus, not relevant to determining what the norms of
reasoning are. Scientific evidence—in particular, physical, chemical,

psychological, and other facts about the brain—should play a role in the development of a descriptive theory of reasoning competence. But how can such facts play a role in the development of a normative theory of reasoning? Any such attempt seems to be guilty of the *naturalistic fallacy* of deriving 'ought' from 'is'.

Many have suggested, however, that the naturalistic fallacy is not a fallacy at all, that philosophical questions (most notably, epistemological and ethical questions) can and ought to be 'naturalized' (see Chapter 1, Section 2). Perhaps rationality should be naturalized as well. If this is right, then it may be perfectly acceptable for the reflective equilibrium process that determines the normative principles of reasoning to include scientific evidence as input. In fact, included as part of the very scientific evidence relevant to 'naturalizing rationality' would be the results of the reasoning experiments. This is all well and good as far as some of us may be concerned (in Chapter 7, I argue that a naturalized picture of rationality is an appealing alternative to the standard picture of rationality), but it will not be of help to friends of the rationality thesis, for they want to insulate human rationality from the potentially damaging empirical evidence of the reasoning experiments. Advocates of the reflective equilibrium argument for the rationality thesis want to discount the evidence resulting from experiments like the selection task and the conjunction experiment by saying such evidence merely indicates the sorts of performance errors humans typically make and does not illuminate our reasoning competence. This sort of evidence is thus *not* available to them as part of the project of naturalizing rationality. Such evidence is, however, just the sort of evidence that bears on a descriptive theory of reasoning competence once we realize that empirical evidence *is* relevant to such a descriptive theory. This shows the inputs to the reflective equilibrium processes of developing both a descriptive and a normative account of reasoning competence are different; this, in turn, blocks a reflective equilibrium argument for the rationality thesis because such a defence turns on there being the same inputs to both reflective equilibrium processes. Even if (RE2″) is true, the reflective equilibrium process involved in determining the normative principles of reasoning includes inputs that are different from the ones the reflective equilibrium process for determining reasoning competence includes; if this criticism is right, the argument from (RE1) and (RE2) to (RE3) (or their revisions) is invalid.

There is a further problem for the reflective equilibrium argument for the rationality thesis: it is unclear that the process involved in developing a theory of reasoning competence and the one involved in determining the normative principles of reasoning would be the same *even if* their inputs were the same. The goal of the first process is to develop a descriptive psychological account of human reasoning competence while the goal of the second is to develop an account of the normative principles of reasoning. Even if the reflective equilibrium model of developing a descriptive theory of reasoning competence (RE2″) and some version of the reflective equilibrium account of justification are true, and even if the reflective equilibrium processes get the same data as input, there is no reason to think the balancing process involved in developing a psychological theory would parallel the balancing involved in justification. In particular, in light of the different goals of these two processes, their inputs, even if they are the same, would be weighted in different ways as part of the balancing process. Even if an intuition is part of the input to both the reflective equilibrium process for determining the normative principles of reasoning and the reflective equilibrium process for determining human reasoning competence, this intuition will carry different weight in the two different processes. The same is true with a scientific fact. Consider, for example, the fact that the brain contains a specific number of neurons. Even if such a fact is part of the input to both the reflective equilibrium process for determining the norms of reasoning (assuming the legitimacy of naturalizing rationality) and the reflective equilibrium process for determining human reasoning competence, there is good reason to think that this fact would be relevant to the outcome of the two processes in different ways. Given that the inputs (even if they are the same) will probably be weighted in different ways because of the different goals of the two processes, the outcome of the two reflective equilibrium processes will probably diverge. This counts against the reflective equilibrium argument for the rationality thesis; again, it suggests that the reflective equilibrium argument for the rationality thesis, even when revised, is invalid.

This point may be made clearer by considering an example from a different realm. Consider once again the application of reflective equilibrium to ethics. Suppose that the reflective equilibrium model is applied to both the project of determining what is moral and to the project of determining what moral sentiments human have. Further, suppose that the inputs to the two processes are the same. Given all this, a particular input to the reflective equilibrium process, say, for example, the intuition that it is wrong to torture babies, will be weighted in a particular way and will interact in a particular way with other inputs as part of the project of determining what is moral that will almost surely differ from the way the same intuition is weighted and interacts as part of determining what human moral sentiments are. As such, the results of the two reflective equilibrium processes will be different.

The attempt to modify the reflective equilibrium account of reasoning competence fails to be successful because it must include scientific evidence in the input to the balancing process. If this modification is made and scientific evidence is included, the input to the process involved with reasoning competence and the process involved with the norms of reasoning may be different. If both processes do not have the same input, the reflective equilibrium argument for the rationality thesis fails. Even with the same input, however, the argument fails because the input will be weighted in different ways given the different goals of the two reflective equilibrium processes.

6. Conclusion

The reflective equilibrium argument for the rationality thesis turns on there being an isomorphism between how normative principles of reasoning are justified and how a theory of reasoning competence is developed. This isomorphism fails to hold. Cohen's version of the reflective equilibrium argument tries to establish this isomorphism by arguing that both processes fit the narrow reflective equilibrium model of justification. I have argued that neither process is appropriately characterized by narrow reflective equilibrium. With respect to the study of reasoning competence, the reflective equilibrium process involves scientific evidence as input. With respect to the norms of reasoning, the process involved is some version of wide reflective equilibrium. Further, I have shown that an attempt to defend the required isomorphism by arguing that both processes fit a wide reflective equilibrium model fails as well because, even if the two processes do fit the same model (which is far from obvious), they have different inputs, and even if they did have the same inputs, they have different goals.

The conclusion of this chapter is, in a sense, no surprise given the point I made in Section 2 against the general argument for the rationality thesis. My point, against the analogy between developing a theory of linguistic competence and developing a theory of reasoning competence, was that norms of grammaticality are indexed to actual facts about human psychology, neurophysiology, and the like, whereas norms of reasoning are not. Because the process of developing a descriptive theory of reasoning competence is, regardless of whether it involves either wide or narrow reflective equilibrium, indexed to empirical facts about humans, we should expect the results of such a process to diverge from an account of what the normative principles of reasoning are.

Norman Daniels has made an interesting and somewhat parallel point.[50] He argues that the analogy suggested by Rawls[51] between linguistics and ethics is mistaken: linguistics involves *narrow* reflective equilibrium while ethics involves *wide* reflective equilibrium. While it is not obvious that linguistics (or cognitive science) is appropriately characterized as involving *narrow* reflective equilibrium, I think that Daniels is on the right track in pointing to the distinction. Ethical principles—*like* principles of reasoning and *unlike* linguistic principles and psychological descriptions—seem independent of physiological facts about humans. Justifying principles of ethics or reasoning involves general philosophical reflection in a way that justifying psychological or linguistic principles does not. If Daniels is right about ethics and I am right in thinking that justifying principles of reasoning is like justifying principles of ethics in the relevant ways, even if a wide reflective equilibrium account of the justification of principles of reasoning can be developed, the analogy between this process and the psychological project of determining actual human reasoning competence does not hold.

In Chapter 1, I suggested that one reason why we might think the question of whether humans are rational is a conceptual question is because the normative principles of reasoning are dependent on humans for their existence and character, in particular, on human reasoning competence. The reflective equilibrium argument for the rationality thesis is an attempt to fill in the details of such a defence of the rationality thesis. In this chapter, I have argued that this attempt fails.

[50] Daniels, 'On Some Methods of Ethics and Linguistics'.
[51] Rawls, *A Theory of Justice*, 46–8.

6

Evolution

THE arguments for the rationality thesis that I have considered thus far have mostly been conceptual arguments. In contrast, the arguments I consider in this chapter say that the rationality thesis is an empirical truth. The general argument, based on evolutionary theory, is initially quite appealing and many philosophers have (at least implicitly) endorsed it.[1] This evolutionary argument involves two parts. The first is the claim that evolution, through natural selection, will select for cognitive mechanisms that generate true beliefs. This seems reasonable because natural selection has selected other (non-cognitive) mechanisms that help in the production of true beliefs. For instance, it selected the human visual system that typically does an excellent job of helping to generate true beliefs about the world (for example, there is a tiger over there). Further, although the visual system does sometimes generate false beliefs, these tend to be rare, to occur in identifiable ranges of situations (such as in the dark or in situations involving optical illusions), and to be compensated for fairly easily. We should expect natural selection to have done a similarly good job selecting our cognitive mechanisms. The second part of the evolutionary argument posits a connection between rationality and the use of mechanisms that produce true beliefs. It seems quite reasonable to think a system that generates

[1] See Daniel Dennett, 'Making Sense of Ourselves', in *The Intentional Stance* (Cambridge, Mass.: MIT Press, 1987), 96; Jerry Fodor, 'Three Cheers for Propositional Attitudes', in *Representations* (Cambridge, Mass.: MIT Press, 1981), 121; Alvin Goldman, *Epistemology and Cognition* (Cambridge, Mass.: MIT Press, 1986), 98; William Lycan, 'Epistemic Value', in *Judgment and Justification* (Cambridge: Cambridge University Press, 1988), 142; Ruth Millikan, 'Naturalist Reflections on Knowledge', *Pacific Philosophical Quarterly*, 65 (1984), 317; ead., *Language, Thought and Other Biological Categories* (Cambridge, Mass.: MIT Press, 1987), *passim*; David Papineau, *Reality and Representation* (Oxford: Blackwell, 1987), 77–8; Karl Popper, 'Evolutionary Epistemology', in J. W. Pollard (ed.), *Evolutionary Theory* (London: Wiley, 1984), 239; W. V. O. Quine, 'Natural Kinds', in *Ontological Relativity and Other Essays* (New York: Columbia University Press, 1969), 126; and Elliott Sober, 'The Evolution of Rationality', *Synthese*, 46 (1981), 98. Not all of these people consistently support the evolutionary argument but each has been more or less tempted by it at some time. For example, Fodor, *Psychosemantics* (Cambridge, Mass.: MIT Press, 1987), now eschews Darwinian explanations in cognitive science and philosophy of mind.

true beliefs is rational; what could be more rational than to infer true beliefs about the world? Simply put, the two-step evolutionary argument moves from a connection between evolution and truth on the one hand and a connection between truth and rationality on the other, to a connection between evolution and rationality. The evolutionary argument is supposed to provide a strong reason for seeing humans as rational: that humans have evolved is a good reason to believe they are rational. If the evolutionary argument is successful, it provides good reason for interpreting the reasoning experiments in such a way that all divergences from the normative principles of reasoning are construed as performance errors, in other words, it provides good reason for interpreting the reasoning experiments in such a way that they are consistent with the rationality thesis.

In this chapter, I will develop the evolutionary argument and then argue that it fails to provide support for human rationality. My discussion will focus on the first step of the evolutionary argument—the claim that evolution will select for cognitive mechanisms that produce true beliefs. First, I will consider an intuitive argument in favour of this step of the evolutionary argument. This argument tries to establish the connection between evolution and truth by way of natural selection and optimality: evolution is driven by natural selection and natural selection will select for optimal principles, namely, those principles that select true beliefs. I will discuss four objections to this argument: first, that natural selection is not the only force that drives evolution; second, that even when natural selection explains why we have a certain trait, it does not guarantee that the trait was selected *because* of its selective advantage; third, that even if the trait was selected for because of its selective advantage, the trait may not be the most optimal; and, fourth, that natural selection can only choose between available traits, and sometimes the optimal traits are not available. I will argue that the first objection—an objection that is in favour these days, particularly in philosophical circles—is impotent. Although other evolutionary forces exist, natural selection is the only one that can plausibly explain something as complex as human reasoning competence. The other three objections pose more serious challenges to the first step in the evolutionary argument (although the second objection can be partially answered and the fourth objection rests on an unclear matter of burden of proof). In the last two sections, I will consider two variations on the evolutionary argument: one replaces biological evolution with conceptual evolution in the attempt to use truth to forge the link between evolution and human rationality; the other attempts to use reproductive success to replace truth as the link between evolution and rationality. I shall argue that neither of these attempted modifications proves adequate to save the evolutionary argument for human rationality.

1. The Basic Evolutionary Argument

The evolutionary argument in its general form has two parts: the first part establishes a connection between evolution and truth; the second part establishes a connection between truth and rationality. To begin, why should we believe that there is a connection between evolution and truth? In general, the answer is that having true beliefs seems a good thing in terms of reproductive fitness. If I have true beliefs about what food is nourishing for me and my offspring, about where to find it, how to consume it, and so on, then I will do better at getting fed than I would if I had random false beliefs about these things. While this seems a plausible defence of the claim that biological evolution favours mechanisms that produce true beliefs (what I call truth-tropic mechanisms), there is more structure to this argument. The basic idea is that evolution is driven by natural selection, that natural selection selects optimal cognitive mechanisms, and that these mechanisms, since they are optimal, will be truth-tropic. This seems plausible when compared to typical evolutionary theorizing about other human systems, for example, the human visual system. Natural selection is the driving force in the standard story of the evolution of the visual system. The particular visual system that gets selected is chosen because it is the best at doing what visual systems are supposed to do. The evolution of cognitive mechanisms, in general, and human reasoning competence, in particular, is supposed to work the same way—natural selection drives their evolution and, thus, the best cognitive mechanisms are selected. From here, there remains only a small step in the argument: truth-tropic cognitive mechanisms are the best ones, a truth-tropic reasoning competence is the best kind. This seems, at first glance, an indisputable step; what could be a better system for belief selection than one that selects true beliefs?

Adding the second step of the evolutionary argument—namely, that there is a connection between truth and rationality—to this argument for the connection between evolution and truth produces the following argument for the rationality thesis:[2]

---

[2] Parts of this argument are adapted from parts of an argument sketched in Stephen Stich, *The Fragmentation of Reason* (Cambridge, Mass.: MIT Press, 1990), 55–74.

(1) Biological evolution is caused by natural selection.

(2) Natural selection favours optimal traits.

(3) The optimal cognitive mechanisms are those that are good at producing true beliefs.

(4) Therefore, biological evolution favours cognitive mechanisms that are good at producing true beliefs.

(5) A rational cognitive mechanism is one that is good at producing true beliefs.

(6) Therefore, biological evolution favours rational cognitive mechanisms.

(7) Human cognitive mechanisms are the result of biological evolution.

(8) Therefore, there is a strong reason to believe that humans are rational—in particular, there is a strong reason *not* to interpret the reasoning experiments as demonstrating human irrationality.

In the discussion that follows, I will focus primarily on the argument for (4), the first part of the evolutionary argument.

2. The Origin of Cognitive Mechanisms

Consider (1), the claim that evolution is caused by natural selection. Although this may seem like an obvious truth, it is false; there are a variety of forces that drive evolution including *random genetic drift* (sampling error in evolution that is introduced by the finite size of populations), *variable mutation rates* (the phenomenon whereby if one allele[3] mutates into another less frequently than the other mutates into it, then—whether or not it would otherwise be favoured by natural selection—the allele might dominate its competitor), *laws of development* (for example, the correlation of head size and body size that holds for most animals), *accidents of history*, *macromutations*[4] (the sudden appearance of totally new traits due to large-scale mutations; also known

---

[3] 'Rival' traits, that is, traits that can occur in the same place in chromosomal material, are called alleles. For example, the alleles for human eye colour include a blue allele, a green allele, and so on. Only two alleles for the same feature (for example, eye colour) can be present in a single organism—one allele from the person's father and one from the person's mother—and only one of the two alleles can be exhibited.

[4] Richard Goldschmidt, *The Material Basis of Evolution* (New Haven: Yale University Press, 1940).

as 'hopeful monsters'), and *environmental factors* (for example, natural selection does not need to be invoked to explain why flying fish have evolved so that they return to the water after entering the air since gravity will explain the evolution of such behaviour[5]).[6] The existence of this variety of forces that drive evolution threatens to undermine the argument for (4),[7] the claim that biological evolution favours truth-tropic principles, because this claim seems plausible only in light of natural selection (as indicated by the role that appeal to natural selection plays in the argument from (1) and (2) to (3)).[8]

By way of beginning to reply to this argument, notice that the evolutionary argument for the rationality thesis need not be committed to a claim as broad as (1), the claim that biological evolution is caused by natural selection. Really all that is needed to make the argument for (4) go through is the premiss that the evolution of our cognitive mechanisms in general (or our reasoning competence, in particular) is caused by natural selection. The strategy for replying to the objection to (1) is to find some way to restrict the premiss: (1) could be modified so as to be immune to the objection that there are other forces besides natural selection that drive the evolution of cognitive mechanisms—the existence of a variety of forces that drive evolution only counts against (4) if there is reason to believe these other forces play a role in the evolution of cognitive mechanisms. A promising way to do this involves the observation that natural selection is the only explanation for the evolution of

---

[5] George C. Williams, *Adaptation and Natural Selection* (Princeton: Princeton University Press, 1966), 11–12.

[6] For a discussion of some of these non-selectionist evolutionary forces, see Steven J. Gould and Richard Lewontin, 'The Spandrels of San Marcos and the Panglossian Paradigm: A Critique of the Adaptationist Programme', *Proceedings of the Royal Society of London*, 205 (1978), 281–8; repr. in Elliott Sober (ed.), *Conceptual Issues in Evolutionary Biology* (Cambridge, Mass.: MIT Press, 1984); see also Elliott Sober, *The Nature of Selection* (Cambridge, Mass.: MIT Press, 1984), 20–31.

[7] In contrast, Lycan, 'Epistemic Value', 153, suggests that even if non-selectionist evolutionary forces are responsible for our cognitive mechanisms, the rules that our mechanisms follow would be basically the same as those we would have had if natural selection were the sole cause of them. The two very brief arguments he gives for this claim are not convincing.

[8] This argument against the conclusion that biological evolution favours truth-tropic mechanisms is similar to one made in Stich, *The Fragmentation of Reason*, 63–4. Sober, 'The Evolution of Rationality', 110–11, expresses concern that non-selectionist forces might undermine the evolutionary argument. Richard Lewontin, 'The Evolution of Cognition', in Daniel Osherson and Edward E. Smith (eds.), *Thinking: An Invitation to Cognitive Science*, iii (Cambridge, Mass.: MIT Press, 1990), also suggests that, in light of various non-selectionist forces of evolution, our cognitive mechanisms might have evolved but not be the result of natural selection.

complex structures.[9] The suggestion involves modifying premiss (1) as follows:

(1′) The biological evolution *of functionally complex structures* (including the mechanism underlying our reasoning competence) is caused by natural selection.[10]

My defence of the modified first premiss of the evolutionary argument for the rationality thesis proceeds as follows: first, I will defend the claim that natural selection is the only explanation for the evolution of complex structures; then I will argue that human cognitive mechanisms are complex structures.

Consider some functionally complex structure S that is the result of biological evolution. As a functionally complex structure, S has many interacting parts, each with an articulated and intricate structure. Each part of S serves some particular purpose that plays a role in the overall function of the structure. An especially good example of such a structure is the human eye.[11] The eye has many parts, each of which is intricately designed. Together, these parts perform a remarkable function—they enable their possessor to see—with great precision and efficiency. The evolution of such a complex structure, one with so many interacting parts, requires the feedback that is the earmark of natural selection. Natural selection is able to retain minutely small modifications to a structure on the basis of how these modifications improve the functioning of the structure; it is the only evolutionary force capable of doing this. It is this selective retention on the basis of merit that is required for random mutations to lead to the production of complex structures like the eye.

[9] Williams, *Adaptation and Natural Selection*, see esp. chs. 1, 2, and 9. This point is adapted from Williams and eloquently articulated in Richard Dawkins, *The Blind Watchmaker* (New York: W. W. Norton, 1986) and Steven Pinker and Paul Bloom, 'Natural Language and Natural Selection', *Behavioral and Brain Sciences*, 13 (1990), 707–84. My discussion here draws upon Dawkins and Pinker and Bloom.

[10] This thesis applied to human cognitive mechanisms has been defended by evolutionary psychologists (among others); see Ch. 8, Section 2. Also see John Tooby, 'The Emergence of Evolutionary Psychology', in David Pines (ed.), *Emerging Synthesis in Science* (Redwood City, Calif.: Addison-Wesley, 1988); and Leda Cosmides and John Tooby, 'From Evolution to Behavior: Evolutionary Psychology as the Missing Link', in John Dupré (ed.), *The Latest on the Best: Essays on Evolution and Optimality* (Cambridge, Mass.: MIT Press, 1987); and the essays in Jerome Barkow *et al.* (eds.), *The Adapted Mind* (New York: Oxford University Press, 1992). Evolutionary psychologists do not necessarily endorse (4) or the argument for it from (1′), (2), and (3).

[11] See Dawkins, *The Blind Watchmaker*, esp. ch. 4, for a vivid discussion of the evolution of the eye.

This is not to deny that there are non-selectionist evolutionary forces like genetic drift, accidents of history, and so forth, but these forces are woefully ill-equipped to produce a structure like an eye. The chances are infinitesimally small that a non-selectionist force could produce a structure that can do all the things that eyes can do—for example, focus an image, control incoming light, respond to the presence of edges, and react differentially to colours. The only way such an unlikely arrangement of biological stuff could come into existence in the right place to perform some very specially designed functions is through a process that involves selective retention on the basis of how well this collection of stuff performs functions, that is, through the process of natural selection. Non-selectionist evolutionary forces can explain *some* features of organisms. Variable mutation rates might explain why a certain eye colour is common while another is rare. Laws of development might explain certain patterns in overall body shape and size. Only natural selection has what it takes to provide an account of the presence of functionally complex evolved structures.

For the fact that natural selection is the only good scientific explanation for the evolution of functionally complex structures to be relevant to the evolutionary argument for rationality, one needs to show that human reasoning competence is both functionally complex and the result of evolution. In Chapter 2, I argued that our reasoning competence is a mental organ and sketched some evidence that it is innate. If this is right, then our reasoning competence is also the result of evolution. If our reasoning competence is not innate, then this version of the evolutionary argument for the rationality thesis is, of course, a nonstarter (in Section 7 below, I discuss a version of the evolutionary argument that at least gets off the ground even if our reasoning competence is not innate). For evolution to possibly guarantee the rationality of our reasoning competence, our reasoning competence must be the result of evolution. For the evolutionary argument for the rationality thesis to look plausible, I need to show that reasoning competence is functionally complex.

The argument is a straightforward one. Our ability to reason is flexible, general, and intricate. We reason quickly, regularly, in a variety of domains (some of which are quite complex), and—the reasoning experiments aside—we reason consistently and reliably. Whatever mechanism is behind our ability to reason, it will require many detailed and interacting parts. No simple mechanism could enable its possessor to do all the things that we can do in terms of reasoning; our reasoning competence must be a complex mechanism. This is not to say that our reasoning behaviour provides evidence that we have a particular reasoning mechanism; there are many possible mechanisms that could explain our reasoning behaviour. My point here is that any mechanism that could possibly underlie our reasoning behaviour has to be complex.

Given this fact, the chances are infinitesimally small that a random set of molecules would come together to form a structure that could perform the functions the reasoning organ performs. Think of the set of mechanisms that could possibly underlie our reasoning ability. This set of mechanisms can be thought of as a set of Turing machines. A Turing machine is an abstract mathematical model of a computational process. There is a Turing machine equivalent for every possible computational system and there are an infinite number of Turing machine configurations, many of which do nothing of any functional significance. The odds that some randomly selected Turing machine will do *anything* of interest are quite small; more to the point here, the odds that a randomly selected Turing machine would be in the set of Turing machines that characterize our ability to reason are infinitesimally small. This is not just because there are so many possible Turing machines but because the Turing machines that are functionally equivalent to our reasoning ability are quite complex and thus constitute a quite narrow range of the set of all possible Turing machines. Only a process that involves the selective retention of changes (that is, changes due to feedback between a process and the environment in which the process takes place) could produce such a system with any marginally significant degree of probability. This sort of feedback is the fingerprint of natural selection; none of the other evolutionary forces can explain such functional complexity. The mechanism underlying our reasoning competence is functionally complex. Assuming such a complex mechanism is primarily innate, then it must be the result of natural selection. (1'), the claim that our reasoning mechanism evolved as a result of natural selection, is thus well supported.

3. The Natural Selection of Cognitive Mechanisms

The argument for (4)—the claim that evolution favours truth-tropic mechanisms—currently under consideration is:

(1') The biological evolution *of functionally complex structures* (including the mechanism underlying our reasoning competence) is caused by natural selection.

(2) Natural selection favours optimal traits.

(3) The optimal cognitive mechanisms are those that are good at producing true beliefs.

(4) Therefore, biological evolution favours cognitive mechanisms that are good at producing true beliefs.

So far, I have argued that there is good reason to believe (1'). Consider now (2), the claim that if some trait is the result of natural selection, there is good reason to believe it is optimal. An objection to this premiss is that even if a trait is the result of natural selection, it is not always the case that the trait was itself selected for, and, if a trait was not selected for, there is no reason to believe that it is optimal. Consider the distinction between selection *of* and selection *for*.[12] A trait can be the *result* of natural selection without the effects of that trait having caused it to be selected. If this is the case, there has been selection *of* that trait without there being selection *for* it—'selection of does not imply selection for'.[13] If, in contrast, a trait is selected because of its effects, then there is selection *for* this trait (there is, of course, selection *of* this trait as well—selection for *does* imply selection of). I call the process whereby there is selection *of* a trait without there being selection *for* it *free-riding*.[14] Examples of free-riders include a *spandrel*[15] (a trait that is just an architectural by-product of a set of traits that was selected for), a *piggyback trait* (a trait that was selected because it is associated with some other trait that was selected for, for example, a trait that is the result of pleiotropy in the standard genetic sense), and an *exaptation*[16]

[12] Sober, *The Nature of Selection*, 97–102; see esp. the helpful picture on 99. See also Williams, *Adaptation and Natural Selection*, 9, for a similar distinction between designating something as 'the means or mechanisms for a certain goal or function or purpose' compared to designating something using 'words appropriate to fortuitous relationships such as a cause and effect'.   [13] Sober, *The Nature of Selection*, 100.

[14] Sober, ibid. 24, uses the word 'pleiotropy' for the process I call free-riding. In particular, Sober uses 'pleiotropy' to refer to situations in which a *cluster* of genes has more than one effect on the phenotype. One problem with this term is that its standard genetic sense denotes situations in which a *single* gene has multiple phenotypic effects. Sober's use of 'pleiotropy' for the broader notion could be derived by combining the standard genetic account of pleiotropy with the non-standard definition of a gene used by Richard Dawkins, *The Selfish Gene* (Oxford: Oxford University Press, 1976), 30—namely, Dawkins defines a gene as a 'portion of chromosomal material which potentially lasts enough generations to serve as a unit of selection'. I adopt the term 'free-riding' to avoid confusion due to the use of 'pleiotropy'.

[15] Gould and Lewontin, 'The Spandrels of San Marcos and the Panglossian Paradigm'.

[16] Steven Jay Gould and Elizabeth Vrba, 'Exaptation—a Missing Term in the Science of Form', *Paleobiology*, 8 (1982), 4–15.

(a trait that emerges when a trait previously selected for is used to perform some new function).

One might argue that the existence of these phenomena causes problems for the claim that evolution favours truth-tropic cognitive mechanisms because it undermines the premiss that natural selection will choose optimal traits (2). If a trait is the result of one of the aforementioned evolutionary phenomenon (that is, if the trait is a free-rider), then it was *not* selected for because it is optimal. Consider the example of the chin.[17] Why do we have a chin? On the naïve adaptationist view of natural selection, *because* we have a chin, having a chin must be selectively advantageous. The chin, however, is simply the result of the selective advantage of two different jaw-related growth fields (the alveolar and mandibular growth fields). Having these jaw-related growth fields was selected *for* and having a chin of a certain type was simply an architectural side-effect of them, that is, the chin is a spandrel. The chin, while unquestionably the result of evolution, was *not* selected for by natural selection. The point about cognitive mechanisms is that even if we can be sure that our cognitive mechanisms are the result of natural selection, we cannot be sure that they were selected for as a result of these traits themselves exhibiting selective advantage; after all, they might be free-riders. Lewontin suggests that all of our cognitive mechanisms might be spandrels:

there may have been no direct selection for cognitive ability at all. Human cognition may have developed as the purely epiphenomenal consequence of the major increase in brain size, which, in turn, may have been selected for quite other reasons.[18]

Gould makes a similar claim. He says that he does not doubt that:

the brain's enlargement in human evolution had an adaptive basis mediated by selection. But I would be more than mildly surprised if many of the specific things it now can do are the product of direct selection 'for' that particular behaviour. Once you build a complex machine, it can perform so many un-anticipated tasks.[19]

Note the difference between the argument against (2) that appeals to free-riders and the argument against (1) (from Section 2 above) that

---

[17] Gould and Lewontin, 'The Spandrels of San Marcos and the Panglossian Paradigm', in Sober (ed.), *Conceptual Issues in Evolutionary Biology*, 256.

[18] Lewontin, 'The Evolution of Cognition', 244.

[19] Steven Jay Gould, 'Panselectionist Pitfalls in Parker and Gibson's Model of the Evolution of Intelligence', *Behavioral and Brain Sciences*, 2 (1979), 386.

appeals to non-selectionist evolutionary forces. The argument I considered and rejected in Section 2 is that natural selection is not the cause of our having the innate cognitive mechanisms that we have because other evolutionary forces besides natural selection might have been the cause of the evolution of cognitive mechanisms. The argument I am currently considering grants that natural selection is the cause of our having the innate cognitive mechanisms that we do but challenges the claim that this means the mechanisms are optimal. This challenge turns on the existence of processes of natural selection that cause certain traits to be selected without their having been selected for.[20]

A defender of (2), the claim that natural selection favours the most optimal traits, might deny that any trait that is supposed to be the result of selection *of* but not selection *for* is a trait at all. Support for this claim might be drawn from a critique of the way that adaptationists atomize organisms into traits.[21] In the case of the chin, the defender of (2) could deny that the chin is a separate trait at all. In general, this move would deny that anything that was not selected for is a trait. This would have the result that every trait would be selected for, thereby blocking the objection to the premiss that natural selection selects optimal traits (2) based on the claim that some selected traits might not be optimal since they were not selected for. This response fails because only through a definitional fiat—that is, by simply not counting non-optimal cognitive mechanisms as traits—does it save the claim that every trait is selected for. The important issue, however, is not what counts as a trait but whether any cognitive mechanisms are non-optimal. Changing the definition of a trait does nothing to settle this question.

Before evaluating the objection to (2) based on the distinction between selection of and selection for, I will broaden it. There are other ways besides being a free-rider that a trait could be selected without it being optimal. The trait might be a *neutral trait*[22] (that is, it might have been selected not because of any features it has but because it had no negative features), it might be the result of *meiotic drive*[23] (a phenomenon

---

[20] Stich, *The Fragmentation of Reason*, 63–90, discusses variants of both objections—to (1) and (2)—but fails to be clear about the difference between non-selectionist evolutionary forces and selectionist evolutionary forces that might cause the selection of non-optimal traits.

[21] Gould and Lewontin, 'The Spandrels of San Marcos and the Panglossian Paradigm', 256.

[22] See Mooto Kimura, 'The Neutral Theory of Evolution', *Scientific American*, 240/5 (1979), 98–126.

[23] J. Crow, 'Genes that Violate Mendel's Rules', *Scientific American*, 240/2 (1979), 134–46.

that occurs when an allele 'stacks the deck' in its own favour by making copies of itself in more than the usual 50 per cent of the cells that are involved in meiosis, the process that makes gametes, for example, in human, sperm and eggs), or it might have been selected because of *heterozygote superiority*[24] (a phenomenon whereby even if a homozygous trait is the most selectively advantageous, it might not be selected if it is a recessive allele and if its associated heterozygote trait is less adaptive than the homozygote pair of the dominant allele[25]). Unlike the non-selectionist forces discussed earlier, these evolutionary phenomena (including free-riding) have much to do with natural selection. Natural selection can explain why we have, for example, a trait that results from its having 'ridden piggyback' on some *other* trait, but this explanation does not invoke selection *for* this trait; rather, natural selection explains selection *for* some other trait that in turn explains the selection *of* the piggyback trait.

With all of these various evolutionary phenomena that undermine a simple picture of natural selection, (2), the claim that evolution selects for optimal traits, seems to be in trouble. A possible way of saving this claim—a move that parallels my answer to the above objection to (1) by modifying it to get (1′)—would be to admit that natural selection sometimes, due to the evolutionary phenomena discussed above, fails to select optimal traits, but deny that these phenomena play a role in the evolution of functionally complex structures such as human cognitive mechanisms. This would save the claim that cognitive mechanisms resulting from natural selection are optimal. Thus (2) could be replaced with:

(2′) With respect to functionally complex structures (such as human cognitive mechanisms), natural selection favours optimal traits.

But what reason is there for thinking that such evolutionary phenomena as pleiotropy, heterozygote superiority, meiotic drive, and the like (phenomena that, unlike, for example, genetic drift, are part of natural selection) do not operate in the evolution of functionally complex structures? A plausible answer parallels the one given above to the objection

---

[24] See Philip Kitcher, *Vaulting Ambition* (Cambridge, Mass.: MIT Press, 1985), 215, and A. R. Templeton, 'Adaptation and the Integration of Evolutionary Forces', in R. Milkman (ed.), *Perspectives on Evolution* (Sunderland, Mass.: Sinauer, 1982).

[25] These technical terms need explaining. If an organism has the same allele from both parents, it is said to be a *homozygote*; if an organism has a different allele from each parent, it is said to be a *heterozygote*. Some alleles are dominant and others are recessive. If an organism is a heterozygote, the dominant allele will be expressed while the recessive allele will not be. For example, if brown eyes are dominant and the person is a brown eye–blue eye heterozygote, then she will have brown eyes.

that non-selectionist evolutionary forces sometimes explain the evolution of cognitive mechanisms. In the previous section, I argued that natural selection is the only explanation for the evolution of functionally complex structures. The parallel response to the challenge that traits resulting from natural selection are not always selected for (and thus not necessarily optimal) is that the evolution of functionally complex structures can only be explained by these traits having been selected *for* because only natural selection can explain the sort of functional complexity that they exhibit.

Note that this response does not require that there has been selection *for* the properties associated with every *possible* way of describing every part of the reasoning faculty. There are an infinite number of ways to describe an organ or its parts that do not correspond to a function it performs. Dr Pangloss's example of the nose being made to hold eyeglasses is such an example, as are the examples of the redness of blood and the fact that humans typically have a prime number of digits of each limb.[26] Clearly, such 'traits' are not selected for. Most traits of this sort are non-functional, but even those that are functional cannot play a function that is complex or that is an important function for the organ. For example, one might say that the nose does, in fact, serve the function of holding eyeglasses. This function is not a complex one (the nose is not intricately designed to hold eyeglasses—in fact, the relationship goes in the opposite direction) and, further, the nose was clearly *not* selected for this function. These points are not relevant to the case of reasoning because the reasoning organ and its functional parts *are* functional. A highly specialized structure like reasoning competence must be the result of selection for its functions. The specificity with which reasoning competence matches specific cognitive tasks that are important for humans to perform makes it highly unlikely that this faculty is simply the result of something like an increase in brain size.

While this response works against seeing the evolution of human reasoning competence as a spandrel or other non-selectionist force, it does not work against a more specific account of how a cognitive mechanism could have been selected without having been selected *for*. Suppose that a cognitive mechanism is selected for because it performs a particular function in certain circumstances. The same mechanism might well perform a function that was *not* selected for in other circumstances. This function, not having been selected for, might well be non-optimal.

---

[26] Pinker and Bloom, 'Natural Language and Natural Selection', 710.

To make this concrete, imagine that the mechanism for making *plausibility* judgements (for example, whether it is more *plausible* that Linda, a former philosophy major, is now (1) a bank teller or (2) both a feminist *and* a bank teller) is selected for because of its use for making plausibility judgements. This mechanism might also be called into use in making *probability* judgements (for example, whether it is more *probable* that Linda is a bank teller or both a feminist and a bank teller). Having *not* been selected for to make probability judgements, the mechanism may not be the optimal principle for making such judgements. In fact, the mechanism for plausibility is probably *not* the optimal principle for probability judgements, because, while it might be more *plausible* that a philosophy major would be a feminist bank teller than a bank teller (whether or not she is a feminist), it cannot be more *probable* that anyone (regardless of her major) would be a feminist bank teller than that she would be a bank teller, because all feminist bank tellers are necessarily bank tellers. The general point is that a principle that was selected but not selected for can be *non*-optimal; the selection forces behind this fact undermine the simple picture of natural selection and count against (2′). While selection for is the only plausible explanation of the evolution of functionally complex structures, that such a structure has been selected for does not guarantee that every functional feature of it will have been selected for.

This discussion of the evolution of reasoning competence is usefully compared to discussions about the evolution of language. By the evolution of language, I mean the evolutionary development of the language organ, rather than the development of a particular natural language like English. Many linguists, cognitive scientists, and philosophers think that the ability to speak and understand language is biological in nature and that this biologically based capacity for language is a distinct mental organ, an underlying mechanism that embodies linguistic knowledge (see my discussion in Chapter 2, Section 1). Some of those who share this picture claim that the evolution of language is *not* the result of natural selection.[27] Steven Pinker and Paul Bloom argue that natural selection is the only explanation for the evolution of the linguistic competence.[28] For reasons quite similar to those I presented in Section 2 above, they argue that none of the other forces that drive

---

[27] Noam Chomsky, *Language and Problems of Knowledge* (Cambridge, Mass.: MIT Press, 1980); and Massimo Piattelli-Palmarini, 'Evolution, Selection and Cognition', *Cognition*, 31 (1989), 1–44.

[28] Pinker and Bloom, 'Natural Language and Natural Selection'.

evolution can explain the intricate structure of the innate mental organ responsible for our ability to speak and understand natural languages. It is interesting to note a difference between Pinker and Bloom's argument concerning the evolution of the language faculty and my argument about the evolution of reasoning competence. While Pinker and Bloom argue that the language organ was selected for, they are not troubled by the fact that various functional features of the language organ—not ones that perform central functions of that organ, but ones that perform the linguistic equivalent of holding eyeglasses—were *not* selected for.[29] When, however, the argument is made in the context of the evolution of the reasoning faculty, such an admission becomes problematic. Admitting that a feature of reasoning competence (for example, a mechanism behind a particular principle of reasoning) was selected but *not* selected *for* opens up the possibility that this feature is not optimal and thus could be the source of irrationality.

Natural selection is the only explanation for the evolution of functionally complex structures like the mechanism that underlies our reasoning competence. Further, selection *for* such complex structures is the only plausible story behind this natural selection process—the suggestion that our cognitive mechanisms might result from selection for an increase in brain size is incredibly implausible. That selection for is the only plausible story behind complex structures does not, however, mean that *every feature* of our cognitive mechanisms was selected for; such features may well result from selection for other features of the reasoning faculty, and, as such, these features may fail to be optimal.

4. Natural Selection and Optimality

Nothing I said in the previous section proves that in fact those cognitive mechanisms produced by natural selection are not optimal. Suppose that, for the sake of argument, all of our cognitive mechanisms have been selected for and that all of the traits of such mechanisms were selected for because of the functions they perform. Even granting this, there remains the further question of whether this entails that human cognitive mechanisms are optimal, more particularly, whether they will be optimal in the sense that they will produce true beliefs (3). I will

---

[29] Pinker and Bloom, 715–20.

discuss this question in terms of the metaphor of a filter.[30] The question is whether natural selection provides a filter of the appropriate grain size to select principles that produce true beliefs. (Here and in the rest of this chapter unless otherwise noted, by 'natural selection' I mean natural selection when it is selecting *for* traits; this is a legitimate shorthand to adopt for this section because I am assuming, for the sake of argument, that natural selection has selected for every functional feature of our cognitive mechanisms.) The question can be seen as a challenge to either (2) or (3): if directed at (2), the challenge is that natural selection, even setting aside the objections of the previous section, will not be able to select the optimal principles; if directed at (3), the challenge is that truth-tropic principles are not optimal. For simplicity, I will not distinguish between these different ways of describing the challenge; rather, I will characterize it as directed at the conjunction of (2) and (3), namely, the claim that natural selection favours principles that yield true beliefs. I will consider the objection that natural selection provides a filter of inappropriate size and shape to select for truth-tropic principles of reasoning. It says, on the one hand, that the filter of natural selection is too coarse-grained in that it selects some principles that mostly produce false beliefs and, on the other, that it is too fine-grained in that it selects some principles that produce very few true beliefs.[31]

Even at its best, biological natural selection, for all its power, is not omnipotent; rather it is pragmatic, that is, result-oriented. To simplify the picture, when faced with two mutually exclusive alternatives in a particular environment, natural selection will choose the alternative that will do better in that environment. Being better may amount to being faster or more precise, or some combination thereof, depending on the situation. How do these facts carry over to the case of cognitive mechanisms? If natural selection favours those mechanisms that produce true beliefs, then a mechanism that produces true beliefs (call it M_T) ought to be selected for over a mechanism that does not (call it M_F). But since natural selection selects on the basis of effects, if M_T and M_F have the *same* effects, natural selection will not be able to choose between them, that is, either *neither* will be selected for—in which case natural

<hr/>

[30] For more on the filter as a metaphor, see Peter Lipton and Nicholas Thompson, 'Comparative Psychology and the Recursive Structure of Filter Explanations', *International Journal of Comparative Psychology*, 1 (1988), 215–44.

[31] These objections can be seen roughly as abstracted versions of the three specific problems discussed in Sober, 'The Evolution of Rationality', 98, concerning the question why natural selection involves a filter that is too coarse-grained (my term, not Sober's) to select for the scientific method. See also Stich, *The Fragmentation of Reason*, 60–3.

selection will prove too fine-grained to produce truth-tropic mechanisms
—or *both* will be selected for—in which case natural selection will not
be fine-grained enough, or natural selection will choose between them
at random. Biological evolution cannot simply select for those mechanisms that are truth-tropic because whether a mechanism is truth-
tropic is underdetermined by its effects in a particular environment. It
is even underdetermined by its effects in general. It follows from the
fact that natural selection is unable to distinguish between two mechanisms with the same effects in *any* given environment that natural
selection is unable to distinguish between two mechanisms with the
same effects in *every* possible environment.[32]

As an illustration of the problem that the pragmatic nature of natural
selection causes for the conjunction of (2) and (3)—namely, the claim
that natural selection favours principles which yield true beliefs—
consider the following principles of reasoning:

> INDUCTION: If p per cent of the observed As have been B, infer
> that p per cent of the remaining As are Bs.

> COUNTER-INDUCTION: If p per cent of the observed As have been
> B, infer that $1-p$ per cent of the remaining As are Bs.

> MIXED STRATEGY: Use induction if you are making an inference
> before the year 2000; use counter-induction if you are making an
> inference after the year 2000.[33]

> ADDING STRATEGY: If p per cent of the observed As have been B,
> add up the first 10^{10} integers. From this total subtract the first 10^{10}
> integers. Take the resulting number and add it to p and infer that
> this number represents the percentage of the remaining As which
> are B.[34]

Before the year 2000, natural selection cannot, on the basis of the
beliefs these principles would yield, differentiate between induction
and the mixed strategy. Suppose that, in fact, induction is more truth-
tropic than the mixed strategy. Natural selection is unable to choose
between these principles on the basis of the extent to which they are
truth-tropic because they have the same effects before the year 2000.

---

[32] Sober, 'The Evolution of Rationality', 102.

[33] The mixed strategy is based on Nelson Goodman's well-known 'grue' paradox; see
Goodman, *Fact, Fiction and Forecast*, 4th edn. (Cambridge, Mass.: Harvard University
Press, 1983), 59–83.

[34] These four strategies are adapted from Sober, 'The Evolution of Rationality',
101–2.

The worry is that the filter of natural selection is too coarse-grained to allow just truth-tropic principles to pass through; other principles that have desirable effects will be in the precipitate as well.

4.1. Natural Selection Considers Internal Effects

A potential answer to this worry would be to say that natural selection is more fine-grained than critics of the conjunction of (2) and (3) would have us imagine. Natural selection not only looks at the output of various strategies, it also looks at the way these strategies get to the output. Natural selection selects for more than just *external effects* (that is, what the trait does with respect to the environment); it also selects for *internal effects* (that is, how the trait operates from the *processing* point of view).[35] Natural selection can be thought of as drawing on considerations similar to those that humans use, say, when buying a computer: besides comparing what functions one computer can perform compared to another, we also consider the computers' size, speed, cost, as well as other features. These features are analogous to the internal effects of a trait that natural selection considers. While induction and the mixed strategy have the same *external* effects, they have different *internal* effects—the mixed strategy requires the use of a calendar of some sort to tell whether the year 2000 has been reached, while induction does not. Induction also has the same external effects as the adding strategy (both before and after the year 2000), but their internal effects are quite different; the adding strategy requires a large amount of processing-time and a sophisticated adding machine while induction requires neither. Given the relative internal effects, induction is preferable to the adding strategy and the mixed strategy since it is more efficient and better focused on the task it is supposed to accomplish.

How is including consideration of internal effects supposed to save the claim that natural selection favours truth-tropic mechanisms from the objection that the filter of natural selection is too coarse-grained to select for truth-tropic mechanisms? Natural selection is fine-grained enough to look at internal effects such as speed, memory used, efficiency, and the like; in general, internal economy is a virtue, a virtue that natural selection will recognize. Internal economy is not, however,

---

[35] The distinction between internal and external factors comes from Sober, 'The Evolution of Rationality'. The idea of focusing on the processing point of view when looking at natural selection comes from Williams, *Adaptation and Natural Selection*, *passim*, esp. 33.

preferable if it involves the sacrifice of a great deal of external performance. In this sense, natural selection is also like a person on the market
for a computer: all else being equal, a person would choose the smaller,
cheaper, faster computer, but would not opt for such internal economy
if doing so required that the computer would be unable to function as
a word processor.

4.2. The Garcia Effect

Natural selection is fine-grained enough that internal factors can play a
role in selection. This does not, however, show that natural selection is
fine-grained enough to select for truth-tropic cognitive mechanisms. In
fact, internal effects are often in tension with truth-tropicity; natural
selection will often prefer the quick-and-dirty approach to solving a
problem posed by the environment rather than the truth-tropic one.
While internal effects are no doubt involved in natural selection, it is
wrong to think that consideration of these effects guarantees—or even
makes it more likely—that truth-tropic cognitive mechanisms will be
selected for while non-truth-tropic ones will not be.

I will now consider a ubiquitous example that is supposed to show
that natural selection might select a non-truth-tropic mechanism over a
truth-tropic one.[36] In an experiment performed by John Garcia and his
colleagues, rats were shown to develop a strong aversion to food of a
distinct flavour that they had been fed before being subject to sickness-
causing doses of radiation (I call this the *Garcia effect*).[37] Independently,
Martin Seligman discovered (the hard way) a similar effect in humans,
which he called the *sauce béarnaise effect*.[38] Six hours after eating filet
mignon with *sauce béarnaise*, Seligman got sick because of a stomach
virus; subsequently, he was unable to eat the sauce (although he had no
problem eating filet mignon, eating in the same environment, eating off
the same plates, and so forth). One natural way to describe this phenomenon is to say that humans and rats seem to be following a principle such as:

---

[36] The example is discussed for similar purposes in Stich, *The Fragmentation of
Reason*, 61–3, among other places.

[37] John Garcia *et al.*, 'Biological Constraints on Conditioning', in Abraham Black and
William Prokasy (eds.), *Classical Conditioning*, ii (New York: Appleton-Century Crofts,
1972).

[38] Martin Seligman and Joane Hager, *The Biological Boundaries of Learning* (New
York: Appleton-Century Crofts, 1972), 8.

CAUTIOUS PRINCIPLE: If I eat food with a distinct taste and subsequently get sick, infer that food which tastes like this will make me sick.

Although the *sauce béarnaise* did not in fact *cause* Seligman to get sick, the cautious principle would explain why he subsequently became unable to eat *sauce béarnaise*—he inferred, from the conjunction of the sauce and his sickness, that the sauce caused the sickness. This is a bit of a simplification. The Garcia effect and the *sauce béarnaise* effect seem to be non-cognitive principles roughly akin to reflexes. We have no reason to think that Seligman *inferred* that the *sauce béarnaise* caused his sickness in the same way that I often infer q from p and **if** p, **then** q; in fact, we have no reason to believe that any conscious inferences were involved in the development of Seligman's aversion to the sauce. For my purposes, however, I want to discuss a (perhaps imaginary) effect like the Garcia effect and the *sauce béarnaise* effect except that the imaginary effect is a conscious cognitive one. All of these effects— the Garcia effect, the *sauce béarnaise* effect, and the imaginary effect —can be characterized as fostering *over-detection*; principles of this form are more likely to misidentify non-poisonous foods as poisonous (make 'false positives') than to fail to identify as poisonous foods that actually are (make 'false negatives').[39] Henceforth, I will call the resulting behaviour of the imagined cognitive principle the 'Garcia effect' since it has the same general form as the Garcia effect in rats. The important point is that natural selection might select a cognitive mechanism that gives rise to the Garcia effect and, as I will discuss below, contrary to the conjunction of (2) and (3), such a mechanism would not be truth-tropic.

Returning to the (possibly imaginary) cognitive version of the Garcia effect, let us suppose (as seems true) that greater than 50 per cent of the

---

[39] For other discussions of principles of this form, see Jerry Fodor, 'Psychosemantics', in William Lycan (ed.), *Mind and Cognition* (Oxford: Blackwell, 1990), 330–2. For a critique of 'Psychosemantics', see Ned Block, 'Advertisement for a Semantics for Psychology', in P. A. French *et al.* (eds.), *Midwest Studies in Philosophy*, x (Minneapolis: University of Minnesota Press, 1986), 673–4 n. 65. In 'Psychosemantics', Fodor is concerned with giving an evolutionary account of *meaning*—an account he subsequently rejects in, for example, Fodor, 'A Theory of Content', in *A Theory of Content and Other Essays* (Cambridge, Mass.: MIT Press, 1990)—rather than an evolutionary argument for rationality, but some of the points he makes are relevant here. For a more sophisticated version of an evolutionary account of meaning, see Millikan, *Language, Thought and Other Biological Categories*, Papineau, *Reality and Representation*, and Dennett, *The Intentional Stance*. There is not necessarily a connection between the truth of an evolutionary theory of meaning and the success of the evolutionary argument for the rationality thesis.

sicknesses that affect humans have nothing to do with food, distinctly˘ flavoured or otherwise, and that the Garcia effect is to be explained by the cautious principle. If this is true, then a mechanism that instantiates the cautious principle will tend to produce more false beliefs than true beliefs. (This was the case with Seligman: the sauce did not cause him to be sick—it was the virus—but he was cautious and 'blamed' the sauce.) The cautious principle is thus not truth-tropic. The crucial point is that despite all this, the cautious principle could still be a perfectly good principle for natural selection to choose; it might be more adaptive (that is, it might do a better job of fostering reproductive success) in some environments for an organism to be cautious when it comes to the threat of food poisoning. Natural selection will thus sometimes fail to produce truth-tropic cognitive mechanisms; the conjunction of (2) and (3) is thus false.

4.3. Interpreting the Garcia Effect

There is a general problem with interpreting cognitive mechanisms that arises here: it is difficult to characterize a cognitive mechanism on the basis of the behaviours it causes because behaviour underdetermines the underlying mechanism.[40] If Seligman avoids eating *sauce béarnaise* because of some cognitive process, he might be following the cautious principle. He might, however, be following one or the other of the following principles:

> PROBABILISTIC PRINCIPLE: If I eat food that has a distinctive taste and subsequently get sick, I should believe that food with this taste is more likely to make me sick than most food I encounter.

> TWO-CONDITIONAL PRINCIPLE: If I eat food that has a distinctive taste and subsequently get sick, I should believe that food with this taste will make me sick; if I do not get sick, I should believe that food with this taste will *not* make me sick.[41]

---

[40] Dennett, *The Intentional Stance*, 103–16, raises another worry that would cause trouble for interpreting the Garcia effect. Dennett holds the view that we cannot say what the nature of a mental state or a mental mechanism is. If he is right, there is no determinate answer to whether the Garcia effect is caused by the cautious principle being instantiated in humans even if the relevant neurophysiological mechanism were isolated. Answering such a radical position about mental states is beyond the scope of this project and is not ultimately relevant to the matter at hand.

[41] The probabilistic principle is modification of what Richard Feldman, 'Rationality, Reliability and Natural Selection', *Philosophy of Science*, 55 (1988), 221, calls strategy A. He says that I should believe that this taste *might* make me sick, but this seems

Both of these principles would explain Seligman's behaviour as effectively as the cautious principle.

The problem of how to interpret the principle behind the Garcia effect interacts with whether the Garcia effect is properly explained by the cautious principle and is, hence, an example of a non-truth-tropic mechanism that has been selected by natural selection. A friend of the conjunction of (2) and (3) could defend it against this problem by criticizing the cautious principle analysis of the Garcia effect. This could be done by noting that the probabilistic and the two-conditional principles *are* truth-tropic and would explain the Garcia effect as well as the cautious principle.[42]

The cautious principle is not truth-tropic because it produces false beliefs in most of the cases in which it is used to generate beliefs. It is invoked only when I have eaten food with a distinct flavour and I subsequently get sick. It will lead to false beliefs in those cases where I get sick but not because of distinctly flavoured food I have eaten. The probabilistic principle will be used in the same instances as the cautious one (that is, when distinctly flavoured food is followed by sickness), but the probabilistic one will almost always yield true beliefs (it will yield true beliefs even in cases where the cautious principle leads to false ones). This is because distinctly flavoured food consumed before getting sick is more likely to be a source of sickness than food whose consumption does not precede sickness. The two-conditional principle will be used far more frequently than the cautious one (it will be used whenever any distinctive-tasting food is eaten, not just when such food causes sickness), but it will generate true beliefs most of the time because it will usually yield the inference that food with a distinctive taste that does not cause sickness after one consumption does not cause sickness in general.

The argument against the conjunction of (2) and (3) is that sometimes natural selection overlooks truth-tropic mechanisms in favour of non-truth-tropic ones. It proceeds by example: the cautious principle is not truth-tropic yet mechanisms that instantiate it get selected. The response under consideration is that there is no reason to think that we have cognitive mechanisms that instantiate the cautious principle;

---

trivially true since any food *might* make me sick. Fodor's version of this strategy applied to another context is: 'that just might be a predator and I'm taking no chances' ('Psychosemantics', 330). The two-conditional principle is a paraphrase of what Feldman, 'Rationality, Reliability and Natural Selection', 222, calls strategy B.

[42] Feldman, 'Rationality, Reliability and Natural Selection'.

the same evidence that points to the cautious principle also points to the probabilistic and the two-conditional principle. The latter two are truth-tropic, so there is no reason to think humans have a non-truth-tropic cognitive mechanism. The opponent of the conjunction of (2) and (3) thus has failed to produce an adequate counter-example to the claim that natural selection produces truth-tropic mechanisms.

A critic of (2) and (3) might, however, reply that this response misses the general point. The particulars of the example of the Garcia effect are not important. Even if it turns out that the two-conditional principle is what causes the Garcia effect, natural selection *could* have chosen a mechanism that instantiates the cautious principle over some more truth-topic principle *if* the cautious principle was selectively advantageous, that is, if it led to greater reproductive success. In fact, natural selection could opt for cognitive mechanisms that generally produce false beliefs so long as they produce true beliefs in the most important situations. The point is that natural selection selects for mechanisms that are adaptive and it is certainly possible for mechanisms that are not truth-tropic to be the most adaptive; whether or not the cautious principle is actually what is behind the Garcia effect, it remains possible that a non-truth-tropic principle might be preferred over a truth-tropic one.

What might a defender of the argument for (4), the claim that biological evolution favours truth-tropic principles, say in response to this objection? I see three possible responses. The first is to try to generalize from the above response to the cautious principle case. The general response would be that, when presented with a set of behaviours that is supposed to be caused by a mechanism that is claimed to be adaptive but not truth-tropic, try to argue that the proposed mechanism is not in fact the mechanism that causes the behaviour. Argue instead that the mechanism that is really behind the behaviour is truth-tropic. Call this the *different mechanism strategy*. The two-conditional and the probabilistic principles are examples of this strategy: some behaviour (for example, Seligman's avoidance of and expressed distaste for *sauce béarnaise*) is explained by a mechanism that instantiates the cautious principle, which is not truth-tropic; the two-conditional and the probabilistic principles are offered as alternative principles that might be instantiated by the mechanism that explains the relevant behaviour.

The second response is to accept the proposed mechanism but argue that it can be construed as truth-tropic. An example of this would be that even if the mechanism behind the Garcia effect exhibits the behaviour that it would if it instantiated the cautious principle, the mechanism can be construed as a taste-that-once-preceded-sickness detector rather than a poison detector. Call this the *reconstrual strategy*. The third response to the criticism of the defence of the conjunction of (2) and (3) is to weaken (3) so that it does not claim that all optimal mechanisms produce true beliefs. I will consider each of these responses in turn.

Consider first the different mechanism strategy. Suppose, as an objection to the conjunction of (2) and (3), someone proposes a mechanism that is behind a set of behaviours and claims that it is an optimal, non-truth-tropic mechanism. A friend of (2) and (3) could use the different mechanism strategy to come up with a description of an alternative mechanism that is consistent with the behaviour of the proposed mechanism but that *is* truth-tropic. Without loss of generality, cognitive mechanisms can be characterized by principles of the form:

If p occurs/is believed/etc., then do/believe/infer/etc. q.

Alternative mechanisms can be characterized, for example, by weakening the consequent of the conditional (as in the probabilistic principle) or by coupling the conditional with another principle (as in the two-conditional principle). There are other possible ways of proposing alternative truth-tropic mechanisms when presented with non-truth-tropic ones. There is, however, a problem with this strategy. This sort of reinterpretation may not always be motivated—why should we think that truth-tropic mechanisms are more likely to be selected than those that are not truth-tropic? What possible reason do we have for believing that humans (or rats) use the probabilistic or two-conditional principle rather than the cautious one? Besides the principle of charity—which I argued in Chapter 4 is unable to serve this purpose—the only general motivation I can see for believing that truth-tropic mechanisms are more likely to be possessed is if one *already* believes that truth-tropic mechanisms are more likely to be selected by biological evolution. But this is precisely what is at issue here.[43] Further, whatever interpretation is offered, it remains a possibility that a non-truth-tropic mechanism will be more selectively advantageous than another that is truth-tropic.

To review, I am considering the claim that natural selection favours truth-tropic mechanisms. I am examining the Garcia effect as a possible counter-example to this claim as well as the attempt to defuse the

---

[43] This is similar to an objection raised in Block, 'Advertisement for a Semantics for Psychology', 673–4, against Fodor, 'Psychosemantics'.

example by denying that the Garcia effect constitutes a counter-example at all. Maybe the defusing attempt works in the particular example, but the general difficulty remains: sometimes the most adaptive mechanisms might not be truth-tropic. The first answer to the general difficulty I considered was that it is always possible and plausible to come up with mechanisms that are truth-tropic to explain the behaviours that are supposed to be produced by non-truth-tropic mechanisms. But, there are two problems with this answer. First, it just begs the question because there is no reason for believing such a reinterpretation is justified in general unless you already believe that natural selection favours truth-tropic mechanisms. Second, all that matters for the objection to go through is the *possibility* that a less truth-tropic mechanism will be selected over a more truth-tropic one; the different mechanism strategy has nothing to say to this problem.

The reconstrual strategy, the second response to this general difficulty, has the virtue of addressing the second problem with the different mechanism strategy. Recall that the second problem is that whatever the cognitive mechanism is, it can be interpreted as truth-tropic. The mechanism behind the Garcia effect is truth-tropic if it is characterized as a taste-that-once-preceded-sickness detector (rather than a poison detector). This reply, in effect, challenges the claim that it is possible for a non-truth-tropic mechanism to be selected over a truth-tropic one by claiming that seemingly non-truth-tropic mechanisms can always be construed as truth-tropic.

Suppose that the mechanism behind the Garcia effect is in fact truth-tropic (namely, that it is a taste-that-once-preceded-sickness detector). This does not mean that, in general, natural selection selects for truth-tropic mechanisms. Neither does the fact (if it is a fact) that any mechanism can be interpreted as truth-tropic show that natural selection selects for truth-tropic mechanisms. What needs to be defended is the claim that the mechanisms resulting from natural selection *must* be interpreted as truth-tropic. Only by establishing this stronger claim can the conjunction of (2′) and (3) be supported. I know of no successful way of defending this stronger claim. The reconstrual strategy thus fails.

The third attempt to support the argument for (4), the claim that biological evolution favours truth-tropic mechanisms, retreats from the claim that natural selection selects for truth-tropic mechanisms. The defender of (4) might admit that sometimes natural selection selects non-truth-tropic mechanisms and sometimes it fails to select truth-tropic mechanisms but deny that this happens very often. This could be done by modifying (3), the claim that optimal cognitive mechanisms are truth-tropic, as follows:

(3′) A very high percentage of optimal cognitive mechanisms are truth-tropic.

This premiss, together with the claim that natural selection favours the most optimal cognitive mechanisms (2′), entails the conclusion that a high percentage of the mechanisms produced by natural selection will be truth-tropic. If this conclusion is right, then the argument for (4) might be salvageable.

This change to the argument for (4), the claim that evolution favours truth-tropic mechanisms, specifically addresses the objection discussed above, where I made the claim that the defender of the conjunction of (2′) and (3) needs to show that the mechanisms resulting from natural selection *must* be interpreted as truth-tropic. Replacing (3) with (3′) makes it possible to avoid this task—to support (3′), one need not establish that all mechanisms possibly produced by natural selection are truth-tropic, only that most of them are. If the previous objection to the conjunction of (2) and (3)—that there is no strong reason to believe that any particular mechanism is truth-tropic—goes through, then, short of some particular reason to the contrary, the same is true for the high percentage of the mechanisms that (3′) claims are truth-tropic. Whether there is such a reason to the contrary is a question I will not explore since the argument for (4), even so modified, faces another serious objection. I turn to this objection in the next section.

5. The Availability of Optimal Traits

Natural selection, even when it selects *for* a specific trait, can only choose among available alternatives; the best alternatives are, however, not always among the available ones.[44] If this is true, then the conjunction of (2) and (3) is false. A trait is available to an organism if it is physically possible for an organism of that species to possess it. Consider two examples. Having a nervous system that uses fibre optics would be faster and more efficient than the nervous system of any known organism,

---

[44] Stich, *The Fragmentation of Reason*, 64–6; Sober, 'The Evolution of Rationality'; and Feldman, 'Rationality, Reliability and Natural Selection'.

yet no organism has evolved such a super-fast nervous system.[45] Similarly, having the ability to become completely invisible at will would be a very useful trait for organisms to have, but no organisms have ever evolved this trait (though many organisms have the ability to blend into their surroundings and thus to be *less* visible to their predators).[46] Why have these better (perhaps the best) alternatives not evolved? The answer is that no mutations have ever caused an organism to synthesize fibre optics; therefore, fibre optics have never been able to compete against axons and dendrites as a form of neuronal communication. The raw material that natural selection has to work with is limited by the genes organisms have. There is no mutation path[47] (that is, no series of mutations) that has a non-infinitesimally small chance of being followed that goes from any organism that exists or has existed to an organism that uses fibre optics for neuronal communication or that has the ability to turn completely invisible. Further, given the available pre-existing traits, it is not surprising that neither a nervous system made of fibre optics nor the ability to turn invisible ever evolved. These examples show how natural selection is only able to choose between available alternatives and how the best traits may be biologically unavailable. A trait cannot be selected unless it is available and it will not be available unless there are *mutationally accessible* genes that code for the trait.

How then is the fact that natural selection only chooses between available mechanisms relevant to the argument that biological evolution selects for truth-tropic mechanisms? This fact, presented in the form of what I call the *availability objection*, is supposed to count against the claim that a high percentage of the mechanisms produced by natural selection will be truth-tropic (the conjunction of (2') and (3')). If truth-tropic mechanisms are not, in general, available, then natural selection will not be able to produce a significant percentage of them.

Why should we think that truth-tropic mechanisms will be unavailable? For example, why should we think that a truth-tropic mechanism is genetically inaccessible in the way that a mechanism for turning invisible is? Even if we assume that we do not have the conjunction principle in our reasoning competence, it is difficult to show that the mechanisms that embody this principle are inaccessible or even likely to be. In fact, there seems to be no guarantee that in general the most optimal traits

---

[45] The example is similar to one used in Stich, *The Fragmentation of Reason*, 65.

[46] I owe this example to Paul Bloom.

[47] See Dawkins, *The Blind Watchmaker*, ch. 4, for a discussion of this idea.

will be unavailable to natural selection. In the case of our reasoning competence, it seems that our descendants may be capable of evolving a reasoning competence that is equivalent to virtually any Turing machine, from the most to the least optimal. I am not sure where the burden of proof should lie here: should friends of the argument for (4) have to show that mechanisms that embody truth-tropic principles will be available or should friends of the availability objection have to show that they will not be? The availability objection does raise a serious worry against the evolutionary argument, but I am not sure if the worry sticks.

Another approach open to a defender of the claim that biological evolution produces truth-tropic mechanisms is to try to modify (4) and the argument for it in order to take the availability objection into account. At this point, the argument for (4) is as follows:

(1′) The biological evolution *of functionally complex structures* (including the mechanism underlying our reasoning competence) is caused by natural selection.
(2′) With respect to functionally complex structures (such as human cognitive mechanisms), natural selection favours optimal traits.
(3′) A very high percentage of optimal cognitive mechanisms are truth-tropic.
(4) Therefore, biological evolution favours cognitive mechanisms that are good at producing true beliefs.

In order to save this argument in the face of the availability objection, (2′) might be modified in the following fashion:

(2″) With respect to functionally complex structures (such as human cognitive mechanisms), natural selection favours the most optimal *of the available* cognitive mechanisms.

But now (3′) needs to be modified as well:

(3″) A very high percentage of the most optimal *of the available* cognitive mechanisms are truth-tropic.

The argument for (4) from (1′), (2″), and (3″) seems valid, but it is not sound. Compare (3′) to (3″). The claim that optimal mechanisms will be truth-tropic is more plausible than that the most optimal *of the available* mechanisms will be truth-tropic. The latter claim is contingent on there being truth-tropic mechanisms in the set of available ones. As I have pointed out above, it is not clear if this will be the case. A more plausible premiss is:

(3‴) A very high percentage of the most optimal of the available cognitive mechanisms will be more truth-tropic than the other available mechanisms.

Together with (1′) and (2″), this premiss produces the following conclusion:

(4′) Biological evolution favours *the most truth-tropic of the available mechanisms.*

This argument is (by design) immune from the availability objection. The question is whether this conclusion is an adequate replacement for (4), the claim that biological evolution favours truth-tropic mechanisms.

Recall that (4) is the first part of the two-step evolutionary argument for (6), the claim that biological evolution produces rational cognitive mechanisms. For this argument to be valid with (4′) taking the place of (4), (5) will have to be modified as follows:

(5′) The most truth-tropic of the available mechanisms is a rational mechanism.

Together (4′) and (5′) entail (6), the claim that natural selection favours rational cognitive mechanisms. But are these premisses true?

To begin, what is it for a mechanism to be the *most* truth-tropic of those that are available? A tempting account is that a mechanism is the *most* truth-tropic of those available if it generates more true beliefs than any other available mechanisms. This, however, cannot be right because, on this account, a mechanism characterized by the following principle would be the most truth-tropic (or at least *as* truth-tropic as any other) of *any* set of available mechanisms in which it was included:

ALL-INCLUSIVE PRINCIPLE: If A is a possible belief, believe A.

No other mechanism could be more truth-tropic (on the account under consideration) than one that instantiates the all-inclusive principle since no mechanism could possibly generate more true beliefs. But the all-inclusive principle is clearly not a rational strategy since this strategy will sometimes sanction believing in p and **not-p** at the same time. If the all-inclusive strategy is what is meant by being the most truth-tropic, then (5′) is false, since (5′) says that the most truth-tropic of the available mechanisms is rational. But if (5′) is false, then the argument for (6) is not sound. The all-inclusive principle must not be what is meant by being the most truth-tropic.

A better account of what the most truth-tropic mechanism is would be one that says the most truth-tropic mechanism is the one that can generate the best combination of the most true beliefs and the least false beliefs. But is there a general account of what such a best combination would consist in? Supposing such an account could be developed, would (5'), the claim that the most truth-tropic of the available mechanisms is rational, be at all plausible? The Garcia effect is an example of why such a claim is unlikely to be true. Recall that it seemed pragmatic to follow the cautious principle (if I eat food with a distinct taste and subsequently get sick, infer that food which tastes like this will make me sick) given that the result of a false negative (death by poisoning) is severe and the result of a false positive (aversion to a particular taste) is not, particularly given an environment where there is a great variety of food flavours available. The general point is that whether or not a principle is rational seems to be connected with something more than whether it generates true beliefs. Even if an account could be developed of what would be the best combination of accepting true beliefs and rejecting false ones, (5'), the claim that the most truth-tropic of the available mechanisms is a rational one, seems untenable because it deems rational the best of what might be a paltry set of mechanisms (that is, those that are available). Thus, the attempt to save (4), the claim that biological evolution favours truth-tropic mechanisms, by modifying it to be immune to the availability objection fails because the modified premiss (4') is not strong enough to support (6), the conclusion that biological evolution produces rational mechanisms.

6. Rationality and Reproductive Success

I began this chapter by spelling out a two-part evolutionary argument for human rationality. Up to this point, I have focused on the first part, the attempt to establish a connection between biological evolution and truth. The evolution of cognitive mechanisms is, I have argued, driven by biological natural selection, but, for at least three reasons, natural selection will not necessarily produce truth-tropic mechanisms: biological natural selection does not guarantee that traits have been selected *for*; it can opt for some mechanisms that are *not* truth-tropic and can *fail* to opt for some that are; and it can only choose from those mechanisms that are available (though, as I have pointed out above, this might not

be a problem). These reasons suffice to break the connection between
evolution and truth that the evolutionary argument tries to establish.
There are two further modifications to this argument that I will turn to
respectively in this and the subsequent section. The first attempts to
make the connection between evolution and rationality through reproductive success rather than truth; the second attempts to get to rationality through truth but to make the link with conceptual rather than
biological evolution.

The evolutionary argument failed because natural selection cannot
guarantee that the cognitive mechanisms it selects are truth-tropic. There
might, however, be another way to deduce the rationality of cognitive
mechanisms from the fact that they are the result of evolution, that is,
there might be some way to make an evolutionary argument that does
not involve truth. A plausible candidate is to make the link between
evolution and rationality through reproductive success—although natural
selection might not be a reliable producer of mechanisms that detect
truth, it surely is a reliable producer of mechanisms that increase reproductive success. It seems, then, reasonable that biological evolution
will produce cognitive mechanisms that tend to increase reproductive
fitness. Further, it seems rational to follow principles that increase
reproductive fitness. From these two observations, it follows that
evolution will tend to produce rational cognitive mechanisms.

This argument seems a straightforward one when the effects of
evolution on other realms are considered. Consider, for example, the
visual system. Evolution favours visual mechanisms that lead to reproductive success. The only way to explain complex mechanisms like the
human eye is to appeal to forces of natural selection that lead to increased
reproductive success for the species.[48] Further, it seems rational for an
organism to behave in accordance with the mechanisms that increase
reproductive success; it is clearly better and more rational to see with
the visual system that natural selection picked for us than to try to see
with some biological visual system that natural selection selected against.
We seem therefore to have good reason to think that evolution will
select the best visual system. The same seems true with respect to
cognitive mechanisms.

This argument can be formalized as follows:

(RS4) Biological evolution favours mechanisms that lead to the great-
       est reproductive success.

[48] See Dawkins, *The Blind Watchmaker*, and Williams, *Adaptation and Natural Selection*.

(RS5) A rational mechanism is one that leads to the greatest reproductive success.

(RS6) Therefore, biological evolution favours rational mechanisms.

(RS7) Human cognitive mechanisms are the result of biological evolution.

(RS8) Therefore, there is a strong reason to believe that humans are rational—in particular, there is a strong reason not to interpret the reasoning experiments as demonstrating human irrationality.

This argument shares the general (and the initially appealing) structure of the original evolutionary argument: it concludes that we have good reason to think humans are rational on the basis of the fact that the cognitive mechanisms we use for reasoning are the result of biological evolution. At the same time, this modified argument avoids some of the problems of the original evolutionary argument, namely, it does not invoke truth or truth-tropicity—and thus it is not open to objections that the filter of evolution is too wide to precipitate truth-tropic mechanisms.

What, in particular, do we make of (RS4) and (RS5)? Given my arguments that many or most of our principles of reasoning are innate and constitute a complex mental organ, we have reason to believe that these principles are the result of natural selection. Because natural selection selects the trait that produces greater reproductive fitness, (RS4) seems strong. There is, however, as before, the problem of whether the best trait (in terms of reproductive fitness) is *available*. It may be that the cognitive mechanism that would lead to the greatest reproductive advantage compared to its competitors has yet to evolve and, as a result, is not available for natural selection to choose. The idea is to modify (RS4) as follows:

(RS4′) Biological evolution favours mechanisms *from among those that are available* that lead to the greatest reproductive success.

As before with the modification to produce (2″), there is a problem here. Although this premiss, by design, is immune to the availability objection, for the argument to go through with this modified premiss, (RS5) needs to be modified as follows:

(RS5′) A rational mechanism is one that leads to the greatest reproductive success *among those principles that are available*.

The problem with this premiss is that rationality (according to the standard picture of rationality) is not relative to biological factors such as what mechanisms are available to a particular species.

Supposing, however, that the availability objection can be answered, perhaps because there are good reasons to believe that the best cognitive mechanisms in terms of reproductive success are in fact available. Even so, the claim that a rational mechanism is one that leads to the greatest reproductive success, (RS5) or (RS5'), is not as plausible as it may seem. Recall the sense of 'rational' that is of interest to most friends and foes of the rationality thesis (what I call the standard picture of rationality): humans are rational if they reason in accordance with the normative principles of reasoning. The sense of 'rational' involved in (RS5) is not normative in the same way because we can imagine the mechanism that leads to the greatest reproductive success diverging from the normative principles of reasoning. It might be that making *plausibility* judgements in situations where *probability* judgements are called for leads to the greatest reproductive success (perhaps because plausibility judgements can be made more quickly), but, even so, it is not *rational* to make plausibility judgements when probability judgements are called for (see my discussion of plausibility versus probability in Section 3 above). So (RS5) and (RS5') are false—a mechanism that leads to the greatest reproductive success may well not be rational.

This argument against (RS5) or (RS5') is even stronger if reproductive success is understood in more precise terms. Strictly speaking, natural selection is driven by reproductive success from the point of view of genes. Organisms, to borrow a provocative phrase from Richard Dawkins, are merely survival machines for genes.[49] But if reproductive success is measured from the point of view of genes, it is even less likely that a mechanism that leads to the greatest reproductive success will be rational—in the sense favoured by the standard picture—for *supra*-genetic entities like humans. The attempt to save the evolutionary argument by linking evolution to rationality using reproductive success thus fails.

A friend of the rationality thesis might reply to my objections to the reproductive success version of the evolutionary argument by *defining* rationality in terms of reproductive success. On this account, a cognitive mechanism is rational if it increases reproductive success. This account of rationality is an alternative to the standard picture of rationality that

---

[49] Dawkins, *The Selfish Gene.*

I am taking for granted at this point. I consider alternatives to the standard picture in Chapter 7.

7. Conceptual Evolution

Suppose that the reasons I gave in Chapter 2 for thinking that human reasoning competence is innate were mistaken and that human reasoning competence is not primarily innate but is instead mostly learned. If this is right, the argument for the rationality thesis based on biological evolution is—even if all the objections I have considered are set aside— a non-starter. Still, if, as some have argued, the development of knowledge fits the general model of natural selection, an evolutionary argument for the rationality thesis might be salvageable; such an argument, because it does not involve biological evolution, might be immune to the objections I have raised to the versions of the evolutionary argument considered so far. The idea of using natural selection as a model for the development of knowledge—sometimes called conceptual evolution—goes under the name of *evolutionary epistemology*. As part of articulating the conceptual evolution version of the evolutionary argument for the rationality thesis, I shall turn to an exposition of evolutionary epistemology.

Evolutionary epistemology is an approach to the theory of knowledge that sees a significant similarity between the growth of knowledge and biological evolution. An evolutionary epistemologist claims that the development of human knowledge proceeds through some natural selection process analogous to Darwin's theory of biological natural selection. The three major components of the model of natural selection are variation, selection, and retention. According to Darwin's theory of natural selection, variations are not pre-designed to perform certain functions. Rather, those variations that perform useful functions are selected while those that do not are not selected; such selection is responsible for the appearance that variations intentionally occur. In the modern theory of evolution, genetic mutations provide the blind variations (blind in the sense that variations are not influenced by the effects they would have—the likelihood of a mutation is not correlated with the benefits or liabilities that mutation would confer on the organism), the environment provides the filter of selection, and reproduction provides the retention. Fit is achieved because those organisms with features that make them less fit for survival do not survive in competition with other organisms in the environment that have fitter features. Evolutionary epistemology applies this blind variation and selective retention model to the growth of scientific knowledge and to human thought processes in general. According to this view, the development of human knowledge is governed by a process analogous to biological natural selection, rather than by natural selection itself.[50] This version of evolutionary epistemology sees the (partial) fit between theories and the world as explained by a mental process of trial and error. Roughly, evolutionary epistemology explains the development of knowledge through a process of the survival of the best (that is, most fit) beliefs.[51]

With this picture of evolutionary epistemology in hand and recalling the original appeal of the evolutionary argument for rationality, it is easy to see the structure and strength of the evolutionary epistemological argument for the rationality thesis. The straightforward version of the evolutionary argument for rationality attempts to forge a link between biological evolution and rationality via truth but this failed because biological evolution cannot deliver truth; if evolutionary epistemology provides the right account of the origin of beliefs—that is, if human knowledge develops by selecting for the best beliefs—then there is a connection between evolution (in the general, *not* the biological, sense of the term) and truth, and thus there is hope for an evolutionary argument for rationality.

[50] There is another view sometimes called evolutionary epistemology; it is the *literal* version of evolutionary epistemology rather than the analogical version. The literal version sees biological evolution as the primary cause of the growth of knowledge. This view dovetails nicely with the claim that our cognitive mechanisms are innate. On this view, the growth of knowledge occurs through blind variation and selective retention because biological natural selection itself is the cause of conceptual variation and selection. A plausible version of the literal view need not hold that all human *beliefs* are innate but rather can hold that the mental mechanisms that guide the acquisition of non-innate beliefs are themselves innate and the result of biological natural selection. (For more on this point, see Edward Stein and Peter Lipton, 'Where Guesses Come From: Evolutionary Epistemology and the Anomaly of Guided Variation', *Biology and Philosophy*, 4 (1989), 33–56.) This version of evolutionary epistemology is not directly relevant to the argument for the rationality thesis currently under consideration. Michael Ruse, *Taking Darwin Seriously* (Oxford: Blackwell, 1986), ch. 5, defends a version of literal evolutionary epistemology which he links to sociobiology.

[51] The classic essays on evolutionary epistemology are Donald Campbell, 'Evolutionary Epistemology', in Paul Schilpp (ed.), *The Philosophy of Karl Popper*, i (LaSalle, Ill.: Open Court, 1974); repr. in Gerald Radnitsky and W. W. Bartley III (eds.), *Evolution, Theory of Rationality and the Sociology of Knowledge* (LaSalle, Ill.: Open Court, 1987); Karl Popper, *Conjectures and Refutations* (New York: Basic Books, 1962); and id., *Objective Knowledge* (Oxford: Oxford University Press, 1972).

The argument can be laid out as follows:

(EE4) Conceptual evolution favours principles that are good at producing true beliefs.
(EE5) A rational principle is one that is good at producing true
beliefs.
(EE6) Therefore, conceptual evolution favours rational principles.
(EE7) Humans follow principles which are the result of conceptual
evolution.
(EE8) Therefore, there is a strong reason to believe that humans are
rational—in particular, there is a strong reason not to interpret
the reasoning experiments as demonstrating human irrationality.

This argument is not open to some of the same sorts of objection that
counted against the original evolutionary argument, because it is independent of the biological details of our beliefs. These worries aside, is
(EE4) plausible? First, (EE4)'s plausibility rests partly on the plausibility of evolutionary epistemology, a philosophical programme that
has come under much scrutiny.[52] Assessing the various criticisms of it
is, however, beyond the scope of this project. The second question,
which *is* within the scope of this project, is whether conceptual evolution
is, as some evolutionary epistemologists claim, a reliable producer of
truth. I shall ask this question in terms of whether evolutionary epistemology is compatible, as it seems initially to be, with convergent
realism, the view that as human beliefs change they make progress
towards the truth. This will determine if (EE4) is true because conceptual
evolution can only be truth-tropic if our beliefs get closer to the truth
as they develop.[53]

I begin with a question about biology: does biological evolution
progress towards a goal? Early theories of the origin of species included
belief in a chain of being, a hierarchy of living things ranging from the
most primitive to the most advanced. In its early incarnation, the chain
of being was believed to be static and to have been created by a god.

---

[52] For discussions of some of the criticisms of evolutionary epistemology, see Ruse,
Taking Darwin Seriously; Michael Bradie, 'Assessing Evolutionary Epistemology', *Biology and Philosophy*, 1 (1986), 401–59; and Edward Stein, 'Evolutionary Epistemology',
in Jonathan Dancy and Ernest Sosa (eds.), *A Companion to Epistemology* (Oxford:
Blackwell, 1992).
[53] These issues are discussed at length in Edward Stein, 'Getting Closer to the Truth:
Realism and the Metaphysical and Epistemological Ramifications of Evolutionary Epistemology', in Nicholas Rescher (ed.), *Evolution, Cognition and Realism* (Lanham, Md.:
University Press of America, 1990).

In its later conceptions (most notably, those defended by Charles Bonnet
and Jean-Baptiste Robinet in the middle of the eighteenth century), the
chain of being hierarchy was seen as pre-planned but gradually unfolding
through time. This picture of a temporalized chain of being sees biological progress as heading towards a final particular and attainable
goal. Darwin was responsible for the shift away from the belief in a
divine and teleological view of the origin of species. Two of the most
revolutionary insights of his theory were its move away from teleology
(the view that the evolution of species progresses towards an ultimate
goal) and its elimination of a designer without the elimination of design. Darwin argued that speciation could occur by natural selection
through time: it does not require a goal or the design of an all-powerful
creator. He saw evolution as a branching process: an original species
gave rise to a variety of organisms within the species, which in turn
gave rise, through speciation, to further distinct species. He did, however, want to preserve the notion that humans are more advanced than
most other existing species because we appear later in the branching
process. Today, most of us agree with Darwin in viewing evolution
as non-teleological and independent of a designer. We also share with
Darwin the intuitive sense that, in some way, we are more advanced
than other species. From the perspective of modern biology, however,
this last belief is doubtful—it is far from clear that in any qualitative,
biological sense we are more advanced than other species.[54] What is
clear is that, contrary to the chain of being view, there need be no ideal
species towards which evolution progresses—in fact, progress towards
an ideal species is inconsistent with contemporary evolutionary biology.

With this discussion as background, I turn to conceptual evolution.
Whereas in the case of biological evolution we postulate no goal to
progress towards, prima facie there does seem to be a goal for conceptual evolution, namely truth. It seems, for example, that scientific
knowledge progresses towards a correct theory of the world. If so, this
fact gives rise to a dramatic disanalogy between biological and conceptual
evolution. (In spite of the threat of disanalogy, many evolutionary epistemologists seem to believe in convergent realism, that is, even if science can never get to the truth, it can at least approach it.[55]) I will propose

[54] Francisco Ayala, 'The Concept of Biological Progress', in Francisco Ayala and
Theodosius Dobzhansky (eds.), *Studies in the Philosophy of Biology* (Berkeley: Univer-
sity of California Press, 1974). See also Matthew Nitecki (ed.), *Evolutionary Progress*
(Chicago: University of Chicago Press, 1988).

[55] See e.g. Campbell, 'Evolutionary Epistemology', 447–8, and Popper, *Objective
Knowledge*, 58.

two arguments that undermine the analogy between biological evolution and conceptual evolution that is the crux of evolutionary epistemology, namely arguments that evolutionary epistemology is not consistent with convergent realism. The first argument, which I call the *no goal-directed progress argument*, says that conceptual evolution, if it is to be analogous to biological evolution, cannot get closer to the truth because there is no goal in biological evolution. The force of this argument can be avoided if, as seems reasonable, some disanalogy between biological and conceptual evolution is allowed. The second argument, which I call the *veil of selection argument*, says that conceptual evolution cannot progress towards the truth because the criterion of selection, since it is pragmatic, is too broad. This argument counts against (EE4) because it shows that conceptual evolution cannot be relied upon to produce truth-tropic principles.

An essential feature of biological evolution is that it has no goal to approach—there is no ideal state towards which it progresses. An epistemology modeled on biological evolution cannot progress towards a goal if the analogy is to hold. If epistemology does not approach a goal, then both convergent realism and (EE4) are false because both require that conceptual evolution progresses towards truth. This is the no goal-directed progress argument.

A response to this argument is that the mere absence of progress towards a goal does not mean there can be no progress; giving up on progress towards truth does not entail giving up on progress completely. For example, Thomas Kuhn and Larry Laudan reject convergent realism, but do not thereby reject every sense of progress.[56] Kuhn, for example, removes the notion of a fixed truth from science, replacing it with an *environmentally dependent* notion of optimality, a notion that includes 'maximum accuracy of predictions, degrees of specialization and number of concrete problem solutions'.[57] While Kuhn and Laudan do not think the development of scientific knowledge progresses *towards truth*, they do see it as progressing in some sense. I agree; progress is directional change towards a better state,[58] but knowing the truth is not the only possible better state—the development of theories could progress by increasing the number of phenomena explained, the number of

[56] Thomas Kuhn, *The Structure of Scientific Revolutions* (Chicago: University of Chicago Press, 1970); and Larry Laudan, *Progress and its Problems* (Berkeley: University of California Press, 1977).
[57] Thomas Kuhn, 'Reflections on my Critics', in Imre Lakatos and Alan Musgrave (eds.), *Criticism and the Growth of Knowledge* (London: Cambridge University Press, 1970), 264.   [58] Ayala, 'The Concept of Biological Progress'.

problems solved, the number of bridges built, and so on. Although work needs to be done to develop a precise notion of scientific progress to take the place of getting closer to the truth, strides have been made towards a (non-truth-tropic) notion of progress suited to evolutionary epistemology. I am not, however, as confident as Kuhn is that it would be 'easy'[59] to develop such a notion. Consider, for example, how difficult it is to talk about progress in biological evolution, where the mechanisms of variation and selection are far better characterized and understood than in conceptual evolution. Thus, while the no goal-directed progress argument allows for progress in conceptual evolution, it does not allow for progress towards the truth.

Even granting, then, that there can be progress without progress towards a goal and progress in conceptual evolution without progress towards truth, there cannot be progress towards truth in an evolutionary epistemology, and that is what is at issue in (EE4). There are certain types of progress that can occur without a goal, while there are others that cannot—some processes require a goal in order to have a metric of progress, while others do not. The distinction I am drawing is between *convergent progress* and *non-convergent progress*. Convergent progress involves getting closer to a goal while non-convergent progress involves improvement but without a goal. The sort of progress that involves truth is convergent progress; the only possible metric for getting closer to the truth requires a true account of the world to get closer to. The no goal-directed progress argument thus counts against (EE4).

Some friends of evolutionary epistemology favour a variant of the view called *natural selection epistemology* that might defuse this argument. Some evolutionary epistemologists, rather than arguing for a close analogy with biology, argue that change in both epistemology and biology are distinct instances of 'selection processes'.[60] A natural

---

[59] Kuhn, 'Reflections on my Critics', 264.

[60] See e.g. Donald Campbell, 'Selection Theory and the Sociology of Scientific Validity', in Werner Callebaut and Rik Pinxten (eds.), *Evolutionary Epistemology* (Dordrecht: Reidel, 1987); Donald Campbell and Bonnie Paller, 'Extending Evolutionary Epistemology to "Justifying" Scientific Beliefs', in Kai Hahlweg and C. A. Hooker (eds.), *Issues in Evolutionary Epistemology* (Albany, NY: State University of New York Press, 1989); and David Hull, 'A Mechanism and its Metaphysics', *Biology and Philosophy*, 3 (1988), 123–55. I have my doubts about the move to a natural selection epistemology. If the notion of selection theory is made too much broader it will include almost every developmental process. Broadening the notion of selection theory is supposed to save evolutionary epistemology from the force of various disanalogies that some have argued hold between conceptual and biological evolution. It seems to me that these disanalogies are too quickly admitted by many evolutionary epistemologists; rather than embracing

selection epistemology thus need not match biological evolution in every feature so long as it exemplifies 'general' selection theory. A natural selection epistemologist could, thus, respond to the no goal-directed progress argument by saying that there are at least two sorts of selection process, those that have a goal and those that do not—biological evolution does not have a goal but conceptual evolution does—and that while both sorts of evolutionary process fit the model of natural selection, they differ in at least this one way. The move to a natural selection epistemology may save (EE4) and the evolutionary epistemologist's attempt to embrace convergent realism, but, even if it does, it does so only momentarily.

I will now proceed to my second argument that evolutionary epistemology is incompatible with convergent realism and hence that (EE4) is false. Evolutionary epistemology attempts (as does natural selection epistemology) to apply the natural selection model of blind variation and selective retention to conceptual evolution. Put simply, in biological evolution (focusing on just the selection part of the process), the organism that fits better in the environment than its competitors is the organism that is selected. This does not mean the organism is *ideally* suited to that particular environment—only that it is well enough suited to survive and better suited than its competitors. The same sort of account is given to explain why a belief or scientific theory is selected—the belief selected is more fit than its competitors. Here 'more fit' amounts to better behavioural consequences or closer correlation with the data. As a result, according to evolutionary epistemology, selection cannot distinguish between knowledge and mere useful opinion, that is, it cannot distinguish between (locally) optimal behaviour based on truths and equally optimal behaviour based on falsehoods. If we read 'better fit' to mean better fit with the data, the same point can be made by appealing to underdetermination of theory by data: the data are consistent with many more theories (beliefs) than just the true one. There is, in other words, a veil of selection in evolutionary epistemology—the selection criterion of optimality fails to guarantee that true beliefs and truth-tropic principles will be selected. If we think of selection as a filter, in the case of conceptual evolution, the filter is too coarse-grained to precipitate only true beliefs and truth-tropic principles—other beliefs and principles will pass through the filter as well. Evolutionary epistemology,

these disanalogies, many of them should be attacked head on. Stein and Lipton, 'Where Guesses Come From', addresses some of the supposed disanalogies between biological and conceptual evolution.

since it holds that belief selection is neutral with respect to truth (that is, selection is for good results not for truth), is not consistent with guaranteed progress towards truth. Selection is based on optimality but, since there are many false beliefs that will work just as well as any true one, and many non-truth-tropic principles that will work just as well as truth-tropic ones, optimality does not amount to truth. The conclusion of the veil of selection argument is that, since selection in evolutionary epistemology is based on pragmatic criteria, it cannot guarantee progress towards the truth.

The no goal and the veil of selection arguments count against (EE4), the claim that our beliefs will get closer to the truth as they develop. This undermines the evolutionary epistemology argument for the rationality thesis by blocking the link between evolution and truth that seemed a promising route to connect evolution to rationality. The evolutionary epistemology argument for the rationality thesis thus fails.

8. Conclusion

In the first several sections of this chapter, I argued that biological evolution cannot be relied upon to produce principles of reasoning that are truth-tropic. In the most recent section, I argued that the same is true for conceptual evolution. That conceptual evolution fails to produce true beliefs and truth-tropic principles may seem unconnected to why biological evolution fails to do so, because biological evolution fails to do so for reasons that seemed connected with the details of biological evolution. Conceptual evolution, however, fails to produce true beliefs because the filter of natural selection is not fine-grained enough to select for truth (or rationality). This is similar to why biological evolution fails to produce true beliefs. This similarity indicates that there is a deeper reason—one having to do with the model of natural selection in its abstract form—why the evolutionary argument for rationality, in both its biological and conceptual forms, does not work. This feature is, as emphasized above, that the filter of selection (whether natural or otherwise) is designed to precipitate pragmatic results and not truth. This shows that evolutionary arguments, when they try to establish connections with truth, will not suffice to defend the rationality thesis.

I began this chapter by comparing the mechanisms of cognition to the mechanisms of vision. I suggested that just as natural selection has done an excellent job selecting a visual system that helps us generate true beliefs about the world, so natural selection should be expected to have selected a cognitive system that generates true beliefs about the world. Much of the burden of this chapter has been to show that natural selection cannot, in fact, be relied upon to do so with respect to cognition. This might indicate that something is wrong with my comparison between cognition and vision. Actually, I think the comparison was apt but the characterizations of the relation between natural selection and cognition, on the one hand, and natural selection and vision, on the other, are mistaken. I originally characterized the visual system as doing an excellent job of generating true beliefs about the world. Although this may well be true, it is a mistake to confuse this with the claim that the visual system was selected *for* generating true beliefs. In fact, the visual system, like our cognitive mechanisms, was selected for because of its pragmatic effects. If the visual system is good at producing true beliefs, this is a (happy) side-effect of its contribution to the selective advantageousness of genes for eyes, the visual cortex, and so on, not because natural selection has selected for truth-tropic visual mechanisms. Thus, the ramifications of this chapter go beyond the evolutionary argument for the rationality thesis; they show that the attempt to connect natural selection to truth or rationality in any realm—not just cognition— will fail.

7

The Standard Picture

IN the last few chapters, I have been considering arguments for the view that humans are rational. These arguments tried to support the rationality thesis by providing reasons for interpreting the reasoning experiments so that they are only about performance errors. Interpreted in this fashion, these experiments lend no support to the irrationality thesis. None of the arguments presented in the previous chapters established that this interpretation of the reasoning experiments is the right one. As a result, in so far as the reasoning experiments suggest that humans systematically violate the normative principles of reasoning, the irrationality thesis seems in good shape.

There is another strategy that can be used against the irrationality thesis. Rather than argue that the reasoning experiments do not provide evidence about human reasoning competence, friends of the rationality thesis can argue that the standard picture of rationality is mistaken. According to the standard picture of rationality, there are normative principles of reasoning and these principles are (at least, for the most part) what we think they are, that is, they stem from principles of logic, probability, and the like. If the standard picture of rationality is wrong and the normative principles of reasoning do not match principles of logic, probability, and the like but, rather, match the principles embodied in our reasoning competence, then the rationality thesis would be true. Or, perhaps an argument for the rationality thesis could be developed if there are no normative principles of reasoning that apply to everyone. In any event, if they are willing to sacrifice the standard picture of rationality, friends of the rationality thesis could be vindicated.

There are, then, two general strategies for arguing against the irrationality thesis in the face of the evidence of the reasoning experiments. First, one might try to show that the reasoning experiments do not in fact support the irrationality thesis, that is, that they do not show that human reasoning competence diverges from the normative principles of reasoning. Second, one might try to undermine the standard picture of rationality, that is, the view that there are normative principles of reasoning and that these principles are based on rules of logic, probability, and the like. The second strategy seems a tougher road to travel, so I started with the first. In Chapter 3, I considered some specific attempts to undermine the reasoning experiments. I found that, while some such attempts might work in a piecemeal fashion (for example, subjects in the conjunction experiment might not be violating the conjunction principle but instead might be misinterpreting the experimental task as asking them to assess *plausibility* rather than *probability*), in order to undercut the irrationality thesis, a more general strategy is needed to counter the prima facie plausible interpretation of the reasoning experiments. In the previous three chapters, I have considered and rejected arguments for interpreting the reasoning experiments as consistent with the rationality thesis, in particular, for interpreting them as being exclusively about performance errors. In light of my discussion thus far, it seems reasonable to interpret them as showing that we fail to reason in accordance with the normative principles of reasoning. This suggests that if one wants to resist the irrationality thesis, the second strategy for arguing against it—namely to undermine the standard picture of rationality—is the more promising strategy, even though it seems the more difficult one.

In Chapter 1, I sketched three arguments why human rationality might be a conceptual matter. The three arguments address themselves to the normative principles of reasoning. The first claims that relativism is true for the norms of reasoning, the second claims that the norms of reasoning are dependent on our reasoning competence, and the third claims that we have no access to the norms of reasoning. All three arguments can be used against the standard picture of rationality and thus can also be used against the irrationality thesis and in support of the rationality thesis. The first argument attempts to undermine the irrationality. thesis by denying that there are normative principles of reasoning that apply to everyone; the normative principles of reasoning are indexed to individuals rather than to humans in general. If this is right, then each human thereby reasons in accordance with her own normative principles and hence is rational. The second argument attempts to undermine the irrationality thesis by denying that it is possible for the normative principles of reasoning to diverge from human reasoning competence. In so far as the reasoning experiments show that we diverge from what we think the norms of reasoning are, they show that we must be mistaken about what the norms of reasoning are. According to the second argument, norms of reasoning are not independent of reasoning competence. The third argument attempts to undermine the irrationality thesis by denying that we have access to the norms of reasoning. If we cannot know what the norms of reasoning are, then we cannot reasonably claim that people diverge from them; the irrationality thesis is, on this view, unsupportable.

In each of the first three sections of this chapter, I will consider these three arguments from the least to the most critical of the standard picture of rationality, namely in the reverse order from which I have just presented them. I will argue that none of these arguments successfully undermines the irrationality thesis. These arguments, however, do not leave the standard picture of rationality unscathed. In the remaining sections of this chapter, I turn my attention to the standard picture of rationality. I say what its virtues are and consider the serious objections that can be raised against it. I also consider a serious alternative to it, what I call the *naturalized picture of rationality*. Having said some things in favour of naturalized rationality, I explore the connections between the conclusions of the previous chapters and this way of looking at rationality.

1. The No Access Argument

The first argument against the irrationality thesis is based on the observation that to inquire whether humans are rational, we must use the very reasoning capacities that we are attempting to assess. If we are irrational, then our inquiry into human rationality (as well as our other scientific and philosophical inquiries) is suspect because engaging in this inquiry requires that we reason, but, as reasoners, we make systematic errors. As a result, if the irrationality thesis is true, we cannot know that it is true; in so far as evidence leads us to believe the irrationality thesis, this evidence suggests that we cannot be justified in believing this thesis. According to this argument, which I call the *no access argument*, the irrationality thesis is roughly self-refuting: if the irrationality thesis is true, we cannot know that it is.[1]

The rationality thesis does not face a parallel problem. If we are rational, then it is at least possible that our inquiry into human rationality will not be suspect; if, through reasoning, we come to the conclusion that humans are rational, our conclusion is consistent with the reliability

---

[1] John Macnamara, *A Border Dispute* (Cambridge, Mass.: MIT Press, 1986), 184, sketches an argument that seems similar to this one.

of the methods used to discover it. The rationality thesis is not self-refuting—it is compatible with its own truth. If the first argument shows that the irrationality thesis is self-refuting but the rationality thesis is not, then this argument amounts to a *reductio ad absurdum* argument for the rationality thesis.

The general form of a *reductio ad absurdum* argument is as follows: begin with some assumption *A*; show that *A* entails a contradiction; this constitutes a deductively valid argument for the negation of *A*. If the irrationality thesis is self-refuting, then it leads to a contradiction (namely, it entails its own truth and the truth of its negation), and, thus, the rationality thesis—the negation of the irrationality thesis—is true. The question then is whether in fact the irrationality thesis is self-refuting. Before I can answer this question, I need to clarify what self-refutation is.

1.1. Self-Refutation

A statement is self-refuting if it contradicts itself. There are three different senses in which a statement can be self-refuting.[2] First, a statement can be *pragmatically* self-refuting. Consider the statement 'George cannot speak' spoken by George. The statement may well be true, for all we know, and it may well be true that the statement can in fact be spoken by George; the statement cannot, however, be true *if* in fact George speaks it. This is a paradigmatic case of pragmatic self-refutation: the statement is only refuted if it is asserted in a certain way. Strictly speaking, however, the *statement* 'George cannot speak' is not self-refuting, but the action of uttering it is (the statement is contradicted by George's *act* of speaking it); that is the fingerprint of pragmatic self-refutation. A shirt popular among lesbians and gay men saying 'Nobody knows I'm a lesbian [gay]' provides a real-life case that is close to pragmatic self-refutation. It might be true of some particular person that no one knows she is a lesbian, but wearing this shirt is likely to make people believe that she is a lesbian, which, if she is, thereby makes it false that nobody knows she is a lesbian. This is not exactly a case of pragmatic self-refutation because (*a*) wearing is not asserting and (*b*) it is possible that no one would believe that the wearer of the shirt is a lesbian.

---

[2] John Mackie, 'Self-Refutation—A Formal Analysis', *Philosophical Quarterly*, 14 (1964), 193–203; repr. in *Logic and Knowledge*, ed. Joan Mackie and Penelope Mackie (Oxford: Oxford University Press, 1985).

Second, a statement can be *absolutely* self-refuting. Consider the statement 'I know that I know nothing'. The statement cannot be true, because the truth of the whole sentence contradicts the claim that it makes. Under no circumstances, under no way of putting forth this statement, can it be consistently asserted.

Third, a statement can be *operationally* self-refuting. Consider the sentence 'I believe that I have no beliefs'. If we assume that putting forth 'I believe X' entails that I have at least one belief, the statement is self-refuting because it denies that I have any beliefs. But unlike statements that are absolutely self-refuting, operationally self-refuting statements, although they cannot be consistently put forth in any fashion, could well be true; I could believe that I have no beliefs (this would be true, for example, if I was an eliminativist about beliefs[3]). Unlike pragmatically self-refuting statements, in which the way that the statement is put forth conflicts with the statement—George cannot say that he cannot speak, but he could use a sign language to communicate it—with operationally self-refuting statements, there is no way that the sentence can be consistently put forth—even if I use a sign language, I cannot consistently assert that I believe that I have no beliefs. A pragmatically self-refuting statement, although it is self-refuting if asserted in a certain way by a person (or set of people), can be consistently asserted in *some* way by those who could not assert it in the first way. A statement is operationally self-refuting if it is not absolutely self-refuting and it cannot be asserted in *any* way by a person or set of persons; a statement that is operationally self-refuting can, however, be true.

Before I consider whether the irrationality thesis is self-refuting, I want to consider a thesis that is even more likely to be self-refuting, namely the thesis that *every* inference humans make violates the normative principles of reasoning—what I call the *maximal irrationality thesis* (the *maximal thesis*, for short). If the maximal thesis is true, then the irrationality thesis is true. The reverse is not true: even if the irrationality thesis is true, the maximal thesis could still be false. If, however, the maximal thesis is not self-refuting, then the irrationality thesis cannot be. This is because the irrationality thesis is entailed by

---

[3] Eliminativism is the view that our common-sense psychological categories and the theory that underlies them are radically mistaken. According to this theory, there are, in fact, no such things as beliefs. See Paul Churchland, *Scientific Realism and the Plasticity of Mind* (Cambridge: Cambridge University Press, 1979); Stephen Stich, *From Folk Psychology to Cognitive Science* (Cambridge, Mass.: MIT Press, 1983); and Daniel Dennett, 'Beyond Belief', in *The Intentional Stance* (Cambridge, Mass.: MIT Press, 1987).

the maximal thesis and because a non-self-refuting statement cannot entail a self-refuting one. If, however, the maximal thesis is self-refuting, this does not entail that the irrationality thesis is self-refuting (though it is consistent with its being so).

Can cognitive science discover that *every* inference humans make is irrational? Can I assert that *every* inference humans make is irrational? The idea is that the answer to these questions is no; the maximal thesis is self-refuting because I must make some inferences in order to arrive at any belief or to make any discovery, but according to the maximal thesis, all inferences humans make violate the norms. In what way is the maximal thesis self-refuting? The claim that humans are maximally irrational is not pragmatically self-refuting: the mode of presentation does not affect the self-consistency of such a statement. Consider the version of the maximal thesis that makes the claim 'I have concluded that every inference humans make violates the norms of reasoning'. My utterance on its own is logically consistent, but my act of putting forth this statement involves contradicting myself; even my *believing* the maximal thesis would be self-refuting. The maximal thesis is not, however, absolutely self-refuting; it could perfectly well be the case that every inference humans make is irrational—the *statement* is not self-contradictory, even though any way that I might put it forth would be. The maximal thesis is then *operationally* self-refuting—my asserting the statement suggests that I have reason to believe it, but if the statement is true, I cannot have any reason to believe it (or anything else for that matter) because, according to the statement itself, every belief that I have as the result of an inference is unjustified. The upshot is that although the maximal thesis could not be consistently proven by cognitive scientists or rationally believed by any human being, it still could be true. This is significantly different from showing that a statement is objectively self-refuting. If a statement is objectively self-refuting, then its negation must be true. The same is not true for a statement that is operationally self-refuting; if a statement is operationally self-refuting, then it is epistemologically inaccessible for those that it applies to. If the maximal thesis is operationally self-refuting, then the maximal thesis is epistemologically inaccessible to humans.

1.2. *Epistemological Inaccessibility*

The epistemological situation of the maximal irrationality thesis that is suggested by the no access argument is similar to a standard account of a person's epistemological situation with respect to other minds and a standard account of our epistemological situation with respect to the mathematical proposition known as Goldbach's conjecture. The problem of other minds has to do with whether a person can know that there are other minds in the world. Of course, I can see there are other bodies, but my only evidence that there are other minds has to do with the behaviour of these other bodies. The observed behaviour of other bodies is perfectly consistent with it being the case that these other *bodies* have no minds and instead are robots or zombies. It is possible that there are other minds, but it is also possible that there are *not*. This question, however, may be unanswerable. There may be no evidence I can have access to that will bear on this question; the sort of evidence that would be relevant (for example, that some other body had conscious experience or felt pain) seems epistemologically inaccessible.'

Goldbach's conjecture says that every even number greater than two can be expressed as the sum of two prime numbers. Although this proposition is true for every number that it has ever been tested on, the conjecture has never been proven, that is, a mathematical proof has never been given to show that it is true for all numbers. Some have argued that no such proof that can be given. If this is true, a proof of Goldbach's conjecture is epistemologically inaccessible; although it may be a fact that every even number greater than two is the sum of two prime numbers, we cannot prove that it is true. The comparison with the knowledge of other minds and with Goldbach's conjecture shows that even if the maximal irrationality thesis is epistemologically inaccessible, it is in good company—we might be able to be as confident in asserting that humans are irrational as I am that there are other minds besides my own and as mathematicians are that Goldbach's conjecture is true.

The irrationality thesis cannot be worse off in terms of self-refutation than the maximal irrationality thesis because the irrationality thesis is contained in the maximal irrationality thesis. Given that the maximal irrationality thesis is operationally self-refuting, the strongest claim of self-refutation that can be made against the irrationality thesis is that it is operationally self-refuting. It follows that the strongest claim the no access argument could make against the irrationality thesis is that it is epistemologically inaccessible. Even if the no access argument establishes that the irrationality thesis is epistemologically inaccessible, this would not in itself—as the analogies with the problem of other minds and Goldbach's conjecture suggest—constitute an argument for the rationality thesis. It would, however, somewhat undermine the main argument for the irrationality thesis, because it undermines the reasoning experiments and, thus, the conclusions based on them. The rationality thesis is not epistemologically inaccessible in the way that the irrationality thesis is; this asymmetry with respect to epistemological accessibility suggests that the rationality thesis is in better shape than the irrationality thesis. If the no access argument is right, we can never have evidence for believing the irrationality thesis, while there is at least the possibility that some evidence will support the rationality thesis.

1.3. Is the Irrationality Thesis Epistemologically Accessible?

To assess the strength of the no access argument better, consider the following version of the argument:

(1) We should believe the irrationality thesis on the evidence of the reasoning experiments. (assumption)
(2) If the irrationality thesis is true, then humans cannot be justified in believing anything that relies on their reasoning processes.
(3) Humans are not justified in believing the irrationality thesis on the basis of the reasoning experiments. (from 1 and 2)
(4) Since (1) and (3) contradict each other, we should reject (1); therefore, the reasoning experiments do not count as evidence for the irrationality thesis.

The crucial step in the argument is (2), which initially seems reasonable. The irrationality thesis says that humans systematically violate the norms of reasoning in the sense that human reasoning competence diverges from the norms of reasoning. The idea behind (2) is that if our reasoning competence diverges from the norms then we can never be justified in any of our beliefs. Is this right?

1.3.1. A Particular Example: The Conjunction Experiment

Unlike the maximal irrationality thesis, the irrationality thesis does not claim that *every* inference humans make is irrational; it only claims that *some* of the principles we have in our reasoning competence diverge from the norms. For example, the irrationality thesis claims that humans do not follow the conjunction principle in certain situations in which we should follow it and that our failure to do so is not due to performance errors. Is the claim that humans do not follow the conjunction principle self-refuting? Consider the no access argument rewritten for the specific case of the conjunction experiment:

(C1) We should believe that humans lack the conjunction principle in their reasoning competence on the evidence of the conjunction experiment. (assumption)

(C2) If humans lack the conjunction principle in their reasoning competence, then humans are not justified in believing any conclusion that requires human reasoning.

(C3) Humans are not justified in believing that humans lack the conjunction principle in their reasoning competence on the basis of the conjunction experiment. (from C1 and C2)

(C4) Since (C1) and (C3) contradict each other, we should reject (C1); therefore, the conjunction experiment does not count as evidence that humans lack the conjunction principle in their reasoning competence.

What do we make of this argument, in particular, what do we make of (C2)? (C2) basically says that if humans lack the conjunction principle, then human reasoning cannot prove anything and cannot be relied upon. The idea is that, given the ubiquity of the conjunction principle in human reasoning, if humans do not reason in accordance with the conjunction principle, then the results of human reasoning cannot be trusted. There are at least two problems with (C2) and this rationale for believing it.

Although there are many situations in which the conjunction principle might be invoked, it is not the case that every time I acquire a new belief I need to invoke the conjunction principle. For example, suppose that I believe that all presidents of the United States have been men and I believe that Oprah Winfrey is not a man. From this, I can infer that Oprah Winfrey has not been President of the United States. In making this inference, I do not need to invoke the conjunction principle. It seems that I am justified in believing the conclusion of my reasoning process even if humans lack the conjunction principle in our reasoning competence. Lacking the conjunction principle does not therefore undermine all of my reasoning processes; perhaps it just undermines reasoning that requires the invocation of the conjunction principle. This suggests that (C2) ought to be rewritten as follows:

(C2′) If humans lack the conjunction principle in their reasoning competence, then humans are not justified in believing any conclusion of a reasoning process that demands the invocation of the conjunction principle.

(C2') seems more plausible than (C2). There is still, however, a problem with it. The conjunction principle says that you should not attach a lesser degree of probability to an event A than you do to both the event A and the (distinct) event B. The conjunction experiment does not show that people *always* fail to attach a lesser degree of probability to an event A than they do to both A and B, only that they *sometimes* do, in particular, that they typically do in situations like the one involving Linda. Although humans may lack the conjunction principle in our reasoning competence, we may have a principle in its place that in certain contexts results in the same inferential behaviour as the conjunction principle does. In such contexts, it seems that we *are* justified in believing the conclusions of such inferences because, in these contexts, inferences in accordance with such principles match the inferences in accordance with the norms. This suggests a further modification to (C2). Consider:

(C2'') If humans lack the conjunction principle in their reasoning competence and instead have some other principle P, then humans are not justified in believing any conclusion that is based on P rather than the conjunction principle unless P and the conjunction principle result in the same conclusion in the particular context.

(C2'') seems true, but it is not at all clear that (C2'') will fill (C2)'s spot in the argument for (C4). The argument for (C4) is a reductio-style argument. (C1) and (C2) were supposed to entail the negation of (C1). Does (C2''), when conjoined with (C1), entail the negation of (C1)? This depends on whether the process of forming the belief that humans lack the conjunction principle requires the use of the conjunction principle in a context in which P—the principle that we have in our reasoning competence in place of the conjunction principle—diverges from the conjunction principle. If the process of forming the belief 'Humans lack the conjunction principle' requires the use of the conjunction principle in contexts in which P diverges from it, then it seems that (C1) and (C2'') will entail (C3). It is not clear, however, that this will be the case.

1.3.2. Does Irrational Mean always Irrational?

Rather than dwell on the particular version of the no access argument that involves the conjunction principle, I want to return to the general version of the argument with these two objections in hand. Recall the no access argument:

(1) We should believe the irrationality thesis on the evidence of the reasoning experiments. (assumption)

(2) If the irrationality thesis is true, then humans cannot be justified in believing anything that relies on their reasoning processes.

(3) Humans are not justified in believing the irrationality thesis on the basis of the reasoning experiments. (from 1 and 2)

(4) Since (1) and (3) contradict each other, we should reject (1); therefore, the reasoning experiments do not count as evidence for the irrationality thesis.

I want to focus on (2) and consider precisely what it says. The irrationality thesis says that humans lack the normative principles of reasoning in their reasoning competence. This entails that there are many contexts in which humans will reason in accordance with their reasoning competence (that is, in which humans will not make any performance errors) but in which we will fail to reason in accordance with the norms. For (2) to be true, *every* instance of human reasoning has to fall into one of these contexts, that is, every instance of human reasoning has to involve a principle of reasoning that diverges from the normative principles of reasoning in a context in which that principle produces an inference that is different from what the relevant normative principle of reasoning would produce. (2) says that if the irrationality thesis is true, then humans cannot be justified in believing anything. The idea is that if we are irrational, any inference we make will be tainted by our irrationality. It seems highly unlikely that this is true.

My discussion of the version of the no access argument for the rationality thesis that involves the conjunction experiments suggests two objections to (2). With respect to the particular version of the no access argument, the first objection was that the conjunction principle is not invoked every time we engage in reasoning. Generalizing this objection, one objection to (2) is that the non-normative principles of reasoning that we have in our reasoning competence are not invoked every time we reason. The reasoning experiments do not provide evidence for the view that *none* of the principles of reasoning in our reasoning competence match the norms, and the irrationality thesis (in its non-maximal form) is not committed to this view. (2) seems in trouble because we can be justified in believing the results of a reasoning process that relies on those normative principles of reasoning that we do in fact have in our reasoning competence.

As an example, consider how a reductio-style argument relating to our visual capacities and to visual illusions might be developed on the model of the no access argument. An experimenter studying the bent-stick-in-water illusion must, of course, use vision to note the results of her experiments. It would be ridiculous to claim that since the experimenter's conclusion is that people are subject to visual illusions as part of their visual competence (that is, the illusions are not the result of performance errors), all visual data is thereby called into question. Visual illusions occur only in certain contexts. The same sort of claim is true with respect to the reasoning experiments; even if we are irrational, it does not follow that all human reasoning is bad reasoning.

The second objection to the particular version of the no access argument was that even though we are reasoning in accordance with some principle other than the conjunction principle we do not *always* fail to make inferences that accord with the conjunction principle. Generalizing this objection, it is possible for me to engage in the same reasoning behaviour I would if I had some normative principle N in my reasoning competence even though I have some non-normative principle P in my reasoning competence. In other words, while I fail to reason in accordance with P in certain contexts, there may well be other contexts in which reasoning in accordance with P will produce the same reasoning behaviour as reasoning in accordance with N.

Consider the selection task as an example. Recall that in some abstract versions of the selection task (such as the one involving the rule 'If a card has a vowel on one side, then it has an even number on the other side'), subjects make the incorrect selections when asked which cards they need to look at to verify that the cards fit the rule. According to the irrationality thesis reading of the selection task, subjects fail to reason in accordance with principles arising from rules of logic (they fail to reason in accordance with some norm N) because humans have some non-normative principle (P) in our reasoning competence and because the task falls in a context where reasoning in accordance with P and reasoning in accordance with N diverge. In some concrete versions of the selection task (such as the one involving the rule 'Every time I go to New York, I travel by train'), subjects make the correct selections. According to one reading of the selection task that is compatible with the irrationality thesis, subjects make the correct selections not because they are reasoning in accordance with a normative principle of reasoning, but because they are reasoning in accordance with a non-normative principle P in a context in which reasoning in accordance with P matches the reasoning behaviour they would produce in that context if they were reasoning in accordance with the associated normative principle N.

All of the non-normative principles of reasoning that the reasoning experiments suggest we have in our reasoning competence are like P in the above example, namely there are some contexts in which these principles of reasoning, even though they are not normative principles of reasoning, produce the same inferential behaviour that norms would produce in the same context. Given this, (2), which says that if the irrationality thesis is true, humans cannot be justified in believing anything that results from our reasoning, seems in deep trouble. According to this objection, we can be justified in believing the results of our reasoning so long as we are relying on principles of reasoning in contexts in which these principles produce reasoning behaviour that matches the reasoning behaviour of normative principles of reasoning.

1.3.3. The 'Careful' Cognitive Scientist

Friends of the no access argument against the irrationality thesis might attempt to revise (2) to respond to these two objections. Consider:

> (2′) If the irrationality thesis is true, then humans are not justified in believing any conclusion based on a non-normative principle of reasoning unless the reasoning based on that principle was done in a context in which reasoning based on it accords with reasoning based on the appropriate normative principle of reasoning.

This premiss is immune to the two objections raised against (2) above. The question, however, is whether (2′) can take the place of (2) in the no access argument against the irrationality thesis. For the argument with (2′) taking the place of (2) to produce the needed contradiction (in (3)), it must be required that, in order to come to believe the irrationality thesis based on the evidence of the reasoning experiments, we must rely on non-normative principles of reasoning in contexts in which they diverge from the reasoning behaviour that would result from the norms. The initial version of the no access argument obtained a contradiction from the premiss that the reasoning experiments provide evidence for the irrationality thesis by arguing that the truth of the irrationality thesis entails that no conclusion based on human reasoning can be justified. I have tried to show that, under closer examination, the irrationality thesis does not entail that human reasoning is so impotent. Conclusions made on the basis of human reasoning can be justified even if the irrationality thesis is true so long as they are based on normative principles of reasoning or on non-normative principles of reasoning in contexts in which inferential behaviour based upon such principles matches the reasoning behaviour based upon normative principles of reasoning. To establish a contradiction between the fact that humans are irrational and the fact that human reasoning is required to come to know this fact, friends of the no access argument need to show that every chain of argument leading to the conclusion that humans are irrational is based on a non-normative principle of reasoning in a context in which it diverges from the inferential behaviour of the associated normative principles of reasoning.

This seems a rather difficult task to accomplish. There are many chains of reasoning that lead to a conclusion. Even if one could show that a particular chain of reasoning to some conclusion requires a normative principle that humans lack, this does not show that there is *no* chain of reasoning to that conclusion which involves inferences based on principles we have in our reasoning competence in contexts in which they match the norms. For the no access argument to work, it needs to be shown that, regardless of the evidence that might be uncovered, *every* chain of reasoning to the conclusion that the irrationality thesis is true requires an inference that can only be based on a principle of reasoning that human reasoning competence lacks.

It seems to me unlikely that all chains of reasoning that lead to the irrationality thesis, regardless of the evidence they invoke, require inferences that can only be based on principles of reasoning that humans lack in their reasoning competence. It seems possible that there could be a careful cognitive scientist who avoided reasoning using principles in contexts in which they diverge from the normative principles of reasoning. Such a cognitive scientist might be able to come to the conclusion that humans are irrational without relying on any principle of reasoning in a context in which it diverges from the normative principles of reasoning. If this is possible, then the truth of (2′) is compatible with humans being justified in believing in the irrationality thesis, and hence that the irrationality thesis is not operationally self-refuting in the way that the no access argument claims.

One might suspect, however, that there is something tricky going on in the careful cognitive scientist example. How could this cognitive scientist reliably know which principles of reasoning to avoid in which contexts? In order to conclude that some principle P produces reasoning behaviour that, in some context, matches the reasoning behaviour that would be produced by the relevant norm N, the cognitive scientist could not rely on any principles of reasoning that produce reasoning behaviours that diverge from behaviours produced by the relevant norms. It seems that if she were careful, she would be able to do this. There is a problem, however: how would the process get started? In other words, in making her *first* conclusion that humans lack some normative principle of reasoning in our reasoning competence, how could the careful cognitive scientist be sure that she is not *already* relying on some non-normative principle of reasoning that undermines her justification for believing this conclusion?

The cognitive scientist cannot be sure that she is not, from the start of her investigation, in some way basing her reasoning on a principle that diverges from the norms. She can, however, decrease the chances that she is doing this. The chances that she is, from the start, using a *non*-normative principle of reasoning as a part of her reasoning method can be reduced if, once her investigation is under way, she checks back over her initial reasoning method to see if the principles she used from the start are non-normative ones. If they are, then some early inferences might be reconsidered, and perhaps altered. The cognitive scientist could increase the chances that the principles she is using are norms if she engages in some kind of self-checking process to make sure that none of the principles of reasoning in our reasoning competence that she has revealed as non-normative are being used as part of her own reasoning process. This process of self-checking will not *guarantee* that the cognitive scientist is not using any non-normative principles of reasoning. The cognitive scientist might be using a principle of reasoning in human reasoning competence that she has not yet discovered is in human reasoning competence or she might be using a principle that is non-normative although she has not yet determined it to be non-normative. Despite these possibilities, the practice of self-checking for irrationality, if done frequently, would dramatically reduce the chances that one is using non-normative principles of reasoning, and thereby dampen even further the strength of the no access argument's blow against the irrationality thesis.

Further, we might imagine an altered version of the careful cognitive scientist example; imagine that not only is the cognitive scientist *careful*, she is also *lucky*. Not only does this cognitive scientist self-check to make sure that she is not using some of the very principles that she has discovered are non-normative and in our reasoning competence, but none of the principles in human reasoning competence that she is reasoning in accordance with as part of her investigation of human rationality do in fact diverge from the norms in the contexts she is using them. For matters to work out this way, she has to be quite lucky, and she will have no way of knowing that she is as lucky as she in fact is. In spite of how much luck is involved, this situation is *possible*. In fact, if enough people are engaging in this kind of research, the odds may be good that *some* cognitive scientist will be both careful and lucky and will, successfully, and without using any non-normative principles of reasoning, prove that humans are irrational in the sense that we violate the normative principles of reasoning. Given this possibility, (3) does not follow from (1) and (2′) and thus the charge of self-refutation (even of the operational sort) that plays a crucial part in the no access argument against the rationality thesis fails to stick.

The careful cognitive scientist example brings out an interesting point. Even if humans lack a normative principle of reasoning in our reasoning competence, we might come to appreciate that this principle is a normative principle of reasoning and even try to bring our reasoning into accordance with it. This point is further supported by an analogy with linguistics.[4] It follows from linguistic theory that there are *conceivable* non-human languages that do not share some of the features all possible *human* languages share. A human child, brought up among beings (call them Martians) who spoke such a non-human language (call it Martian), would not be able to acquire the language of her adoptive parents with the same remarkable speed with which human children, brought up by humans, normally acquire human languages.[5] The crucial difference for humans, between learning Martianese and English, is that we have a specialized capacity for learning languages like English but not for learning languages like Martian. This does not mean that a child brought up by Martians would be unable to learn Martian eventually. There is no reason to think humans would never be able to learn Martian and communicate with Martians—after all, we learn to do lots of things for which we have no specialized competence.

---

[4] I use the same analogy to make a similar point in Ch. 5, Sect. 4.3.

[5] Hilary Putnam, 'The "Innateness Hypothesis" and Explanatory Models in Linguistics', *Synthese*, 17 (1967), 12–22; repr. in Ned Block (ed.), *Readings in the Philosophy of Psychology*, ii (Cambridge, Mass.: Harvard University Press, 1981), 292, makes the stronger and mistaken claim that linguists are committed to the view that humans would be *unable* to learn Martianese.

The relevant point with respect to reasoning is that even if humans lack some principle in our reasoning competence, humans may be able to acquire it and be able to use it on some occasions. For example, it seems possible that, having determined that humans lack the conjunction principle, we might endeavour to teach people to recognize the various situations in which the conjunction principle should be invoked and, then, to apply the conjunction principle in these situations. People trained in this way might still violate the conjunction principle in unfamiliar contexts or when they are being rushed, but they might reason in accordance with it more frequently than untrained people would. Something like this goes on in the case of visual illusions. We learn not to believe our eyes when the stick in the water looks bent. We think to ourselves, 'I know the stick *looks* bent, but this is just one of those visual illusions; the stick is really straight'. People trained to follow the conjunction principle might, when presented with the case of Linda, think, 'I am tempted to say that Linda is more likely to be a bank teller and a feminist than she is to be a bank teller, but I recognize that this is one of those tricky conjunction principle situations; Linda is really more likely to be a bank teller'. That this seems possible lends further support to the view that even if the irrationality thesis is right and we lack certain normative principles of reasoning, it does not necessarily follow that some people will not be able to learn such principles and, when they are being careful and reflective, that they will be able to follow them. For this further reason, the no access argument fails.

To review, there are several problems with the no access argument against the irrationality thesis. First, even if the argument's premises are true, the conclusion it warrants is that the irrationality thesis is epistemologically inaccessible, not that it is false. Second, the irrationality thesis does not entail that all inferential behaviour in accordance with human reasoning competence will always diverge from the normative principles of reasoning; the no access argument seems to require that the irrationality thesis does entail this. For these reasons, the no access argument does not succeed in undermining the irrationality thesis.

2. *No Extra-Human Norms*

The second argument against the irrationality thesis says that the normative principles of reasoning are indexed to human reasoning ability;

there is no standard against which rationality can be assessed beyond human reasoning competence. According to this argument, which I call the *no extra-human norms argument*, whatever human reasoning competence turns out to be, the principles embodied in it are the normative principles of reasoning. Roughly, the two parts of the argument are, first, that humans are rational if we reason as well as we can and, second, that we are doing the best we can if we are reasoning in accordance with our reasoning competence and are avoiding performance errors. In so far as I reason in accordance with my reasoning competence, according to this argument, I am rational.

This argument is more plausible in light of an analogy with ethics. In ethics, ought implies can; if someone has a moral obligation to do something, this implies that she is able to do it. Contrapositively, if someone cannot do something, then it follows that she does not have a moral obligation to do that thing. I, for example, do not have a moral obligation to give a million dollars a year to charity because I earn painfully less than a million dollars a year. The argument that links the normative principles of reasoning to human reasoning competence says that it is absurd to think (as the standard picture of rationality entails) that humans ought to reason in a way that conflicts with and goes beyond our reasoning competence; it is absurd to think that we ought to reason in a way that we are unable to. The present argument says that the best we can do is what we ought to do; rationality cannot prescribe anything more than this. For example, if humans lack the conjunction principle in our reasoning competence, then the norms cannot demand of us that we reason in accordance with it.

This argument sees the reasoning experiments as revealing human reasoning competence, and, thereby, as also revealing the norms. The reasoning experiments, in so far as they reveal that we do not reason in accordance with principles stemming from logic, probability theory, and the like, reveal only that our reasoning competence diverges from our preconceived ideas of the normative principles of reasoning; they do not thereby establish the irrationality thesis. Rather, the reasoning experiments establish that some of our preconceived ideas about the normative principles of reasoning are mistaken—we endorse unrealistic candidates for how we ought to reason. According to this argument, humans are rational and this is a conceptual fact. We do not, on this view, need to do any experiments to determine whether we are rational; we know a priori that we are rational because whatever reasoning competence we have, reasoning in accordance with it is the best we can do.

What is empirical, on this view, are the details of what it means to be rational. The reasoning experiments just give us insight into what our reasoning abilities are; by knowing what these abilities are, we can determine what the normative principles of reasoning are.

2.1. The Similarity Experiment

A clear example of this way of seeing the reasoning experiments comes from an experiment that I call the *similarity experiment*. In one version of this experiment, subjects are given a list of ordered pairs of things from a certain category, for example, they might be given a list of pairs of countries or a list of pairs of birds. Subjects are then asked to say how similar they think the first item of each pair is to the second item. For example, subjects are asked to say how much they think North Korea is like China or how similar are penguins to robins.[6]

There is a rule of similarity that says that if A is similar to B to degree *n*, then B is similar to A to degree *n*. I call this the *symmetricality rule*. There is a corresponding principle of reasoning about similarity that I call the *symmetricality principle* which says that if you believe A is similar to B to degree *n*, then you should believe that B is similar to A to degree *n*. For example, if I think that Rock Hudson is very similar to Cary Grant then I should also think that Cary Grant is very similar to Rock Hudson. The symmetricality principle seems to be a normative principle of reasoning.

Returning to the similarity experiment, you will probably not be surprised to hear, given the other reasoning experiments I have mentioned thus far, that most subjects in the similarity experiment violate the symmetricality principle. For example, subjects rate North Korea as *more* similar to China than they rate China as similar to North Korea. Similarly, they say that penguins are more like robins than robins are like penguins. Subjects violate the symmetricality principle in a variety of domains; the phenomenon seems robust.

A straightforward reading of the similarity experiment is to say that it lends support to the irrationality thesis. Subjects ought to reason in accordance with the symmetricality principle but they fail to; humans therefore lack the symmetricality principle in our reasoning competence and we have more evidence for our irrationality. Amos Tversky, the psychologist who conducted this experiment, does not interpret the

[6] Amos Tversky, 'Features of Similarity', *Psychological Review*, 84 (1977), 327–52.

similarity experiments in this way. Rather, he argues that this experiment shows that similarity is not symmetrical and that the symmetricality principle is not a normative principle of reasoning. Tversky distinguishes between *psychological* similarity, which is not symmetrical, and *logical* similarity, which is. Using this distinction, we have the principle of psychological similarity in our reasoning competence while we lack the principle of logical similarity; further, the principle of psychological similarity is a normative principle of reasoning for us while logical similarity is not. In this case, when human reasoning competence and a presumed normative principle of reasoning diverge, experimenters reject the norm and say that the principle of reasoning that we use is in fact the normative principle. The no extra-human norm argument suggests that we should *always* adopt this strategy—which I call the *reject-the-norm strategy*—when our preconceived idea of what a norm of reasoning is diverges from our actual reasoning competence.

2.2. Not a Mere Reflection of the Reflective Equilibrium Argument

The no extra-human norms argument for the rationality thesis might seem similar to some of the arguments I have previously considered, in particular, the reflective equilibrium argument for the rationality thesis (discussed in Chapter 5). The reflective equilibrium argument tries to show that the same process is used to determine both what the normative principles of reasoning are and what the principles embodied in human reasoning competence are. The present argument has the same conclusion. The crucial difference between the present argument and the argument presented in Chapter 5 is that the reflective equilibrium argument embraces the standard picture of rationality and denies that human reasoning competence can diverge from the normative principles of reasoning (which, on the standard picture, are based on rules of logic, probability, and the like), while the argument under consideration here *rejects* the standard picture of rationality and takes the reasoning experiments as giving insight not just into human reasoning competence but also into the normative principles of reasoning. The reflective equilibrium argument says that the reasoning experiments give insight into the sorts of performance error we make but do not in any way undermine the fact that we are rational and that the principles of reasoning we follow stem from rules of logic, probability, and the like. In contrast, the no extra-human norms argument says that the norms just are what we have in our reasoning competence; if the (actual) norms do not match our preconceived notion of what the norms should be, so much the worse for our preconceived notions.

In Chapter 2, I argued that there is an important difference between the relationship of linguistic norms and linguistic competence, on the one hand, and the relationship of normative principles of reasoning and reasoning competence, namely, linguistic norms are indexed to linguistic competence while norms of reasoning do not seem indexed to reasoning competence. I said that perhaps some arguments will show that, contrary to our intuitions, the norms of reasoning *are* indexed to reasoning competence, but, short of such arguments, there seems to be this important difference between linguistics and the study of reasoning. In Chapter 5, I considered an argument to show that the norms of reasoning and human reasoning competence must match. If that argument succeeded, the important difference between linguistics and the study of reasoning would have evaporated. That argument failed. If the no extra-human norms argument is to succeed in overcoming the apparent asymmetry between the study of language and the study of reasoning, it will have to say more than what has been said so far. In what follows, I attempt to develop the present argument in greater detail.

2.3. The Human Finitary Predicament

As humans, we have only a finite amount of time and limited resources to devote to reasoning. Our reasoning is done in a brain of about the size of a small cantaloup and it has a finite number of neurons with finite space available for memory. Each of us will probably live for less than 100 years, a considerable portion of which will be spent sleeping. Further, we make decisions about all sorts of things very quickly. Given these limitations on human reasoning, which together constitute a *finitary predicament* for humans, we are not able to reason in accordance with what the standard picture of rationality says are the normative principles of reasoning.[7]

Consider, for example, the following principle of reasoning:

> CONSISTENCY PRESERVATION PRINCIPLE: Before adding a new belief to your set of beliefs, you should check to make sure that the candidate belief is compatible with each one of your other beliefs. If the candidate belief is compatible with all your other beliefs,

---

[7] Christopher Cherniak, *Minimal Rationality* (Cambridge, Mass.: MIT Press, 1986), discusses the finitary predicament in some detail.

then it may be added to your belief set; if not, you must either give up the belief that the candidate belief conflicts with or not add the candidate belief to your belief set.

On the standard picture of rationality, this principle seems to be a normative principle of reasoning; failing to follow it could well lead to rampant inconsistency, a disastrous result with respect to reasoning given that anything logically follows from an inconsistency.[8] If, however, you look at this principle from the perspective of the human finitary predicament, you get quite a different perspective. Without getting into the details of an account of what beliefs are, it seems that each one of us has some large but finite set of beliefs. Each one of these beliefs entails a large, possibly infinite, number of other beliefs. To check to see if some candidate belief is compatible with all of your beliefs, you would need to check each one of your beliefs to make sure that it is not logically equivalent to the negation of the candidate belief or anything entailed by the candidate belief. This task quickly explodes. A person who tried to follow the consistency preservation principle would never have enough time to acquire any new beliefs, not to mention to do anything else with her cognitive time and energy (such as figuring out where her next meal is coming from). Wasting all this time on checking the consistency of one's beliefs certainly does not sound like rational behaviour.

2.4. The Pragmatic Picture of Rationality

Without going into any further details of the human finitary predicament and its multifarious implications, I want to explain how this predicament is used as part of the no extra-human norms argument for the rationality thesis. The idea is that, because of our finitary predicament, humans could not possibly execute the principles of reasoning that are based on rules of logic, probability, and the like. It is clearly mistaken to say that we ought to reason in a way that we cannot reason; we therefore must reject the standard picture of rationality and replace

---

[8] As a proof that anything follows from a contradiction, Bertrand Russell offered the following proof that if $2 + 2 = 5$, then he is the Pope: 'If we're assuming that $2 + 2 = 5$, then certainly you'll agree that subtracting two from each side of the equation gives us $2 = 3$. Transposing, we have $3 = 2$ and subtracting one from each side of the equation gives us $2 = 1$. Thus, since the Pope and I are two people and $2 = 1$, then the Pope and I are one. Hence I'm the Pope.' I found the quotation in John Allen Paulos, *I Think, therefore I Laugh: An Alternative Approach to Philosophy* (New York: Columbia University Press, 1985), 20.

it with a picture of rationality that has normative principles of reasoning that are feasible given our finitary predicament.

But what is this *feasible* picture of rationality that is supposed to replace the standard picture of rationality? The answer associated with the no extra-human norms argument is a *pragmatic* one: humans are rational if we are *doing the best we can*, namely we are rational if the principles that we use for reasoning are the best we can use. Described in this way, the pragmatic picture is unclear. When I say that humans reason as best as we can, you might wonder, 'As best as we can *given what*?' Do we reason as best as we can given that we are mammals? Given that we are humans? Given that we have a brain about the size of a cantaloup? You also might wonder, 'As best we can *in terms of what*?' Do we reason as best as we can in terms of speed? In terms of preserving consistency? In terms of increasing our reproductive success?

Let us suppose that we can develop a sensible account of what it is for humans to reason as best as we can. The no extra-human norms argument against the irrationality thesis promises an argument that humans will come out as rational according to this account, even in light of the reasoning experiments. The idea is to combine the pragmatic picture of rationality with an *optimistic* picture of human reasoning competence according to which the principles of reasoning that we have in our reasoning competence are the best principles we can have. Together, the pragmatic picture of rationality and the optimistic view of human reasoning competence produce the following version of the no extra-human norms argument for the rationality thesis:

(1) For humans to be rational is for us to reason as best as we can (the pragmatic picture of rationality).

(2) Humans reason as best as we can (the optimistic picture of human reasoning competence).

(3) Therefore, humans are rational.

Suppose the argument for (1), the pragmatic account of rationality, succeeds due to the human finitary predicament; what remains is to assess the argument for the optimistic view of human reasoning competence.

One potential argument for the optimistic view is that we can only reason in accordance with the reasoning competence that we have, therefore reasoning in accordance with the principles that we do is in fact doing the best we can do. Take, for example, our behaviour on the conjunction experiment. In this experiment, humans systematically violate the conjunction principle. This is supposed to show that humans lack the conjunction principle in our reasoning competence. According to the optimistic view of human reasoning competence, reasoning in such a way that we violate the conjunction principle is reasoning as best as we can. But why is reasoning in violation of the conjunction principle reasoning as best as we can? The answer under consideration is that we cannot reason any better because we do not have the conjunction principle in our reasoning competence. This answer has got to be mistaken.

Consider the following example. Suppose that a school adopts the policy of giving a student an 'A' if she has done as best as she can on an exam. Consider Marvin, who correctly answers only 75 per cent of the questions on the exam. Marvin, however, has a learning disability and, as a result, he reads slowly. Given his reading skills, he was only able to read the first seventy-five questions on the exam in the allotted time; he simply left the remaining twenty-five questions blank because he did not have enough time to read them. It seems right to say that Marvin did the best he could on this exam, so he should get an 'A'. Consider Carolyn, who also correctly answers only 75 per cent of the questions on the exam. Carolyn, it should be noted, is having a difficult time with her family (say, her parents are getting divorced, her brother has a drug problem, and so on). As a result, she was unable to concentrate on studying. Given this, she too did as best as she could on the exam and she should get an 'A'. If we take *all* the factors that contribute both to each student's ability and to his or her performance on the exam, we will see that all of them did the best they could given the various factors. Regardless of how many questions she answered correctly, each student did the best she could and deserves an 'A'. Clearly this is a ridiculous grading system; in fact, it is not a grading system at all because no one actually gets evaluated.

The same sort of phenomenon is taking place when we combine the pragmatic picture of rationality with the optimistic view of human reasoning competence. If whatever way humans reason is the best we can do and being rational is reasoning the best we can, then human reasoning ability is not really being evaluated. Consider monkeys. They have a certain reasoning ability, although there are complex problems that humans can solve that monkeys cannot. Given their reasoning ability, monkeys are reasoning the best they can. If we accept the pragmatic picture of rationality, monkeys turn out to be rational. We would like to be able to evaluate the reasoning ability of monkeys, but the pragmatic picture of rationality coupled with the optimistic view of reasoning competence prevents us from doing so. Evaluation is impossible if we accept the pragmatic picture of rationality combined with an unquestioningly optimistic interpretation of actual practice. Just as a teacher is not evaluating a student who gets an 'A' under the school's policy of giving an 'A' to students who are doing the best they can, we are not evaluating human reasoning ability if we judge humans to be rational according to the pragmatic picture of rationality and the optimistic view of reasoning competence. We cannot adopt the optimistic view of reasoning competence if we adopt the pragmatic picture of rationality and we still hope to evaluate human reasoning ability.

Further, it seems that the reasoning experiments pose a challenge to the optimistic picture of reasoning competence. Simply put, it seems as if we *could* do better on some of the tasks involved in the reasoning experiments. Consider the conjunction experiments. Most subjects say Linda is more likely to be a bank teller and a feminist than she is to be a bank teller. This suggests that humans do not have the conjunction principle in our reasoning competence. The standard picture of rationality says that humans are irrational if we do not have the conjunction principle in our reasoning competence. The pragmatic picture of rationality says that we are rational if we are reasoning as best as we can. Reasoning without the conjunction principle is, on this picture, the best we can do. What we want is an account of why we cannot have the conjunction principle in our reasoning competence. Appeals to the human finitary predicament seem like hand-waving here. It is easy to see why we might not be able to follow the consistency preservation principle—it requires a huge amount of time to execute—but we do not have the same sort of account available for why we are unable to reason in accordance with the conjunction principle. Also, recall that some subjects in the conjunction experiment got the right answer and said that Linda is more likely to be a bank teller than she is to be a bank teller and a feminist. This does not prove that they have the conjunction principle in their reasoning competence (they could have some other principle but be making a performance error), but it does seem to suggest that it is possible to give the correct answer even given the limited reasoning abilities that humans have. The optimistic view of human reasoning competence seems in trouble.

Without the optimistic view of human reasoning, what is the fate of the no extra-human norms argument for the rationality thesis? Recall that the argument tries to show that there are no normative principles of reasoning independent of human reasoning competence. To do this, the argument has to reject the standard picture of rationality because, according to the standard picture of rationality, the normative principles of reasoning stem from rules of logic, probability, and the like, and they seem to do so independent of our reasoning capacities. Some *non*-standard picture of rationality must take the place of the standard one if the no extra-human norms argument is to succeed. A picture that is in some way linked to human reasoning ability holds the most promise for filling this role. For this reason, the pragmatic picture of rationality seems to be a good candidate for replacing the standard picture. The question is whether we can develop an argument for the rationality thesis that makes use of the pragmatic picture of rationality but that does not smuggle in the optimistic picture of reasoning competence.

2.5. *The Reject-the-Norm Strategy*

A friend of the no extra-human norms argument might recall the similarity experiment. In this experiment, when subjects failed to reason in accordance with the presumed norm—the symmetricality principle —Tversky rejected the norm in favour of the principle that subjects seemed to be following. If the reject-the-norm strategy is appropriate in the similarity experiment, why not apply it to all the other reasoning experiments in which subjects violate our preconceived notions about what the normative principles of reasoning are? Applying this strategy across the board would have the result of taking away the support that the irrationality thesis gets from the reasoning experiments. If an experiment showed that we reason in a way that diverges from the norm, then the norm would be rejected and replaced with the principle that we in fact use. The general application of the reject-the-norm strategy would ensure that the rationality thesis would not be undermined by empirical evidence of diverging from the norms. There are three general problems with the reject-the-norm strategy. First, some norms are not as easy to reject as the symmetricality principle. Second, it is not clear why the rejected norms should be replaced by the principles embodied in human reasoning competence. Third, the reject-the-norm strategy itself is in need of justification. I consider these three problems in what follows.

Are the similarity experiments paradigmatic of the reasoning experiments? The question is whether the strategy that seems appropriate with respect to the similarity experiments—the reject-the-norm strategy— can be applied to other experiments. Consider first the conjunction experiment. The norm in question in this experiment is that a person should assign a lower probability to the possibility that the distinct events A and B will both occur than she assigns to the possibility that A will occur (the conjunction principle). Subjects violate this principle by saying that some pair of events A and B are more likely to occur than just that A will occur. In light of this, why not just reject the norm and deny that the conjunction principle is a norm? As discussed in Chapter 3, if a person ignores the conjunction principle with respect to her probability judgements, and is willing to make bets based on these judgements, then she will be susceptible to a Dutch book; in other words, a person who violates the conjunction principle in deciding how likely certain events are will lose all her money if she bets on the basis of these judgements. Further, there is no obvious parallel to Tversky's distinction between psychological similarity (which is not symmetrical) and logical similarity (which is). A distinction between psychological likelihood (for which the conjunction principle does not hold) and (say) physical likelihood (for which the conjunction principle holds) might seem an acceptable move, but this would be to admit that humans are 'Dutch-bookable', and, hence, it is just another way of saying that humans are irrational. However the details of what it is to be rational are filled in, it had better be the case that being rational does not allow one to be in a position where one can be Dutch-booked; a rational person should not be open to being duped by a shrewd bookie. The point is that the reject-the-norm strategy does not seem to work in the case of the conjunction experiments.

A similar though perhaps more serious problem would occur if the reject-the-norm strategy is applied to the selection task. Subjects in this experiment seem to accept that a conditional is not falsified if its antecedent is true and its consequent is false. If this is accepted as a norm, then all of logic tumbles. For example, the conditional **if** p, **then** q is equivalent to **not-**p **or** q, which is falsified if both p and **not-**q are true. If the reject-the-norm strategy were adopted in light of the results of the selection task by denying that a conditional is falsified when its antecedent is true and its consequent false, then either the equivalence between **if** p, **then** q and **not-**p **or** q would have to be denied or the instances that would falsify **not-**p **or** q would have to be changed. In short, this single change would cause a domino effect in logic. Further, it is not clear that a consistent system of logic would result if normative principles of reasoning were derived from actual human behaviour. The reject-the-norm strategy will not work as a way of diffusing the support that the reasoning experiments seem to provide for the irrationality thesis in both the selection task and the conjunction experiment.

Even if the reject-the-norm strategy could be sensibly applied to all of the reasoning experiments, why should the norms in each instance be replaced by the principles that are embodied in our reasoning competence? Consider the following situation. Suppose that there is a certain context in which the rules of logic suggest that we should reason in accordance with some principle N. Further, suppose that N would take too long for creatures with brains about the size of a cantaloup to follow when reasoning in real time. In this context, suppose humans in fact reason in accordance with some principle P. Of course, there are other possible principles that apply to this context as well. Some of these principles are, like N, not implementable on brains the size of ours. Some of these principles do not work very well to attain whatever our goal is in this context. For the no extra-human norms argument for the rationality thesis to succeed, N (the principle that is the norm according to the standard picture of rationality) needs to be replaced as the normative principle of reasoning in this context by P (the principle that we have in our reasoning competence). The reject-the-norm strategy does not, however, guarantee that this substitution will take place. In fact, some other principle Q, which is *not* in our reasoning competence, but which *is* implementable on brains of our size and is better than P for attaining our goal(s) in this context, might replace N as the normative principle of reasoning. If Q, not P, replaces N as the norm, then humans would still not reason in accordance with the normative principles of reasoning and the argument for the rationality thesis would still fail to go through. In general, even if we reject the principle of reasoning that would be the norm according to the standard picture of rationality, we are not obliged to see a principle of reasoning that we have in our reasoning competence as the normative principle of reasoning; there may well be some other principle of reasoning that should count as the norm even though we do not have it in our reasoning competence. This scenario is perfectly plausible but it is not compatible with the no extra-human norms argument according to which our reasoning competence constitutes the normative principles of reasoning. Given this, the no extra-human norms argument seems in further trouble. This does not mean that we have to give up on the pragmatic picture of rationality; it just means that accepting this picture does not produce an argument for the rationality thesis.

Finally, even if we reject the standard picture of rationality and replace it with the pragmatic picture, there is still the further problem that I considered at the end of the last section, namely, we might be able to learn principles that are not in our reasoning competence and follow them on some occasions. For example, even if we lack the conjunction principle in our reasoning competence, we might learn to detect certain situations in which it should be invoked and become pretty good at doing so. According to the no extra-human norms argument, we have no ground from which to compare a principle of reasoning that is not in our reasoning competence with one that is; all we can say is that a principle is not part of our reasoning competence, and therefore it is not rational for us to reason in accordance with it. On any reading of what doing the best we can do means, this does not make sense.

The no extra-human norms argument attempts to undermine the standard picture of rationality and replace it with the pragmatic picture, according to which the normative principles of reasoning are the best possible principles for humans. For this to succeed as an argument for the rationality thesis, the principles in our reasoning competence need to be the best principles we could possibly have. Above I argued that one initially appealing way of reading what it means to reason as best as we can actually prevents the possibility of evaluation and thus eliminates the normativity of rationality. In so far as a more sophisticated version of the pragmatic picture of rationality can be worked out (that is, in so far as we can develop an account of what it is to reason as best as we can), an argument that the way we in fact reason is the best we can do is still required. The no extra-human norms argument thus does not undermine the standard picture of rationality in a fashion that establishes the rationality thesis.

3. No General Norms

The third argument against the rationality thesis is that there are no general normative principles of reasoning. According to this argument, what counts as rational is indexed to each human being, so what counts as rational is (at least potentially) different for each human being. If this is right, no experiment can show that humans are violating the normative principles of reasoning because each of us is always reasoning in accordance with the principles in her reasoning competence and the principles in a person's reasoning competence just are the normative principles of reasoning for her. The reasoning experiments give us access to the principles that individuals have in their reasoning competence, and, in turn, give us access to what the norms are for them. According to this view, humans are rational, and human rationality is a conceptual question, though it is an empirical question what it means to be rational for each individual.[9]

Why should we agree that what is rational is indexed to each individual? In the last section, I presented the facts of the human finitary predicament. Because of the limited time, energy, and brain space that we have, there are certain principles of reasoning we cannot follow. In the previous section, I suggested that some principles of reasoning that are normative principles of reasoning according to the standard picture do seem implementable on our brains in a reasonable amount of time. Still, there are some normative principles of reasoning that we may not be able to implement (for example, the principle of consistency preservation) and this may be enough to reject the standard picture of rationality. Once the standard picture of rationality has been rejected, we need some other way to assess human reasoning ability. The no general human norms argument suggests that the very idea of looking for normative principles of reasoning that apply to all humans is mistaken. Once we reject the standard picture of rationality, we should see that there are no normative principles that apply across all humans. Rather, given the limitations imposed on us in virtue of the finitary predicament, there are norms associated with each individual in virtue of her reasoning abilities and her individual preferences. I call this the *relativistic picture of rationality*. For example, a mathematician might require a different set of principles of reasoning to go about her line of work than a gardener needs to go about his—precise logical reasoning will probably be more important to the mathematician than the gardener. The mathematician will thus want to devote more of her cognitive resources to principles that assure mathematical accuracy than the gardener would. The gardener, in turn, could apply the cognitive resources he saves by not aiming for mathematical precision to other cognitive tasks. The mathematician who, rather than allotting her cognitive resources to maximizing reasoning precision, allotted them in a way that would befit a gardener would be irrational. The relativistic picture of rationality is still normative, but the norms are indexed to individual interests and individual reasoning abilities. The relativistic

---

[9] Stephen Stich, *The Fragmentation of Reason* (Cambridge, Mass.: MIT Press, 1990), 154, attributes to Don Norman an argument with affinities to the one described here.

picture of rationality says that each of us ought to reason in accordance with the particular normative principles suited to our individual abilities and preferences.

This is a bit of a simplification. People cannot choose their reasoning competence according to their needs. Compare how I might choose which car to buy. I would consider the sort of driving I plan to do, the number of passengers I will typically have, the amount of cargo room I will need, the fuel efficiency of the car, its cost, and many other factors. By weighing these factors, I can choose the car that is best suited for me. People do not choose their reasoning competence in this fashion; we do not choose our reasoning competence at all. Some features of human reasoning competence are probably innate (see my discussion in Chapter 2) and you do not get to choose your innate traits. In fact, you do not even get to choose those parts of your reasoning competence that are not innate. This is partly because the principles that I reason in accordance with are unconscious and partly because I do not typically know which principles are in fact the best for my interests and circumstances. In fact, the suggestion that someone decides to become a mathematician and then selects the appropriate reasoning competence to go with her career choice has the story backwards. That someone has a certain reasoning competence has more impact on what sort of reasoning she will do (for example, the mathematical sort or the gardening sort) than the other way around.

On one way of looking at it, the relativistic picture of rationality is a version of the pragmatic picture of rationality. Recall that the pragmatic picture of rationality says that humans are rational if we reason as best as we can. For the purpose of the no extra-human norms argument, I assumed that we could make sense of the idea of there being some principles of reasoning that are the best for all humans given the fact that we share the same reasoning competence, the same finitary predicament, and roughly the same environment. If, however, we focus on the different abilities and interests that individuals have, we might think that the best a person can do varies from individual to individual. In this way, the relativistic picture of rationality is a version of the pragmatic one.

There is one particular advantage of the relativistic picture of rationality compared to the pragmatic picture of rationality as an argument for the rationality thesis. Recall from Section 2 that one problem with the pragmatic picture of rationality is that there is the possibility that the best feasible principle for humans might not be a principle that is

in human reasoning competence; even if the standard picture of rationality is replaced with the pragmatic picture of rationality, this does not
establish the rationality thesis, because the best principle might not be
a principle that is in our reasoning competence. This possibility might
be blocked in the case of the relativist picture of rationality. When
talking about the best possible principle for humans, you have to abstract
from the particulars of the actual reasoning competence of individuals
in order to allow for the possibility of evaluation. Failure to do this leaves
the account open to the charge that monkeys are just as rational as
humans because monkeys reason as best as they can given their capacities
and interests. The thought behind the no general norms argument is that
by focusing on the capacities and interests of individuals rather than on
those of humans in general, we might be able to avoid the possibility
that the best principles of reasoning a person can follow are not contained
in her reasoning competence.

The problem with this suggestion is that in moving away from the
possibility that the best principle for me is not available to me, we
move closer to the problem of eliminating the possibility of evaluation.
The relativistic picture of rationality seems to be committed to saying
that *whatever* principles of reasoning I follow are the best I can follow
given my interests and capacities. This, as I argued above in Section 2,
eliminates the possibility of evaluating people's reasoning capacities.
The objection is the same as the one raised with respect to the pragmatic picture of rationality except that the present objection is at the
level of the individual human rather than at the level of all humans. The
relativistic picture of rationality faces the same problem that the pragmatic picture of rationality faces when brought into the service of an
argument for the rationality thesis—if the norms are linked to actual
competence, then evaluation becomes impossible. This is not surprising
given that the relativistic picture of rationality is a version of the pragmatic one.

A friend of the no general norms argument might deny this charge
by saying that the relativistic picture of rationality is not committed to
the idea that each individual reasons in accordance with the normative
principles of reasoning that are associated with her in virtue of her
interests and capacities. I am not sure how the details of such a view
would be worked out—it seems difficult to have a principled procedure
for indexing norms to each individual that leaves open the possibility
that an individual might not reason in accordance with the normative
principles that are associated with her. Assuming, however, that such

an account could be developed, this does not produce an argument for the rationality thesis. Recall that the no general norms argument is supposed to be an argument for the view that humans are rational that works by replacing the standard picture of rationality with some other picture. The relativistic picture of rationality seemed a plausible picture of rationality on which to base such an argument for the rationality thesis. The relativistic picture seems a plausible candidate, however, only because it seems to link the normative principles of reasoning for an individual to that individual's actual reasoning competence. This virtue of the relativistic picture of rationality has been shown to be only apparent. A version of the relativistic picture of rationality that allows for an individual to fail to reason in accordance with the principles of reasoning that would be the best for her would be of no help in establishing the rationality thesis. The no general norms argument for the rationality thesis thus fails.

4. Assessing the Damage to the Standard Picture

In Sections 1–3 of this chapter, I considered whether friends of the rationality thesis could defend their view by arguing against the standard picture of rationality. I have argued that this approach has little promise. In the process of considering the various arguments for the rationality thesis, I have considered the human finitary predicament and suggested that this might count against the standard picture of rationality. Even if rejecting the standard picture of rationality does not produce an argument for the rationality thesis, arguments against this picture warrant attention; if the standard picture is mistaken, then perhaps the debate between the rationality thesis and the irrationality thesis has been improperly characterized and perhaps such arguments will shed new light on the nature of the issues between them. In this section, I begin by reviewing the virtues of the standard picture of rationality. I will then consider the extent to which the human finitary predicament counts against the standard picture. I also consider a more general worry about the standard picture, namely that the only reason we have for embracing this account of what the normative principles of reasoning are is that these principles are favoured in our culture, our language, and our way of thinking; following Stephen Stich, I call this criticism of the standard picture *epistemic chauvinism.*

4.1. The Virtues

The main virtues of the standard picture of rationality are that it accounts for the (seeming) normativity of rationality, that it is intuitively plausible and simple, and that it coheres well with such well-established disciplines as logic and mathematics. I will say something about each of these interconnected virtues in turn.

The standard picture of rationality says that there are normative principles of reasoning, that these principles apply to all humans, and that the principles stem from rules of logic, probability, and the like. One obvious virtue of this account is that it explains why rationality is, or at least seems to be, a normative concept. This is in contrast to the *nihilistic picture of rationality*, according to which *any* principle of reasoning is as good as any other. The virtue of normativity does not, on its own, distinguish the standard picture from the relativistic or the pragmatic picture of rationality. Both of these rival pictures are normative as well, at least in the versions of them that allow for the possibility of evaluation (those versions of them that do not allow for evaluation are not normative, so they fail to have the first virtue that the standard picture does). The pragmatic picture says we ought to reason in accordance with those principles that are the best principles we can use and the relativistic picture says each of us ought to reason in accordance with those principles that are suited to each of our interests and are available to us given our individual capacities.

A further virtue of the standard picture is that it fits with our intuitions about the way rationality is normative. Intuitively, we expect that an account of rationality will provide us with a detailed account of how everyone ought to reason. The account should have universal applicability and should be fairly specific, that is, it should provide clear guidance on which principles we should follow. The standard picture does both. The pragmatic picture has universal applicability (at least according to non-individualistic versions of it) but, in so far as it allows for the possibility of evaluation, it does not provide much guidance on which principles of reasoning each individual should follow. The relativistic picture of rationality does not have universal applicability and does not provide any specific details of which principles of reasoning we should follow.

Finally, the standard picture has the virtue of cohering with well-established domains of knowledge, namely logic and mathematics. This coherence holds because, according to the standard picture of rationality, normative principles of reasoning can be 'read off' rules of logic, probability, and the like. It is a good thing when our preferred theories in different realms of knowledge cohere; coherence provides the theories with mutual support. For example, when our preferred theory of chemistry fits nicely with our preferred theory of physics, this suggests that both theories are on the right track. Given that logic, probability theory, and the like are firmly established, it will be a virtue of an account of rationality that it coheres with these theories. This is not to say that the pragmatic picture or the relativistic picture conflicts with logic or probability. None of these accounts, however, is as intimately connected with logic, probability, and the like in the way that the standard picture of rationality is.

4.2. The Vices

4.2.1. The Human Finitary Predicament Revisited

Although there is quite a lot to be said in favour of the standard picture of rationality, there are some serious objections that can be raised against it. The first objection emerged in previous sections of this chapter: the human finitary predicament makes it impossible for us to reason in accordance with many of the principles recommended by the standard picture. For example, according to the standard picture of rationality, the consistency preservation principle is a normative principle of reasoning, but, as I have sketched above, humans cannot in fact follow this principle because of the finitary predicament; because it is a mistake to say that one ought to do something that one cannot do, the standard picture of rationality must be wrong. There are two responses to this argument against the standard picture that are worth considering.

First, one might point out that only some of the principles of reasoning that are, according to the standard picture, normative ones seem to face implementation problems in light of our finitary predicament. The principles that subjects seem to violate in the reasoning experiments—for example, the conjunction principle—seem, at first glance, reasonable candidates for implementation on human brains in real time. Following the conjunction principle would not lead to the computational explosion that following the consistency preservation principle would. Additionally, a few of the subjects in the reasoning experiments do give the correct (according to the standard picture) response. This does not prove that they are reasoning in accordance with the relevant norms, but it does suggest that it would be computationally possible for humans to do so.

These considerations are helpful if one is looking to block arguments for the rationality thesis that make use of the human finitary predicament. Such arguments suggest, on the one hand, that it is possible for people to reason in accordance with principles like the conjunction principle, but, on the other hand, they suggest, in combination with the evidence of the reasoning experiments, that humans are not, in fact, reasoning in accordance with such principles. The observation that many principles of reasoning do seem computationally possible for humans even in light of our finitary predicament thus weakens arguments for the rationality thesis that proceed by attempting to discredit the standard picture of rationality (for example, the no extra-human norms argument and the no general norms argument). Here, however, I am trying to defend the standard picture against the charge that it recommends that we should reason using principles that we cannot possibly use. Given this, the charge that *some* of the principles that the picture says are norms cannot be norms is enough to pose a serious objection to the standard picture of rationality, even if this charge does not directly lead to an argument for the rationality thesis.

Another reply to the finitary predicament objection to the standard picture of rationality draws on linguistic theory. According to linguistic theory, all sentences of the form

$$(\text{If})^n \text{ snow is white (then grass is green)}^n$$

are grammatical when n is greater than or equal to zero.[10] There are an infinite number of sentences of this form, namely:

$n = 0$: Snow is white.
$n = 1$: If snow is white then grass is green.
$n = 2$: If if snow is white then grass is green then grass is green.
$n = 3$: If if if snow is white then grass is, green then grass is green then grass is green.

. . .

Nearly all of these sentences would be judged ungrammatical by English speakers. In fact, only 'Snow is white', 'If snow is white then grass is green', and *maybe* (though probably not) 'If if snow is white then grass

---

[10] The example comes from Noam Chomsky, *Syntactic Structures* (The Hague: Mouton, 1957), 23–5.

is green then grass is green' would be accepted. Most linguists, however, claim that all of the strings generated by this rule are grammatical and should count as part of the linguistic competence of English speakers. That sentences generated by this rule when n is greater than two are not accepted by English speakers is supposed to be due to the non-linguistic fact that humans have limited computational space for sentence processing. If I judge that the sentence which results from the above linguistic rule when n is equal to three is ungrammatical, I would be seen as making a performance error rather than a competence error because, according to linguistic theory, the mistake is not due to my failing to have the right rule in my linguistic competence, but rather is due to my not having enough memory to apply it. Friends of the standard picture of rationality might try to make a similar move. They might admit that one cannot always and fully apply the consistency preservation principle because this would involve a huge amount of computational time and energy, more time and energy˙than a person could possibly devote to the matter of whether to add a new belief to her belief set. They could proceed to say that this is not a problem with human reasoning competence. It is, rather, a problem with the memory capacities and the time constraints that each of us has available for the purpose of applying a principle in our reasoning competence (namely, the consistency preservation principle). Given memory and time constraints, the fact that we sometimes fail to apply the consistency preservation principle does not show that this principle is not a normative principle of reasoning for humans. This move is a perfectly general one: for any principle ,that it seems we cannot implement due to the finitary pre-dicament, one could argue that the principle is in fact a norm and that it is possible for humans to have this principle in our reasoning competence while admitting that it is not always possible to reason in accordance with this principle due to the finitary predicament.

I am not convinced that this is a completely plausible response to the finitary predicament argument. In the case of the consistency principle, it seems that we never apply this principle; at best, we test a candidate belief to see if it is consistent with a subset of our current beliefs, typically beliefs that seem in some sense related to the candidate belief. Does it make sense to say that I have the consistency preservation principle in my reasoning competence even if I can never actually apply it when I reason (because it would take too much time and memory)? In the case of the linguistic rule discussed above, we make linguistic judgements that accord with the rule in a few simple cases (when n equals zero, one, and perhaps two); the same is not true for the consistency preservation principle. There is a deeper point to make here as well.

The suggestion under consideration is that the competence–performance distinction, a distinction that we are used to invoking with respect to describing reasoning competence, also comes into play with respect to normative matters involving reasoning. Given this parallel, it is useful to recall from Chapter 2, Section 2.3 and Chapter 3, Section 3.1 that simply invoking the competence–performance distinction does not show that what we think are the normative principles of reasoning are actually embodied in reasoning competence. Similarly, simply noting that a principle can be a normative principle of reasoning even if performance factors (broadly construed to include memory size and time constraints) make it impossible to follow it does not show that the principle in question is a norm, only that its being a norm is consistent with the evidence we have. To take the consistency preservation principle as an example, just because it is *possible* for this principle to be a normative principle of reasoning, even though the principle is computationally inaccessible to humans, does not mean that the consistency preservation principle *is* a norm. This leads nicely to the second objection to the standard picture of rationality.

4.2.2. Epistemic Chauvinism

In the last chapter of his book *The Fragmentation of Reason*, Stephen Stich writes:

If the principal reason that our evaluative epistemic concepts, concepts like rationality and justification, stand out from the crowd is that they happen to be the evaluative notions passed on by our language and culture, it's hard to see why anyone but an epistemic chauvinist would much care whether his cognitive processes were sanctioned by those notions.[11]

Stich's idea applies directly to the standard picture of rationality. The standard picture of rationality says that our intuitions about the normative principles of reasoning are basically correct; the principles of reasoning that we think are the norms—principles that stem from logic, probability theory, and the like—are in fact the norms. But why should we trust our intuitions about the normative principles of reasoning? What reasons do we have for thinking that the best source of insight

---

[11] Stich, *The Fragmentation of Reason*, 130. The objection is developed at length ibid., chs. 4 and 5, but not in ways that I necessarily agree with.

into what the normative principles are is our intuitions about what the normative principles are? Our preferences for the principles that stem from logic, probability, and the like are, according to this objection, the result of epistemic chauvinism. Given that our intuitions are among the strongest arguments for the standard picture, epistemic chauvinism is a serious objection to this picture. This fits with the point that I made at the end of the discussion of the previous objection to the standard picture: proving that a principle *might* be a norm does not show that it is a norm. Both objections challenge friends of the standard picture of rationality to spell out why this picture is. true, why it is right about which principles are the norms. Friends of the standard picture of rationality need to go beyond mere possibility and the support of our intuitions to give an explanation of why the normative principles of reasoning are what this picture claims they are.

The friend of the standard picture might try to reply to this objection with arguments that intuitions are all that are relevant to determining the normative principles of reasoning. Some arguments that I made in Chapter 5 apply here: intuitions alone will not lead us to the normative principles of reasoning. Untutored intuitions are notoriously unreliable and even considered intuitions could easily fail to endorse principles that are in fact normative principles. A more sophisticated account of why the standard picture of rationality is the right picture needs to be provided.

Another reply in defence of the standard picture of rationality is to point out that rejecting the standard picture leads to such undesirable results as rampant inconsistency, Dutch-bookability, and so forth. Any picture of rationality that rejects the conjunction principle, the modus ponens principle, and similar principles of reasoning—principles of reasoning that the standard picture says are norms—is sure to run into profoundly problematic results such as those mentioned. These results are not just bad in that they fail to fit with our intuitions; they are bad in that they seem to threaten the very practice of reasoning. What is left of reasoning if we reject modus ponens and allow, for example, that if you believe A and you believe **if** A, **then** B, you can believe that **not-B**, or if we make bets that we will always lose because we are open to Dutch books (which is what will result if rules of probability are systematically violated)? This is supposed to answer the request for a more detailed defence of the standard picture: the standard picture is the only picture of rationality that allows for the possibility of reasoning as we know it.

I want to consider briefly two replies to this defence of the standard picture of rationality. First, it is certainly not the case that all the principles of reasoning endorsed by the standard picture are required for reasoning to occur. Some principles that the standard picture says are norms—for example, the symmetricality principle—are not crucial to reasoning. As my discussion of the similarity experiment (Section 2.1, above) shows, it is perfectly consistent with the practice of reasoning not to reason in accordance with the symmetricality principle.

Second, one might ask whether *some* inconsistency (or Dutch-bookability) is as bad as the above defence of the standard picture suggests. Given the human finitary predicament, some inconsistencies are going to infiltrate our belief set. Recall that, due to the finitary predicament, we are unable to apply the consistency preservation principle. This means, for example, that I will sometimes acquire a belief that is inconsistent with other beliefs I have. If inconsistency is already such a live possibility, the threat of some additional inconsistency is not as worrisome. Given that humans must reason in the context of the finitary predicament, goals such as perfect consistency, complete avoidance of Dutch books, and so forth become less important.

These two replies suggest that the standard picture of rationality is still vulnerable to the objections based on the human finitary predicament and epistemic chauvinism. What seems needed is a picture of rationality with the virtues of the standard picture but that incorporates some response to these two objections. In the next section, I attempt to present such a picture.

5. The Naturalized Picture of Rationality

In Chapter 5, Section 3, I argued that wide reflective equilibrium is a quite plausible account of how we can determine what the normative principles of reasoning are. According to this theory, a principle is a normative principle of reasoning if it results from balancing—that is, bringing into agreement—(1) our first-order judgements about what counts as good reasoning, (2) our more general intuitions about what are the abstract principles of good reasoning, (3) various philosophical theories, and, possibly, (4) various scientific theories (see Chapter 5, Section 5). In this section, I will argue that wide reflective equilibrium with scientific evidence included in the input is at the core of a picture of rationality that is the best alternative to the standard picture of rationality.

Reflective equilibrium is an account of justification that says a set of beliefs and a set of abstract rules that underlie them are justified if the rules provide a coherent and explicit characterization of those judgements. My belief that '2 + 2 = 4' is justified against the background of the set of other first-order mathematical judgements ('1 + 1 = 2', '4 − 2 = 2', and so on) and the set of abstract mathematical rules that define number, addition, and so forth (for example, Peano's axioms of arithmetic). Wide (as opposed to narrow) reflective equilibrium adds general philosophical theories to the considerations that need to be brought into balance with the set of beliefs and rules. In the case of mathematics, theories of number, mathematical knowledge, and perhaps theories of truth and meaning would be among the philosophical theories that are included. With respect to the principles of reasoning, the idea—introduced and defended at length in Chapter 5, Section 3—is that the normative principles of reasoning come from a process of bringing into agreement through critical reflection our first-order beliefs about what counts as good reasoning, our intuitions about what the normative principles of reasoning are, and general philosophical theories.

In Chapter 5, Section 5, while assessing the reflective equilibrium argument for the rationality thesis, I considered a modification to the wide reflective equilibrium account of the normative principles of reasoning whereby scientific evidence would be included as part of the input into the balancing process that is supposed to justify principles of reasoning. At the time, I argued that the inclusion of scientific evidence would be bad news for the reflective equilibrium argument for the rationality thesis because the very evidence that would be most relevant would come from the reasoning experiments and that evidence seems to count *against* the rationality thesis rather than in favour of it. At present, I am not considering an argument for the rationality thesis, but rather am considering an alternative to the standard picture of rationality. Here, I will argue that including scientific evidence as input to the wide reflective equilibrium process of justifying the normative principles of reasoning is useful; including it produces a picture of rationality that preserves the virtues of the standard picture while addressing the two objections I raised against it. I call the picture of reasoning that results the *naturalized picture of rationality*. The naturalized picture of rationality says that there are normative principles of reasoning, that they apply to all humans, and that these principles come from a process of wide reflective equilibrium that balances our first-order judgements about what counts as good reasoning, our more general intuitions about what the normative principles of reasoning are, and various philosophical and scientific theories. In the remainder of this section I first show that this view takes the human finitary predicament and the charge of epistemic chauvinism into consideration and I then show that this view preserves the virtues of the standard picture of rationality.

5.1. Why the Naturalized Picture is Better than the Standard One

Above I argued that a principle should not be a normative principle of reasoning for humans if we are unable to reason in accordance with it. Some candidate principles of reasoning are not implementable on brains like ours given the amount of time we take to reason. Some principles that are norms according to the standard picture of rationality might be computationally inaccessible to us. This is the objection to the standard picture that arises from the human finitary predicament. The naturalized picture of rationality avoids this objection by taking into consideration scientific evidence about humans that bears on which principles of reasoning are computationally accessible to us. This will include: evidence about the neurological structure of the human brain and the capacities that the brain has in virtue of this structure; evolutionary evidence about the circumstances under which our reasoning competence evolved that will suggest what sorts of innate capacity we are likely to have; and evidence from computational theory about the sorts of memory and time constraint our brains impose.[12] Given that this sort of evidence is taken into consideration, principles of reasoning that are deemed norms by the naturalized picture of rationality will be feasible for us given the human finitary predicament.

There is a potential worry that arises from the fact that the naturalized picture of rationality takes scientific evidence into consideration. Recall from Section 2 of this chapter that if too many factors affecting a person's actual reasoning behaviour are taken into consideration, the possibility of evaluating her reasoning behaviour disappears. If all the neurological, evolutionary, and computational evidence (plus the other relevant scientific evidence) is included as part of determining what the normative principles of reasoning are, the worry is that only those principles of reasoning that humans have in our reasoning competence will count as normative principles of reasoning. While we do not want to foreclose the possibility that the principles in our reasoning competence will match the normative principles of reasoning (that is, to

---

[12] See Ch. 5, Sect. 4.3 for a discussion related to the present one.

foreclose the possibility that the rationality thesis is true), the naturalized picture of rationality should not *entail* the truth of this possibility.

While this worry is interesting, it is not well founded. Scientific
evidence is only one of many inputs to wide reflective equilibrium.
Such evidence will be brought into agreement with philosophical considerations, with our intuitions about what counts as good reasoning,
and with our intuitions about what general principles underlie these
first-order intuitions about what counts as good reasoning. These intuitive considerations—considerations that, on their own, would favour
the standard picture of rationality—will ensure that the normative principles of reasoning will not simply be read off scientific evidence about
our reasoning competence. Consider the following example. Suppose
that scientific evidence shows that humans have an 'inferential blind
spot',[13] namely that there are some specific inferences we cannot make
in certain contexts. Suppose, for example, that scientific evidence
shows that, while humans typically reason in accordance with the conjunction principle, in contexts involving bank tellers, we fail to do so.
According to the naturalized picture of rationality, general philosophical and other theoretical considerations could lead us to embrace the
conjunction principle as a normative principle of reasoning in spite of
the fact that we have a context-dependent principle in our reasoning
competence. This shows that, according to the naturalized picture of
rationality, we can embrace a principle as a norm even if it is not in
our reasoning competence. Given this, the naturalized picture of rationality does not undermine the possibility of evaluating human reasoning
behaviour.

The other objection to the standard picture of rationality is that it is
guilty of epistemic chauvinism, namely, that it gives undue weight to
our intuitions about what is rational, intuitions that may be grounded
in our culture, our language, and so forth. The naturalized picture of
rationality does give some weight to our intuitions about rationality,
but our intuitions are being brought into balance with philosophical
theories and scientific evidence. Our intuitions are continually being
evaluated, re-evaluated, and modified in light of these considerations.
Given this, whatever epistemic chauvinism is initially present in our
intuitions about rationality is likely to be cancelled out by considerations that are not chauvinistic, namely philosophical and scientific

---

[13] For a general and detailed philosophical discussion of blind spots, see Roy Sorensen,
Blindspots (Oxford: Oxford University Press, 1988).

considerations. It is possible that these considerations are chauvinistic too—science and philosophy might be biased because they give undue weight to our 'local' intuitions. This is a possibility that we should take seriously, but full consideration of it is beyond the scope of the present project. For now, suffice it to say that since critical reflection, evidence, and argumentation are central parts of both philosophy and science, epistemic chauvinism is likely to be discovered and weeded out through the wide reflective equilibrium process involved in the naturalized picture of rationality. Note that my reply to the way that the naturalized picture of reasoning is subject to epistemic chauvinism parallels my reply to the objection that the naturalized picture of rationality makes it impossible to evaluate a person's reasoning ability. According to the naturalized picture of rationality, neither scientific evidence nor our intuitions about reasoning play the primary role in determining the normative principles of reasoning. Both play a significant role, but neither on its own trumps the other.

A comparison with mathematics would be useful at this point. When I come to believe a mathematical theorem because I have seen a mathematical proof of it, why am I now justified in believing in this theorem? Presumably, I am justified in believing this theorem because the methods of proof have themselves been justified. But why am I justified in believing in the meta-proofs, namely, the proofs that have been used to justify the methods for justifying theorems? Presumably, I am so justified because our first-order mathematical intuitions have been brought into balance with more general mathematical principles as well as with various philosophical theories and, perhaps, with various scientific theories (for example, some people think that relativity theory provides evidence that non-Euclidean geometry is true). Whatever biases were in our first-order mathematical intuitions are cancelled out by the balancing process; that is, the theoretical, philosophical, and, per-haps, scientific input to the reflective equilibrium process ensure that any mistakes in our original intuitions will be rejected. The same sort of cancelling out of biases (but with greater weight on scientific input) will occur as part of the wide reflective equilibrium process involved in naturalizing rationality and should take care of whatever epistemic chauvinism is involved in our first-order intuitions about what counts as good reasoning.

The naturalized picture of rationality thus takes into consideration both objections to the standard picture of rationality. In addition, it has the virtues of the standard picture. Recall that the virtues of the standard picture were that it is normative, intuitive, and it coheres with well-established theories in other realms. First, then, the naturalized picture of rationality is normative. It provides an account of which principles of reasoning we ought to follow—we ought to follow those principles of reasoning that are in wide reflective equilibrium. Second, it fits with our intuitions about the way that rationality is normative, namely it provides an account of how everyone ought to reason. Finally, the naturalized picture of rationality coheres with logic, probability, and the like—although in a different way from that in which the standard picture of rationality coheres with them—as well as with scientific evidence. The standard picture of rationality coheres with logic, probability, and the like, because the standard picture basically 'converts' rules of logic, probability, and the like into principles of reasoning. For example, according to the standard picture of rationality, the rule of logic that says A and **if** A, **then** B together entail B (modus ponens) gives rise to the principle of reasoning that says if you believe A and you believe **if** A, **then** B, you should believe B (the modus ponens principle). The naturalized picture of rationality does not make such a simple conversion. It coheres with logic, probability, and the like, because these are included in the input to the wide reflective equilibrium process involved in the naturalized picture. This means, for example, that modus ponens will be part of the input to the reflective equilibrium process that produces the normative principles of reasoning, but it does not guarantee that the modus ponens principle will be among the principles that the naturalized picture of rationality endorses as norms. The modus ponens principle might conflict with some well-supported philosophical theory or be computationally inaccessible for humans (although both of these possibilities seem unlikely), in which case it might not turn out to be a normative principle of reasoning according to the naturalized picture. The naturalized picture of rationality thus does cohere with logic and mathematics, but not in the same way that the standard picture does. Additionally, unlike the standard picture, the naturalized picture coheres with scientific theories as well. Coherence with a wider set of theories is another advantage that the naturalized picture has over the standard one.

5.2. *Objections*

I now turn my attention to some objections to the naturalized picture of rationality. The first objection concerns the amount of detail provided by it. The standard picture of rationality has the virtue of saying exactly what (at least some of) the norms of reasoning are (for example, the modus ponens principle and the conjunction principle). All I have said specifically about the principles that the naturalized picture would sanction is that it might not sanction the modus ponens principle if this principle conflicted with an established philosophical or scientific theory. But this hardly provides an account of what the normative principles are according to the naturalized picture. 'Where's the beef?', a critic of the naturalized picture might justifiably ask.

Such a critic has a point. The naturalized picture of rationality is short on the specific details of what the normative principles of reasoning are. This is not, however, a serious objection. The naturalized picture is connected to the wide reflective equilibrium account of justification. A feature of this account is that it describes the *process* that produces justification but not the *principles* that will be justified. In order to determine what the normative principles of reasoning are according to the naturalized picture of rationality, one has actually to go through the wide reflective equilibrium process. To look at the description of the wide reflective equilibrium account for the normative principles of reasoning is like demanding that a recipe for a cake be edible. You do not look for an actual cake in the instructions of a recipe. Rather, you carry out the recipe's instructions and then you have your cake (and can eat it too). Similarly, you have to go through the process of bringing all the inputs to wide reflective equilibrium into balance to find the normative principles of reasoning.

A critic might reply that this is easier said than done; carrying out the process is far from simple. The critic is right again, but again the criticism is not serious. I never said that it would be *easy* to determine what the normative principles of reasoning are. To complete the wide reflective equilibrium process may well involve knowing scientific facts we have not yet discovered, settling philosophical questions we have not yet settled, and so on. The naturalized picture of rationality gives an abstract account of what it is to be a normative principle of reasoning, how you determine what the normative principles of reasoning are, and what evidence is relevant to this process, but not a detailed list of what the normative principles of reasoning are. Given that the naturalized picture of rationality has its roots in Goodman's reflective equilibrium account of the principles of induction,[14] this should not be surprising.

---

[14] Nelson Goodman, *Fact, Fiction and Forecast*, 4th edn. (Cambridge, Mass.: Harvard University Press, 1983), 63–4; see my discussion in Ch. 5, Sect. 2.

Goodman does not provide a list of the inductive principles his account would endorse. He just describes the process of reflective equilibrium and leaves us to figure out what principles it would justify.

It is worth noting that the naturalized picture of rationality is not worse off on this count than the standard picture of rationality (or any of the other pictures of rationality that I have considered). The standard picture does give some specifics but does not give anything like a complete list of which principles it endorses as normative. Besides our intuitions, which act as a guide to which principles the standard picture will endorse, all that we know concretely about which principles it will endorse is an implicit sketch of an algorithm that generates some small subset of the principles that the standard picture considers are normative. The algorithm takes rules of logic and probability such as modus ponens and the conjunction rule and produces principles of reasoning such as the modus ponens principle and the conjunction principle.[15] The algorithm only generates a subset of what the standard picture says are normative principles of reasoning; there are some principles of reasoning (for example, the symmetricality principle) that are normative according to the standard picture but that are not generated by the algorithm. The standard picture of reasoning gives only a partial list of the principles of reasoning it endorses as norms while the naturalized picture of reasoning gives no such list. The naturalized picture does describe a process—wide reflective equilibrium—that will generate and justify all the principles that it takes to be normative principles of reasoning, while the standard picture only describes a process that will generate some of the principles it takes to be normative. The naturalized picture of rationality does not provide substantially fewer details than the standard picture of rationality does.

The second objection to the naturalized picture of rationality is that it is circular. According to the naturalized picture, philosophical and scientific theories are part of the input to the process of determining what the normative principles of reasoning are. We cannot, however, do science or philosophy successfully without already having an account of the normative principles of reasoning. If we start without an account of what the norms of reasoning are, how can we hope to develop any good theories of science or philosophy? If we cannot do science or philosophy, we will not have the requisite theories to use as input to the wide reflective equilibrium process to determine what the norms are.

---

[15] See Ch. 1, Sect. 5.1 for some more details of the algorithm.

This seems to be a catch-22 situation; the naturalized picture of rationality does not seem able to get off the ground.

The friend of the naturalized picture would respond to this objection by saying that one of the virtues of the wide reflective equilibrium process is that it can get started with our current scientific and philosophical theories. These theories will continually be evaluated and re-evaluated in light of our intuitions, new scientific evidence, and new philosophical arguments. The naturalized picture assumes that we start our examination of what the normative principles of reasoning are with well-formed beliefs about science, philosophy, and reasoning. In this way, it is like naturalized epistemology: both processes start, to return to Neurath's metaphor, at sea; that is, both inquiries start, not with a clean slate like the one Descartes wanted to have at the start of his (traditional) epistemological reflections, but with some of our most trusted beliefs taken for granted, at least provisionally.

In light of this response, the objection to the naturalized picture of rationality can be revised. Imagine, as seems likely, that our first-order intuitions about what counts as good reasoning include some principles that (by assumption) are not normative principles of reasoning. Further, suppose that some of these non-normative principles of reasoning have been used—implicitly or explicitly—to develop our currently favoured scientific and philosophical theories. If this is the case, it seems likely that these non-normative principles of reasoning will wind up being in wide reflective equilibrium and hence will wind up being endorsed as normative principles of reasoning by the naturalized picture of rationality.

This objection is similar to the one I considered in Chapter 5, Section 3. I argued there that it underestimates the resources of wide reflective equilibrium. Rather than repeat that discussion here, I want to consider some more specific replies in defence of the naturalized picture of rationality. Before doing so, I want to make the objection more concrete. Suppose, then, that P is a principle of reasoning that is intuitively plausible and non-normative. Also suppose that P played a role in the reasoning process that led you to believe some scientific theory S and some philosophical theory T. The above objection says that since P, S, and T are inputs to the wide reflective equilibrium process that, according to the naturalized picture of rationality, determines what the normative principles of reasoning are, it seems likely, or at least possible, that P will wind up being endorsed as a normative principle of reasoning by the naturalized picture of rationality. But, because P, by assumption, is not a normative principle of reasoning, the naturalized picture must be mistaken.

This objection gets much of its plausibility from the (assumed) fact that P plays a role in the reasoning process that leads to S and T. This increased plausibility is just an illusion: P is no more likely to be judged a normative principle of reasoning in virtue of the fact that it leads to S and T that it would if it did not. Recall that many non-normative principles of reasoning that are intuitively plausible will be part of the input to wide reflective equilibrium. I argued in Chapter 5, Section 3 that we should not be particularly worried about the possibility that such non-normative principles will wind up being endorsed as normative principles of reasoning because they will be brought into balance with scientific and philosophical theories as well as our considered intuitions. How does the fact that P plays a role in coming to believe S and T make it more likely that P will be endorsed as a normative principle of reasoning? That a principle plays a role in coming to believe a theory does not entail that the theory will support that principle.

By way of a concrete example, consider the following non-normative (on most accounts) principle of reasoning:

> AFFIRMING-THE-CONSEQUENT PRINCIPLE: If you believe B and you believe **if** A, **then** B, you should believe A.

To see why this is not a normative principle, suppose that you believe

> If it rains, then the ground will get wet

and you believe

> The ground is wet

then the affirming-the-consequent principle says you should also believe

> It is raining.

It is, however, perfectly consistent with your two beliefs that it is not raining and that the ground is wet because of a broken water-pipe. This shows that the affirming-the-consequent principle is problematic. Now consider another case. Suppose that a scientist uses the affirming-the-consequent principle to discover a scientific theory that becomes widely believed. This does not mean that her theory will in any way endorse the affirming-the-consequent principle as a normative principle of reasoning. In fact, there is a well-established distinction in philosophy of science between the *context of discovery* and the *context of justification*. The context of discovery is the context, broadly construed, in which a scientific theory was discovered; this includes the background beliefs of the discoverer, the methods she used, and so on. The context of justification is the context, broadly construed, in which we are justified in believing that a scientific theory is true. The fact that penicillin was discovered due to a test-tube getting accidentally knocked over is part of the context of discovery of penicillin, but not part of the context that justifies our belief that penicillin cures certain bacterial infections. To return to the example at hand, the fact that the affirming-the-consequent principle played a role in the discovery of some scientific theory is part of the context of discovery of that theory, but it need not be involved in the justification of the theory. Therefore, the principle will not be supported just because it plays a role in the discovery of an accepted scientific theory. Further, even if the affirming-the-consequent principle somehow did play a role in the *justification* of the theory, the theory still does not necessarily lend weight to the endorsement of the principle by the wide reflective equilibrium account. The affirming-the-consequent principle is thus not likely to be endorsed by a wide reflective equilibrium account, even if it is initially plausible. In general, that a principle P plays a role in the discovery of a theory T does not entail that T will itself provide support for P. The naturalized picture of rationality is well equipped to answer the objection that it will endorse as normative principles of rationality principles that are non-normative.

6. Conclusion

Throughout much of this book, I have assumed that the standard picture of rationality is true. This was a reasonable assumption for two reasons. First, most friends of both the rationality thesis and the irrationality thesis assume the standard picture of rationality; features of the standard picture permeate most of the arguments for and against the view that humans are rational. Second, the standard picture is an intuitively plausible picture with many virtues. These two reasons are related: one of the primary reasons why friends and foes of the rationality thesis assume the standard picture is its intuitive plausibility.

This chapter began with three arguments for the rationality thesis that try to undermine the standard picture of rationality. In the face of the failure of attempts to argue for the rationality thesis that assume the standard picture of rationality, friends of the view that humans are rational might reject the standard picture and replace it with another picture that provides an easier path to the view that humans are rational. Friends of the rationality thesis, after failing to show that humans are rational in the way that the standard picture says rationality should be understood, might prefer to understand rationality in some other way. The three arguments that I considered were inspired by analogies with aesthetics, taste, and sense of humour (these analogies were first discussed in Chapter 1, Section 3.3). Evaluation in these realms seems linked to human faculties in these realms. For example, how funny something is seems linked to the human capacity for sense of humour and to each individual's sense of humour. Perhaps what counts as good reasoning is linked in some way to human reasoning competence and/or to each individual's ability to reason. This consideration gave rise to alternatives to the standard picture of rationality that I called the pragmatic and the relativistic pictures of rationality. Above, I argued that neither of these pictures seems able to ground an argument for the rationality thesis. Although none of the arguments against the standard picture of rationality establish the truth of the rationality thesis, they might still point out problems with the standard picture.

One argument against the standard picture of rationality seemed pretty damaging. For a principle of reasoning to be a normative principle, it must be one that humans could reason in accordance with (because otherwise we would be saying that we ought to reason in a way in which we are unable to reason). Given the various constraints on our actual reasoning, some of the principles of reasoning endorsed by the standard picture might not be feasible for us. Even if no principles of reasoning are ruled out by the human finitary predicament, there is still the possibility that some might have been. The standard picture does not allow for this possibility. For this reason, and others that I discussed in Section 5 above, the naturalized picture of rationality is preferable to the standard picture: it preserves the virtues of the standard picture while not being open to the objections to it. This conclusion shows that we should take more seriously the analogies with aesthetics, taste, and sense of humour. The standard picture does not allow that the normative principles of reasoning are in any way affected by the various constraints on reasoning that humans face. The human finitary predicament shows that this feature of the standard picture is problematic. The naturalized picture of rationality addresses this problem.

Recall from Chapter 1, Section 2 that a naturalized epistemology is an approach to the theory of knowledge that tries to develop an account of how we ought to arrive at our beliefs, while allowing, in contrast to traditional epistemology, that empirical facts can play an important role is this inquiry. The naturalized picture of rationality is a part of naturalized epistemology because it says that empirical facts play an important role in trying determine which principles of reasoning we ought to follow. In the final chapter, I will say more about the relation between naturalized epistemology and the naturalized picture of rationality.

8

Conclusion

SEVERAL years ago, I was a teaching assistant for an undergraduate course entitled 'Introduction to the Problems of Philosophy'. During a class at the end of the semester, the course instructor was conducting a review session for the final exam when one of the students raised his hand and asked, 'Could you put on the blackboard a list of all the problems of philosophy that we have discussed along with the solution to each of the problems?' Several students laughed, but the instructor did not—she was too exasperated. She was exasperated, no doubt, because if the student thought that philosophical problems like the problem of other minds and the problem of induction had straightforward solutions that could be recounted in a few minutes on a blackboard, he must not have been paying attention throughout the course. Although I too was exasperated with the student's question (though I am glad to say the student was not in my section), I identified with his desire to want a succinct summary of what had been accomplished at the end of a course—what the central questions are and what answers we are inclined to give to them. I often have the desire in courses I teach to spend the last day of class reviewing the central questions that we have been discussing during the semester and the various plausible answers to them. In doing so, I try to build on the conclusions of earlier discussions but to put them together in a way that goes beyond any one of the discussions we had during the term. It is no surprise, then, that in the final chapter of this book, I want to do roughly the same thing; namely, review some of the central questions I have discussed and the answers to them that seem right. While most of what follows rests on the arguments on previous chapters, I do make several new points. With apologies to that student from 'Introduction to the Problems of Philosophy', not all I have to say would fit on a blackboard.

1. The Nature of the Question 'Are Humans Rational?'

One of the central questions of this book has been 'Are humans rational?' Before we can hope to answer this question, we need to understand what it means and what sort of question it is. I explained in Chapters 1 and 2 that, in the context of the debate between the rationality thesis and the irrationality thesis, the question is about whether humans have the normative principles of reasoning in their reasoning competence. Given this, it was still not clear whether the question is conceptual or empirical. In particular, it was not clear whether the reasoning experiments are relevant to it. More generally, it was not clear whether empirical considerations are relevant to epistemology.

From the perspective of the end of the book, I can begin to resolve some of these issues. For starters, I turn to two analogies. The question 'Do humans speak grammatically?' can be separated into three questions: 'What are the normative principles of language (grammaticality)?', 'What is human linguistic competence?', and 'Does linguistic competence match the norms of grammaticality?' As I argued in Chapter 2, the norms of grammaticality are indexed to actual linguistic competence. If we figure out what human linguistic competence is, we have thereby figured out what the normative principles of language are. The empirical inquiry of linguistics is thus relevant to determining the normative principles of language. This does not show, however, that the question 'Does linguistic competence match the normative principles of language?' is an empirical one. In fact, that this is a conceptual question follows from the fact that we know humans follow these principles even though we do not know what the principles are. Because the norms are indexed to actual linguistic competence, the norms of grammaticality and the principles that characterize linguistic competence necessarily match; in linguistics, the norms *just are* the principles that characterize linguistic competence.

Similarly, the question 'Are humans moral?' involves the questions 'What are the norms of morality?', 'What is our ethical competence?', and 'Does human ethical competence match the norms of morality?' At least prima facie, developing an account of our ability for moral thought seems to involve empirical issues in psychology (and perhaps biology); we need to examine how we reason about moral questions, what our ethical intuitions are, and so forth. In contrast, determining what the norms of morality are is a question for moral theory that seems to involve primarily conceptual questions. This is a simplification. First, if the wide reflective equilibrium account of moral theory is right and if scientific evidence is included as part of the input to the wide reflective equilibrium process, then empirical considerations will play a greater role than it first seemed. Second, if 'ought' implies 'can' in ethics, then

TABLE 8.1. *The nature of questions about language and ethics*

Question	Language	Ethics	Reasoning
What are the norms in this realm?	What are the norms of grammaticality? *Empirical*	What are the norms of morality? *Conceptual and a bit empirical*	What are the normative principles of reasoning?
What is our competence in this realm?	What is our linguistic competence? *Empirical*	What is our moral competence? *Empirical*	What is our reasoning competence?
Does our competence in this realm match the norms?	Are humans grammatical? *Conceptual*	Are humans moral? *Empirical*	Are humans rational?

evidence about how humans can act is relevant to establishing what the norms of morality are. Table 8.1 lays out the three questions applied to the realms of language, ethics, and reasoning and gives the plausible answers for language and ethics. In the discussion that follows, I use the lessons of the previous chapters to fill in the answers to the questions in the column that applies to reasoning.

Whether or not humans are rational is partially an empirical question. Assuming that we have a clear account of what it is to be rational, we need to find out whether or not humans fit this account. Doing this involves determining how humans reason. At first glance, this seems straightforwardly empirical: just look at human reasoning behaviour and determine whether we are reasoning in a rational manner. As I have discussed above, especially in Chapters 2, 3, and 4, determining how humans reason is hardly so simple. To determine how humans reason, we need to know what mechanisms underlie our reasoning. Human reasoning behaviour underdetermines the human reasoning mechanism. Our reasoning mechanism produces our reasoning behaviour, but since various factors interfere with our reasoning performance, one cannot determine what our reasoning competence is just by looking at reasoning behaviour. Also, one cannot determine what human reasoning competence is simply by looking at the brain (Chapter 3, Section 3.3).

The full resources of an advanced cognitive science are required to produce an account of human reasoning competence. The cognitive scientific study of human reasoning competence will include the study of reasoning behaviour and neuroscience, and, for reasons discussed in Chapter 5, Section 4, evolutionary theory and computational theory will also be relevant. The reasoning experiments will also be relevant because, properly designed and executed, they give insight into the nature of our reasoning competence. Careful theoretical reflection on the methods of research will be important as well. Cognitive scientists need to make sure that they are not relying on principles of reasoning that they contend are unreliable. Like the careful cognitive scientist of Chapter 7, Section 1–3, researchers need to look at their methods in the light of their conclusions about human reasoning. More generally, cognitive scientists should carefully evaluate various conceptual strategies that might guide their research. For example, they should remain flexible about whether to call a particular reasoning behaviour a performance error or to count this behaviour as part of human reasoning competence (namely, they should adopt the neutral strategy about interpreting reasoning behaviour over its competitors—see Chapter 3, Section 3, for a discussion). Adopting this strategy is a conceptual decision. Conceptual considerations thus play a role, albeit not a large one, in determining what human reasoning competence is.

Determining what human reasoning competence is provides only part of the information one needs to determine whether humans are rational. One also needs to know what it is to be rational. Prima facie, it seems that empirical considerations are not relevant to this issue. In Chapter 7, I argued that this prima facie plausible observation is mistaken. The standard picture of rationality says that the normative principles of reasoning are based on rules of logic, probability theory, and the like. This picture ignores the fact that human reasoning is embodied, takes place in real time, and occurs against the background of other human functions—cognitive as well as digestive, reproductive, and so forth. To take these considerations into account, rationality must be naturalized. As I argued in Chapter 7, Section 5, the naturalized picture of rationality has the virtues of the standard picture of rationality while it lacks the standard picture's vices. The naturalized picture of rationality says that the normative principles of reasoning are those that would result from a wide reflective equilibrium process that includes scientific evidence as input. Such a process brings our intuitions and scientific and theoretical considerations into agreement through a balancing process. Determining the normative principles of reasoning is, thus, both a conceptual and an empirical question.

Because reasoning is important and perhaps essential to how we acquire and maintain knowledge, the results of this inquiry bear directly on epistemology. If humans are irrational, then many of our beliefs that seem justified may not be, and, thus, much of what we think is knowledge may not be. Given the intimate connection between reasoning and knowledge, naturalizing rationality leads to naturalizing epistemology. If empirical considerations are relevant to whether or not humans are rational, empirical considerations are relevant to whether we have knowledge and what we know. The results of this inquiry thus support the project of naturalized epistemology, which is normative *and* empirical, rather than traditional epistemology, which is normative but not empirical, or descriptive epistemology, which is empirical but not normative (see Chapter 1, Section 2).

Empirical considerations thus play a major role in determining how humans in fact reason and what it is for humans to be rational. Conceptual considerations are also relevant to both questions. This does not, however, show that the correct account of how humans reason and the correct account of how humans *should* reason must match. As I argued in Chapter 5, Section 5, different sorts of conceptual and empirical consideration are involved in answering the two questions and, further, even when the same consideration is relevant to both, it may be given a different weight in each reflective equilibrium process. The truth of the rationality thesis does not simply follow from rationality being naturalized and from conceptual considerations playing a role in determining what human reasoning competence is. In this respect, reasoning is like ethics and not like language. In the realm of language, once you know what competence is, you know what the norms are. In the realm of language, we know from the start that human competence will match the norms. In the realm of reasoning, even if we know what human competence is, we have to determine what the norms are (and vice versa) before we can assess our abilities. The rationality thesis and the irrationality thesis are, thus, both empirical theses. (The results of this discussion are summarized in the third column of Table 8.2)

The picture of assessing human reasoning that emerges has roots that are deeper than my Chapter 7 discussion of the standard picture of rationality. Traces of this conclusion can be found in Chapters 3–6. In Chapter 3, I considered the question of how to draw borders around reasoning competence, namely how one should decide which cognitive mechanisms ought to count as part of reasoning competence and which ought to count as sources of performance errors with respect to reasoning.

TABLE 8.2. *The nature of questions about language, ethics, and reasoning*

Question	Language	Ethics	Reasoning
What are the norms in this realm?	What are the norms of grammaticality? *Empirical*	What are the norms of morality? *Conceptual and a bit empirical*	What are the normative principles of reasoning? *Conceptual and empirical*
What is our competence in this realm?	What is our linguistic competence? *Empirical*	What is our moral competence? *Empirical*	What is our reasoning competence? *Empirical and a bit conceptual*
Does our competence in this realm match the norms?	Are humans grammatical? *Conceptual*	Are humans moral? *Empirical*	Are humans rational? *Empirical*

(I argued that this question is equivalent to whether the neutral strategy should be adopted when interpreting reasoning behaviour.) This is a particularly tricky question, partly because it is neither straightforwardly empirical nor straightforwardly conceptual. At first, what seems at issue is the empirical question of which cognitive mechanisms are involved in reasoning competence. Underlying this question is a seemingly conceptual question about what counts as reasoning competence. How you answer this question depends on the precise details of your definition of competence, a definition that is hardly arbitrary. In settling this question, conceptual and empirical considerations are deeply intertwined. In Chapter 4, I suggested that the weak principle of charity, which says that humans should be interpreted as rational unless strong empirical evidence suggests otherwise, is a reasonable strategy for interpreting and assessing reasoning competence and cognitive mechanisms. Here again both empirical and conceptual considerations are relevant. In Chapter 5, I argued that philosophical and other theoretical considerations are relevant to determining what human reasoning competence is. I also suggested, towards the end of Chapter 5, that the normative principles of reasoning might be determined by a process of wide reflective equilibrium with scientific evidence included as input. (This suggestion was elaborated in Chapter 7, Section 5.) Yet again, empirical and conceptual considerations are both relevant. Finally, in Chapter 6, I mentioned the reproductive success argument for the rationality thesis. According to this argument, that a cognitive mechanism contributes to the reproductive success of an organism is relevant to whether a reasoning competence that includes such a mechanism is rational. Once we see that rationality should be naturalized, such considerations become relevant to what counts as rational for humans (for more on this point, see my discussion of evolutionary psychology below).

In Chapter 1, Section 3.1, I discussed Quinean worries about the traditional distinction between conceptual and empirical questions. In light of my conclusions thus far, the traditional distinction seems oddly out of place. With respect to rationality and, by extension, epistemology, conceptual and empirical issues are thoroughly intertwined and interdependent. For example, with regard to the question 'What are the normative principles of reasoning?', sometimes empirical considerations can trump conceptual ones and sometimes conceptual considerations can trump empirical ones. Also, the question of where to draw the borders around reasoning competence seems neither obviously conceptual nor obviously empirical. The general picture of the notions of conceptual and empirical that emerges from my discussion fits more with the web of belief picture of these notions than with the traditional way of seeing the distinction between them.

2. Are Humans Rational?

Given this account of the nature of the question 'Are humans rational?', it seems reasonable to turn to answering that very question. Unfortunately, I do not have a clear answer. The reasoning experiments suggest that humans fail to reason in accordance with the best available principles; there are feasible principles of reasoning that seem preferable to the principles humans seem to actually follow. For example, the conjunction principle seems to be a feasible and a desirable principle for reasoning about probabilities, but the conjunction experiment suggests that we do not reason in accordance with the conjunction principle. Given this, we seem irrational.

Matters are not, however, so simple for two related reasons. First, although there is no principled argument that all divergences from the normative principles of reasoning must be due to performance errors, it is possible that features of the various experiments are flawed in such ways that the errors humans appear to be making do not represent actual instances of human reasoning competence diverging from the norms. I discussed some such claims in Chapter 3: Gigerenzer makes such a claim about the conjunction experiment (Section 2), Cosmides makes roughly this claim with respect to the selection task (Section 1), and it is the general sort of claim championed by friends of the mis-interpretation strategy argument for the rationality thesis (Section 3). Gigerenzer, for example, argues that the results of the conjunction experiment are due to the way the experiment is phrased. If the con-junction experiment is phrased in terms of frequency rather than probability (that is, 'How many people out of 100 who fit this particular description will be bank tellers?' rather than 'What is the probability that Linda is a bank teller?'), subjects respond in accordance with the norms.[1] This argument is an incomplete defence of the rationality thesis: showing that subjects do not make systematic errors related to frequencies does not, without further explanation, explain away the errors subjects make on the probability task. Such a further explanation would need to demonstrate that the errors subjects make on the probability version of the conjunction task are not errors caused by having a reasoning competence that diverges from the norms. There is no conceptual argu-ment that will do this. None of the suggested conceptual arguments for the rationality thesis I have discussed suffice to show that human reasoning competence *must not* diverge from the norms. Although the misinterpretation strategy does not work as a general argument for the rationality thesis, this strategy might be well founded in particular cases. For example, Gigerenzer may be right that humans have the conjunction principle in their reasoning competence and that subjects are simply misinterpreting the probability version of the conjunction experiment.

The second reason why the reasoning experiments do not simply prove humans are irrational is that the results which suggest that human reasoning diverges from the normative principles of reasoning might be due to performance errors. Although no successful conceptual argument has been given to demonstrate that *all* divergences from normative principles of reasoning are due to performance errors, no argument has been given that some, most, or even all of such divergences are *not* due

---

[1] Gerd Gigerenzer, 'How to Make Cognitive Illusions Disappear: Beyond "Heuristics and Biases" ', *European Review of Social Psychology*, 2 (1991), 83–115.

to performance errors. To establish the irrationality thesis, one must show that *some* of the divergences from the norms are *in fact* due to human reasoning competence and not to performance errors. It is no simple task to show that an instance of divergence from the norms is really due to reasoning competence and not a performance error. The problem of where to draw the borders around reasoning competence is partly to blame for this.

Reasoning competence is *epistemologically opaque*. It cannot simply be read off behaviour and it cannot simply be read off the neurological structure of the brain. We are now pretty clear what facts would settle the issue between the rationality and the irrationality thesis but these facts are difficult to discover. To do so, the cognitive scientist must try to understand mechanisms of reasoning at an abstract level (that is, at the mental level) with only partial knowledge of the neurological structures (whether primarily innate or primarily acquired through inter-action with the environment) that embody them. Only with guidance from cognitive science—guidance based on these sorts of abstract explanations—can the brain scientist undertake an informed inquiry into the neurological features of the brain responsible for reasoning competence. This inquiry, in turn, can influence the work of the cog-nitive scientist; by better understanding the underlying neurological structures, the cognitive scientist can better characterize the mental mechanisms involved in human reasoning competence.[2]

Friends of sociobiological explanations might object at this point that the task I assign to the cognitive scientist is actually more appropriately assigned to biologists interested in explaining human behaviour.[3] To develop an accurate characterization of human reasoning competence, one must understand the ecological circumstances in which such a com-petence evolved and was selected or in which the capacity to develop such a competence evolved and was selected. It is the sociobiologist, not the cognitive scientist, who is, according to this objection, ideally positioned to undertake such an investigation.

There is something right about this point, though there is more that

---

[2] Some of the points in this paragraph parallel the account of how linguistics must proceed given in Noam Chomsky, *Language and the Problems of Knowledge* (Cam-bridge, Mass.: MIT Press, 1988), 6–7.

[3] See e.g. E. O. Wilson and Charles Lumsden, *Genes, Minds and Culture* (Cambridge, Mass.: Harvard University Press, 1981); and *Promethean Fire* (Cambridge, Mass.: Harvard University Press, 1983).

is wrong about it. Understanding the various selective pressures involved in the development of human cognitive mechanisms, including reasoning competence, would be useful to cognitive science as I describe its project. Because they start with only an account of human behaviour, cognitive scientists need guidance about what reasoning competence is. Evolutionary considerations seem an appropriate place to look for such guidance. A paradigmatic example of drawing on evolutionary considerations is Cosmides' work on the selection task.[4] As a clue to discovering the nature of the principles people are following in the selection task, Cosmides turned to evolutionary theory for guidance about which principles of reasoning would be adaptive given the environmental and information-processing problems humans faced. According to Cosmides, evolutionary considerations suggest in particular that tasks having to do with social exchange would be particularly important problems for humans to reason about; principles that solve social exchange tasks are thus likely to be used in many versions of the selection task.

Just because evolutionary theory is useful for the inquiry into the nature of human reasoning competence does not make such an inquiry the task for a sociobiologist. Sociobiologists typically make a direct leap from genes to behaviour. For example, they might talk about natural selection selecting for certain reasoning behaviours. This sort of talk clearly involves dramatic over-simplification. Natural selection involves selection for genes, but the connection between genes and behaviour is quite complex; at a minimum, the connection is mediated by the process of development (the process through which genes, in the presence of certain environmental inputs, will produce embodied organisms) and by the mind (genes do not cause behaviour; genes cause certain mental mechanisms to develop, which in turn engender certain sorts of behaviour). Focusing on the role of the mind, the point is that what gets selected by natural selection are not behaviours, but genes that lead to the development of mental mechanisms that cause behaviours. Sociobiology is not the right approach for developing an understanding of mental mechanisms; rather cognitive science informed by evolutionary considerations—what is known as *evolutionary psychology*—is.[5]

---

[4] Leda Cosmides, 'The Logic of Selection: Has Natural Selection Shaped how Humans Reason? Studies with the Wason Selection Task', *Cognition*, 31 (1989), 187–276.

[5] On evolutionary psychology, see Leda Cosmides and John Tooby, 'From Evolution to Behavior: Evolutionary Psychology as the Missing Link', in John Dupré (ed.), *The Latest on the Best* (Cambridge, Mass.: MIT Press, 1987); John Tooby, 'The Emergence of

Returning more specifically to the question of whether the reasoning experiments are relevant to the question 'Are humans rational?', the problem is whether these experiments can play a role in the cognitive scientist's abstract research programme to develop an account of human reasoning competence. The answer to this seems obviously yes. The experiments focus on particular features of human reasoning behaviour, and human reasoning behaviour is of course relevant to developing a theory of reasoning competence. The problems of epistemological access to reasoning competence discussed above show, however, that these experiments need to be interpreted with caution. More precisely, they need to be taken in the context of (*a*) the possibility of performance errors, (*b*) evolutionary considerations, (*c*) neurological and computational constraints (for example, constraints resulting from humans having brains of a particular size and humans being able to perform computations in a certain amount of time[6]), and (*d*) to a limited extent, general philosophical considerations. Given these various factors that ought to figure in the development of a theory of human reasoning competence, friends of the irrationality thesis may have spoken too soon when they took the results of the reasoning experiments to establish the irrationality thesis.

A defender of the irrationality thesis might make the following argument. Consider the infinite number of Turing machines (see Chapter 6, Section 2). Even if we eliminate all of those Turing machines that are inconsistent with our observed reasoning behaviour, that cannot be run on brains the size of ours, and that would not have been adaptive in the environments that our brains were selected, there would still be a large number of Turing machines left. Each of the remaining Turing machines represents a possible configuration of human reasoning competence. Given that there are so many possible arrangements of our

Evolutionary Psychology', in David Pines (ed.), *Emerging Syntheses in Science* (Redwood City, Calif.: Addison-Wesley, 1988); John Tooby and Leda Cosmides, 'Evolutionary Psychology and the Generation of Culture, Part I: Theoretical Considerations', *Ethology and Sociobiology*, 10 (1987), 29–49; and the essays in Jerome Barkow *et al.* (eds.), *The Adapted Mind* (New York: Oxford University Press, 1992). Others who have endorsed evolutionary considerations as helpful in understanding mental mechanisms are David Marr, *Vision* (San Francisco: Freeman, 1982), who argues that evolutionary considerations are relevant to developing an account of the visual mechanisms in the brain; and Steven Pinker and Paul Bloom, 'Natural Language and Natural Selection', *Behavioral and Brain Science*, 13 (1990), 707–84, who argue that evolutionary considerations are relevant to our understanding of human language.

[6] For discussion of these sorts of constraints, see Christopher Cherniak, *Minimal Rationality* (Cambridge, Mass.: MIT Press, 1986).

reasoning competence, the chances that we will actually have a reasoning competence that contains all and only the normative principles of reasoning seem rather low. According to this line of thought, while it is a logical possibility that humans are rational, the odds are in favour of us being irrational. A defender of the rationality thesis might reply, however, that this line of argument underestimates the constraints on what our human reasoning competence could be that result from evolutionary pressures, neuroscientific evidence, and human reasoning behaviour and it underestimates how revisionary the naturalized picture of rationality is.

In Oscar Wilde's novel *The Picture of Dorian Gray*, the character of Lord Henry says, 'I wonder who it was defined man as a rational animal. It was the most premature definition ever given.'[7] My conclusion is similar to Lord Henry's. Although I have not concerned myself with those attempts to *define* humans as rational,[8] I have been concerned with those who attempt to *prove* that humans are rational. Their arguments are not premature; they are, I have argued, unsound. It is, however, their rivals—those who have tried to argue from the basis of the reasoning experiments to the conclusion that humans are irrational—who make arguments that are premature. I have argued that rationality (and, thus, epistemology) need to be naturalized. To determine what is required for humans to be rational, we need to know how various factors constrain our reasoning. Even if we know what is required for humans to be rational, to determine whether humans are in fact rational, we need to know more than we do about, for example, human reasoning behaviour, human neurophysiology, and human evolutionary history. Anyone who has confidently asserted either that humans are rational or that humans are irrational does so on the basis of incomplete empirical evidence and unsupported conceptual claims; in other words, she has taken a strong stand on the question of human rationality without good reason.

---

[7] Oscar Wilde, *The Picture of Dorian Gray* (London: Ward, Lock, 1891; repr. London: Penguin Books, 1985), 52.

[8] e.g. Jonathan Bennett, *Rationality* (London: Routledge & Kegan Paul, 1964).

Bibliography

AYALA, FRANCISCO, 'The Concept of Biological Progress', in Francisco Ayala and Theodosius Dobzhansky (eds.), *Studies in the Philosophy of Biology* (Berkeley: University of California Press, 1974).

BARKOW, JEROME, COSMIDES, LEDA, and TOOBY, JOHN (eds.), *The Adapted Mind: Evolutionary Psychology and the Generation of Culture* (New York: Oxford University Press, 1992).

BENNETT, JONATHAN, *Rationality* (London: Routledge & Kegan Paul, 1964).

BERWICK, ROBERT, and WEINBERG, AMY, *The Grammatical Basis of Linguistic Performance* (Cambridge, Mass.: MIT Press, 1980).

BINKERTON, DEREK, *The Roots of Language* (Ann Arbor, Mich.: Karmona, 1981).

BLOCK, NED, 'Advertisement for a Semantics for Psychology', in Peter French, Theodore Uehling, Jr., and Howard Wettstein (eds.), *Midwest Studies in Philosophy*, x: *Studies in the Philosophy of Mind* (Minneapolis: University of Minnesota Press, 1986).

—— (ed.), *Readings in the Philosophy of Psychology*, ii (Cambridge, Mass.: Harvard University Press, 1981)

BONJOUR, LAURENCE, 'Holistic Coherentism', *Philosophical Studies*, 30 (1976), 281–312.

—— *The Structure of Empirical Knowledge* (Cambridge, Mass.: Harvard University Press, 1985).

BRADIE, MICHAEL, 'Assessing Evolutionary Epistemology', *Biology and Philosophy*, 1 (1986), 401–59.

—— 'Should Epistemologists Take Darwin Seriously?', in Nicholas Rescher (ed.), *Evolution, Cognition and Realism* (Lanham, Md.: University Press of America, 1990).

—— 'Epistemology from an Evolutionary Point of View', in Sober (ed.), *Conceptual Issues in Evolutionary Biology*, 2nd edn.

BRAINE, MARTIN, REISER, BRIAN, and RUMAIN, BARBARA, 'Some Empirical Justification for a Theory of Natural Propositional Logic', in Gordon Bower (ed.), *The Psychology of Learning and Motivation*, xviii (Orlando, Fla.: Academic Press, 1984).

BUSS, DAVID, *The Evolution of Desire: Strategies of Human Mating* (New York: Basic Books, 1994).

CAMPBELL, DONALD, 'Evolutionary Epistemology', in Paul Schilpp (ed.), *The Philosophy of Karl Popper*, i (LaSalle, Ill.: Open Court, 1974); repr. in Gerald Radnitsky and W. W. Bartley III (eds.), *Evolution, Theory of Rationality and the Sociology of Knowledge* (LaSalle, Ill.: Open Court, 1987).

—— 'Unjustified Variation and Selection in Scientific Discovery', in Francisco

Ayala and Theodosius Dobzhansky (eds.), *Studies in Philosophy of Biology* (Berkeley: University of California Press, 1974).

CAMPBELL, DONALD, 'Selection Theory and the Sociology of Scientific Validity', in Werner Callebaut and Rik Pinxten (eds.), *Evolutionary Epistemology: A Multiparadigm Program* (Dordrecht: Reidel, 1987).

—— and PALLER, BONNIE, 'Extending Evolutionary Epistemology to "Justifying" Scientific Beliefs', in Kai Hahlweg and C. A. Hooker (eds.), *Issues in Evolutionary Epistemology* (Albany, NY: State University of New York Press, 1989).

CAPLAN, DAVID, and HILDEBRANDT, NANCY, *Disorders of Syntactic Comprehension* (Cambridge, Mass.: MIT Press, 1988).

CARAMAZZA, ALFONSO, HART, JOHN, and BERNDT, RITA, 'Category-Specific Naming Deficit Following Cerebral Infarction', *Nature*, 316 (1985), 439–40.

CARTWRIGHT, NANCY, *How the Laws of Physics Lie* (Oxford: Oxford University Press, 1983).

CHENG, PATRICIA, and HOLYOAK, KEITH, 'Pragmatic Reasoning Schemas', *Cognitive Psychology*, 17 (1985), 391–416.

—— 'On the Natural Selection of Reasoning Theories', *Cognition*, 33 (1989), 285–333.

CHERNIAK, CHRISTOPHER, *Minimal Rationality* (Cambridge, Mass.: MIT Press, 1986).

—— 'Undebuggability and Cognitive Science', *Communications of the Association for Computing Machinery*, 31 (1988), 402–12.

—— 'The Bounded Brain: Toward Quantitative Neuroanatomy', *Journal of Cognitive Neuroscience*, 2 (1990), 58–68.

CHOMSKY, NOAM, *Syntactic Structures* (The Hague: Mouton, 1957).

—— *Aspects of the Theory of Syntax* (Cambridge, Mass.: MIT Press, 1965).

—— *Reflections on Language* (New York: Random House, 1975).

—— *Language and Problems of Knowledge: The Managua Lectures* (Cambridge, Mass.: MIT Press, 1980).

—— *Rules and Representations* (New York: Columbia University Press, 1980).

—— *Knowledge of Language* (New York: Praeger, 1986).

CHURCHLAND, PAUL, *Scientific Realism and the Plasticity of Mind* (Cambridge: Cambridge University Press, 1979).

COHEN, L. JONATHAN, 'On the Psychology of Prediction: Whose is the Fallacy?', *Cognition*, 7 (1979), 385–407.

—— 'Whose is the Fallacy?: A Rejoinder to Daniel Kahneman and Amos Tversky', *Cognition*, 8 (1980), 89–92.

—— 'Can Human Irrationality be Experimentally Demonstrated?', *Behavioral and Brain Sciences*, 4 (1981), 317–70.

—— 'Continuing Commentary', *Behavioral and Brain Sciences*, 6 (1983), 487–533.

—— *The Dialogue of Reason* (Oxford: Oxford University Press, 1986).

—— 'A Reply to Stein', *Synthese*, 99 (1994), 173–6.

COMRIE, BERNARD, *Language Universals and Linguistic Taxonomy* (Chicago: University of Chicago Press, 1981).

CONEE, EARL, and FELDMAN, RICHARD, 'Stich and Nisbett on Justifying Inference Rules', *Philosophy of Science*, 50 (1983), 326–31.

COSMIDES, LEDA, 'The Logic of Selection: Has Natural Selection Shaped how Humans Reason? Studies with the Wason Selection Task', *Cognition*, 31 (1989), 187–276.

—— 'Cognitive Adaptation for Social Exchange', in Jerome Barkow, Leda Cosmides, and John Tooby (eds.), *The Adapted Mind: Evolutionary Psychology and the Generation of Culture* (New York: Oxford University Press, 1992).

—— 'Beyond Intuition and Instinct Blindness: Toward an Evolutionarily Rigorous Cognitive Science', *Cognition*, 50 (1994), 41–77.

—— and TOOBY, JOHN, 'From Evolution to Behavior: Evolutionary Psychology as the Missing Link', in John Dupré (ed.), *The Latest on the Best: Essays on Evolution and Optimality* (Cambridge, Mass.: MIT Press, 1987).

CROMER, RICHARD, 'The Cognition Hypothesis of Language Acquisition', in *Language and Thought in Normal and Handicapped Children* (Cambridge, Mass.: Blackwell, 1991).

CROW, J., 'Genes that Violate Mendel's Rules', *Scientific American*, 240/2 (1979), 134–46.

CUMMINS, DENISE, 'Are Pragmatic Reasoning Schemas Innate?: Some Evidence', paper presented at the Conference on Epistemology and Evolutionary Psychology, Rutgers University, Apr. 1995.

DANIELS, NORMAN, 'Wide Reflective Equilibrium and Theory Acceptance in Ethics', *Journal of Philosophy*, 76 (1979), 256–82.

—— 'On Some Methods of Ethics and Linguistics', *Philosophical Studies*, 37 (1980), 21–36.

—— 'Wide Reflective Equilibrium and Archimedean Points', *Canadian Journal of Philosophy*, 10 (1980), 83–103.

DAVIDSON, DONALD, 'On the Very Idea of a Conceptual Scheme', *Proceedings and Addresses of the American Philosophical Association*, 47 (1974), 5–20.

—— *Inquiries into Truth and Interpretation* (Oxford: Oxford University Press, 1984).

—— 'Incoherence and Irrationality', *Dialectica*, 39 (1985), 345–54.

DAWKINS, RICHARD, *The Selfish Gene* (Oxford: Oxford University Press, 1976).

—— *The Blind Watchmaker* (New York: W. W. Norton, 1986).

DENNETT, DANIEL, *Brainstorms* (Cambridge, Mass.: MIT Press, 1978).

—— *The Intentional Stance* (Cambridge, Mass.: MIT Press, 1987).

DESCARTES, RENÉ, *Meditations Concerning First Philosophy* (1641).

EVANS, JONATHAN, *The Psychology of Deductive Reasoning* (London: Routledge & Kegan Paul, 1982).

FARAH, MARTHA, 'Neuropsychological Inference with an Interactive Brain: A Critique of the "Locality" Assumption', *Behavioral and Brain Sciences*, 17 (1994), 43–104.

FAUSTO-STERLING, ANNE, *Myths of Gender: Biological Theories about Men and Women* (New York: Basic Books, 1985).

FELDMAN, RICHARD, 'Rationality, Reliability and Natural Selection', *Philosophy of Science*, 55 (1988), 218–27.

FIEDLER, KLAUS, 'The Dependence of the Conjunction Fallacy on Subtle Linguistic Factors', *Psychological Research*, 50 (1988), 123–9.

FLANAGAN, OWEN, *The Science of the Mind* (Cambridge, Mass.: MIT Press, 1984).

FODOR, JERRY, 'Introduction: Some Notes on what Linguistics is About', in Block (ed.), *Readings in Philosophy of Psychology*, ii.

—— 'Three Cheers for Propositional Attitudes', in *Representations* (Cambridge, Mass.: MIT Press, 1981).

—— *The Modularity of Mind* (Cambridge, Mass.: MIT Press, 1983).

—— *Psychosemantics* (Cambridge, Mass.: MIT Press, 1987).

—— 'Psychosemantics', in William Lycan (ed.), *Mind and Cognition: A Reader* (Oxford: Blackwell, 1990).

—— *A Theory of Content and Other Essays* (Cambridge, Mass.: MIT Press, 1990).

—— and GARRETT, MERRILL, 'Some Reflections on Competence and Performance', in John Lyons and Roger Wales (eds.), *Psycholinguistic Papers: Proceedings of the 1966 Edinburgh Conference* (Edinburgh: Edinburgh University Press, 1966).

GALLISTEL, C. R., *The Organization of Learning* (Cambridge, Mass.: MIT Press, 1990).

GARCIA, JOHN, MCGOWAN, BRENDA, and GREEN, KEITH, 'Biological Constraints on Conditioning', in Abraham Black and William Prokasy (eds.), *Classical Conditioning: Current Research and Theory*, ii (New York: Appleton-Century Crofts, 1972).

GARDNER, HOWARD, *The Shattered Mind* (New York: Basic Books, 1974).

GETTIER, EDMUND, 'Is Justified True Belief Knowledge?', *Analysis*, 23 (1963), 121–3.

GIGERENZER, GERD, 'How to Make Cognitive Illusions Disappear: Beyond "Heuristics and Biases"', *European Review of Social Psychology*, 2 (1991), 83–115.

—— and HUG, KLAUS, 'Domain-Specific Reasoning: Social Contracts, Cheating and Perspective Change', *Cognition*, 43 (1992), 127–71.

GILLIGAN, CAROL, *In a Different Voice: Psychological Theory and Women's Development* (Cambridge, Mass.: Harvard University Press, 1982).

GIROTTO, V., GILLY, M., BLAYE, A., and LIGHT, P., 'Children's Performance in the Selection Task: Plausibility and Familiarity', *British Journal of Psychology*, 80 (1989), 79–95.

—— LIGHT, P., and COLBOURN, C. J., 'Pragmatic Reasoning Schemas and Conditional Reasoning in Children', *Quarterly Journal of Experimental Psychology*, 40 (1988), 469–82.

GOLDMAN, ALVIN, *Epistemology and Cognition* (Cambridge, Mass.: MIT Press, 1986).

GOLDSCHMIDT, RICHARD, *The Material Basis of Evolution* (New Haven: Yale University Press, 1940).

GOODMAN, NELSON, *Fact, Fiction and Forecast*, 4th edn. (Cambridge, Mass.: Harvard University Press, 1983).

GOPNIK, M., 'Dysphasia in an Extended Family', *Nature*, 374 (1990), 715.

—— and CRAGO, MARTHA, 'Familial Aggregation of a Developmental Language Disorder', *Cognition*, 39 (1991), 1–50.

GORDON, PETER, 'Level-Ordering in Lexical Development', *Cognition*, 21 (1986), 73–91.

GOULD, STEVEN JAY, 'Panselectionist Pitfalls in Parker and Gibson's Model of the Evolution of Intelligence', *Behavioral and Brain Sciences*, 2 (1979), 385–6.

—— and LEWONTIN, RICHARD, 'The Spandrels of San Marcos and the Panglossian Paradigm: A Critique of the Adaptationist Programme', *Proceedings of the Royal Society of London*, 205 (1978), 281–8; repr. in Sober (ed.), *Conceptual Issues in Evolutionary Biology*.

—— and VRBA, ELIZABETH, 'Exaptation—a Missing Term in the Science of Form', *Paleobiology*, 8 (1982), 4–15.

GRANDY, RICHARD, 'Reference, Meaning and Belief', *Journal of Philosophy*, 70 (1973), 439–52.

GREENBERG, JOSEPH (ed.), *Universals of Language* (Cambridge, Mass.: MIT Press, 1963).

—— FERGUSON, CHARLES, and MORAVCSIK, EDITH (eds.), *Universals of Human Language*, 4 vols. (Stanford, Calif.: Stanford University Press, 1978).

GRIFFIN, DONALD, *Animal Thinking* (Cambridge, Mass.: Harvard University Press, 1984).

GRIGGS, RICHARD, 'The Role of Problem Content in the Wason Selection Task and THOG Problem', in Jonathan Evans (ed.), *Thinking and Reasoning: Psychological Approaches* (London: Routledge & Kegan Paul, 1983).

HARDING, SANDRA, *The Science Question in Feminism* (Ithaca, NY: Cornell University Press, 1986).

HAWKESWORTH, MARY, 'Feminist Epistemology: A Survey of the Field', *Women and Philosophy*, 7 (1987), 112–24.

HENLE, MARY, 'On the Relation between Logic and Thinking', *Psychological Review*, 69 (1962), 376–82.

—— Foreword, in Russell Revlin and Richard Mayer (eds.), *Human Reasoning* (Washington: Winston, 1978).

HERNNSTEIN, RICHARD, 'Level of Stimulus Control: A Functional Approach', *Cognition*, 37 (1990), 133–66.

HOOKWAY, CHRISTOPHER, *Quine: Language, Experience and Reality* (Stanford, Calif.: Stanford University Press, 1988).

HUGHES, M. A. M., 'The Use of Negative Information in Concept Attainment', Ph.D. thesis, University of London, 1966.

HULL, DAVID, 'A Mechanism and its Metaphysics', *Biology and Philosophy*, 3 (1988), 123–55.

HUTCHINS, EDWIN, *Culture and Inference: A Trobriand Case Study* (Cambridge, Mass.: Harvard University Press, 1980).

JOHNSON-LAIRD, PHILIP, LEGRENZI, PAOLO, and LEGRENZI, MARIA, 'Reasoning and a Sense of Reality', *British Journal of Psychology*, 63 (1972), 395–400.

KAHNEMAN, DANIEL, and TVERSKY, AMOS, 'Subjective Probability: A Judgment of Representativeness', *Cognitive Psychology*, 3 (1972), 430–54;. repr. in Kahneman *et al.* (eds.), *Judgment under Uncertainty*.

—— SLOVIC, PAUL, and TVERSKY, AMOS (eds.), *Judgment under Uncertainty: Heuristics and Biases* (Cambridge: Cambridge University Press, 1982).

KIM, JAEGWON, 'What is "Naturalized Epistemology"?', in James Tomberlin (ed.), *Philosophical Perspectives*, ii: *Epistemology* (Atascadero, Calif.: Ridgeview, 1988); repr. in Kornblith (ed.), *Naturalizing Epistemology*.

KIMURA, MOOTO, 'The Neutral Theory of Evolution', *Scientific American*, 240/5 (1979), 98–126.

KITCHER, PHILIP, *Vaulting Ambition: Sociobiology and the Quest for Human Nature* (Cambridge, Mass.: MIT Press, 1985).

—— 'The Naturalists Return', *Philosophical Review*, 101 (1992), 53–114.

KORNBLITH, HILARY, 'Introduction: What is Naturalistic Epistemology?', in Kornblith (ed.), *Naturalizing Epistemology*.

—— (ed.), *Naturalizing Epistemology*, 2nd edn. (Cambridge, Mass.: MIT Press, 1994).

KUHN, THOMAS, *The Copernican Revolution: Planetary Astronomy in the Development of Western Thought* (Cambridge, Mass.: Harvard University Press, 1957).

—— 'Reflections on my Critics', in Imre Lakatos and Alan Musgrave (eds.), *Criticism and the Growth of Knowledge* (London: Cambridge University Press, 1970).

—— *The Structure of Scientific Revolutions* (Chicago: University of Chicago Press, 1970).

LAUDAN, LARRY, *Progress and its Problems* (Berkeley: University of California Press, 1977).

LEHRER, KEITH, *Theory of Knowledge* (Boulder, Colo.: Westview, 1990).

——'Coherentism', in Jonathan Dancy and Ernest Sosa (eds.), *A Companion to Epistemology* (Oxford: Blackwell, 1992).

LETTVIN, J. Y., MATURANA, H. R., McCOLLOGH, W. S., and PITTS, W. H., 'What the Frog's Eye Tells the Frog's Brain', *Proceedings of the Institute of Radio Engineers*, 47 (1959), 1940–51.

LEWONTIN, RICHARD, 'The Evolution of Cognition', in Daniel Osherson and Edward E. Smith (eds.), *Thinking: An Invitation to Cognitive Science*, iii (Cambridge, Mass.: MIT Press, 1990).

LIGHT, P., BLAYNE, A., GILLY, M., and GIROTTO, V., 'Pragmatic Schemas and Logical Reasoning in 6- to 8-Year-Old Children', *Cognitive Development*, 4 (1989), 49–64.

—— GIROTTO, V., and LEGRENZI, P., 'Children's Reasoning on Conditional Promises and Permissions', *Cognitive Development*, 5 (1990), 369–83.

LIPTON, PETER, and THOMPSON, NICHOLAS, 'Comparative Psychology and the Recursive Structure of Filter Explanations', *International Journal of Comparative Psychology*, 1 (1988), 215–44.

LYCAN, WILLIAM, *Judgment and Justification* (Cambridge: Cambridge University Press, 1988).

LYONS, WILLIAM, *The Disappearance of Introspection* (Cambridge, Mass.: MIT Press, 1986).

MACKIE, J. L., 'Self-Refutation—A Formal Analysis', *Philosophical Quarterly*, 14 (1964), 193–203; repr. in *Logic and Knowledge: Selected Papers of J. L. Mackie*, ed. Joan Mackie and Penelope Mackie (Oxford: Oxford University Press, 1985).

MCLAUGHLIN, BRIAN, and RORTY, AMÉLIE (eds.), *Perspectives in Self-Deception* (Berkeley: University of California Press, 1988).

MACNAMARA, JOHN, *A Border Dispute* (Cambridge, Mass.: MIT Press, 1986).

MANKTELOW, KEITH, and EVANS, JONATHAN, 'Facilitation of Reasoning by Realism: Effect or Non-effect', *British Journal of Psychology*, 70 (1979), 477–88.

—— and OVER, D. E., *Inference and Understanding: A Philosophical and Psychological Perspective* (New York: Routledge, 1990).

MARR, DAVID, *Vision: A Computational Investigation into Human Representation and Processing of Visual Information* (San Francisco: Freeman, 1982).

MELE, ALFRED, *Irrationality: An Essay in Akrasia, Self-Deception and Self-Control* (Oxford: Oxford University Press, 1987).

MILLIKAN, RUTH, 'Naturalist Reflections on Knowledge', *Pacific Philosophical Quarterly*, 65 (1984), 315–34.

—— *Language, Thought and Other Biological Categories* (Cambridge, Mass.: MIT Press, 1987).

MOSER, PAUL (ed.), *Empirical Knowledge: Readings in Contemporary Epistemology* (Savage, Md.: Rowman & Littlefield, 1986), pt. II, pp. 231–70.

NISBETT, RICHARD, and BORGIDA, EUGENE, 'Attribution and the Psychology of Prediction', *Journal of Personal and Social Psychology*, 32 (1975), 932–43.

—— KRANZ, DAVID, JEPSON, CHRISTOPHER, and KUNDA, ZIVA, 'The Use of Statistics in Everyday Inductive Reasoning', *Psychological Review*, 90 (1983), 339–63.

NITECKI, MATTHEW (ed.), *Evolutionary Progress* (Chicago: University of Chicago Press, 1988).

PAPINEAU, DAVID, *Reality and Representation* (Oxford: Blackwell, 1987).

PARFIT, DEREK, *Reasons and Persons* (Oxford: Oxford University Press, 1984).

PARKER, SUSAN, and GIBSON, KATHLEEN, *Language and Intelligence in Monkeys and Apes: Comparative Developmental Perspectives* (Cambridge: Cambridge University Press, 1990).

PEARS, DAVID, *Motivated Irrationality* (Oxford: Oxford University Press, 1984).

PIATTELLI-PALMARINI, MASSIMO, 'Evolution, Selection and Cognition', *Cognition*, 31 (1989), 1–44.

PINKER, STEVEN, 'Language Acquisition', in Daniel Osherson and Howard Lasnik (eds.) *Language: Invitation to Cognitive Science*, i (Cambridge, Mass.: MIT Press, 1990).

—— *The Language Instinct: How the Mind Creates Language* (New York: Morrow, 1994).

——and BLOOM, PAUL, 'Natural Language and Natural Selection', *Behavioral and Brain Sciences*, 13 (1990), 707–84.

POIZNER, HOWARD, KLIMA, EDWARD, and BELLUGI, URSULA, *What the Hands Reveal about the Brain* (Cambridge, Mass.: MIT Press, 1990).

POLLARD, PAUL, 'Natural Selection for the Selection Task: Limits to Social Exchange Theory', *Cognition*, 36 (1990), 195–204.

POPPER, KARL, *The Logic of Scientific Discovery* (New York: Basic Books, 1959).

—— *Conjectures and Refutations* (New York: Basic Books, 1962).

—— *Objective Knowledge: An Evolutionary Approach* (Oxford: Oxford University Press, 1972).

——'Evolutionary Epistemology', in J..W. Pollard (ed.), *Evolutionary Theory: Paths into the Future* (London: Wiley 1984).

PULLUM, GEOFFREY, 'The Revenge of the Methodological Moaners', in *The Great Eskimo Vocabulary Hoax and Other Irreverent Essays on the Study of Language* (Chicago: University of Chicago Press, 1991).

PUTNAM, HILARY, 'The "Innateness Hypothesis" and Explanatory Models in Linguistics', *Synthese*, 17 (1967), 12–22; repr. in Block (ed.), *Readings in the Philosophy of Psychology*, ii.

—— 'The Meaning of "Meaning"', in *Mind, Language and Reality: Philosophical Papers*, ii (Cambridge: Cambridge University Press, 1975).

QUINE, WILLARD V. O., *Word and Object* (Cambridge, Mass.: MIT Press, 1960).

—— 'Two Dogmas of Empiricism', in *From a Logical Point of View* (Cambridge: Harvard University Press, 1961).

—— *Ontological Relativity and Other Essays* (New York: Columbia University Press, 1969).

—— 'Epistemology Naturalized', in *Ontological Relativity and Other Essays*; repr. in Kornblith (ed.), *Naturalizing Epistemology*.

—— and ULIAN, J. S., *The Web of Belief* (New York: Random House, 1970).

RACHLIN, HOWARD, LOGUE, A. W., GIBBON, JOHN, and FRANKEL, MARVIN, 'Cognition and Behavior in Studies of Choice', *Psychological Review*, 93 (1986), 33–45.

RAWLS, JOHN, *A Theory of Justice* (Cambridge, Mass.: Harvard University Press, 1971).

—— 'The Independence of Moral Theory', *Proceedings and Addresses of the American Philosophical Association*, 48 (1974–5), 5–22.

RESCHER, NICHOLAS, *The Coherence Theory of Truth* (Oxford: Oxford University Press, 1973).

ROSENBERG, JAY, 'About Competence and Performance', *Philosophical Papers*, 17 (1988), 33–49.

RUSE, MICHAEL, *Taking Darwin Seriously* (Oxford: Blackwell, 1986).

SELIGMAN, MARTIN, and HAGER, JOANE, *The Biological Boundaries of Learning* (New York: Appleton-Century Crofts, 1972).

SKYRMS, BRIAN, *Choice and Chance* (Belmont, Calif.: Wadsworth, 1986).

SOBER, ELLIOTT, 'Psychologism', *Journal of Social Behavior*, 8 (1978), 165–91.

—— 'The Evolution of Rationality', *Synthese*, 46 (1981), 95–120.

—— *The Nature of Selection* (Cambridge, Mass.: MIT Press, 1984).

—— (ed.), *Conceptual Issues in Evolutionary Biology* (Cambridge, Mass.: MIT Press, 1984; 2nd edn. 1994).

SORENSEN, ROY, *Blindspots* (Oxford: Oxford University Press, 1988).

—— 'Self-Strengthening Empathy', unpub. MS.

SPELKE, ELIZABETH, 'Where Perceiving Ends and Thinking Begins', in Albert Yonas (ed.), *Perceptual Development in Infancy* (Hillsdale, NJ: Erlbaum, 1988).

—— 'Principles of Object Perception', *Cognitive Science*, 14 (1990), 29–56.

—— 'Initial Knowledge: Six Suggestions', *Cognition*, 50 (1994), 431–45.

—— BREINLINGER, KAREN, MACOMBER, JANET, and JACOBSON, KRISTEN, 'Origins of Knowledge', *Psychological Review*, 99 (1990), 605–32.

STEIN, EDWARD, 'Getting Closer to the Truth: Realism and the Metaphysical and Epistemological Ramifications of Evolutionary Epistemology', in Nicholas Rescher (ed.), *Evolution, Cognition and Realism* (Lanham, Md.: University Press of America, 1990).

—— 'Evolutionary Epistemology', in Jonathan Dancy and Ernest Sosa (eds.), *A Companion to Epistemology* (Oxford: Blackwell, 1992).

—— 'Rationality and Reflective Equilibrium', *Synthese*, 99 (1994), 137–72.

—— and LIPTON, PETER, 'Where Guesses Come From: Evolutionary Epistemology and the Anomaly of Guided Variation', *Biology and Philosophy*, 4 (1989), 33–56.

STERNBERG, SAUL, 'High-Speed Scanning in Human Memory', *Science*, 153 (1966), 652–4.

STICH, STEPHEN, *From Folk Psychology to Cognitive Science: The Case against Belief* (Cambridge, Mass.: MIT Press, 1983).

STICH, STEPHEN, *The Fragmentation of Reason* (Cambridge, Mass.: MIT Press, 1990).

—— and NISBETT, RICHARD, 'Justification and the Psychology of Human Reasoning', *Philosophy of Science*, 47 (1980), 188–202.

—— and RAMSEY, WILLIAM, 'Connectionism and Three Levels of Nativism', *Synthese*, 82 (1990), 177–205.

TEMPLETON, A. R., 'Adaptation and the Integration of Evolutionary Forces', in R. Milkman (ed.), *Perspectives on Evolution* (Sunderland, Mass.: Sinauer, 1982).

THAGARD, PAUL, and NISBETT, RICHARD, 'Rationality and Charity', *Philosophy of Science*, 50 (1983), 250–67.

TIENSON, JOHN, 'About Competence', *Philosophical Papers*, 19 (1990), 19–36.

TOOBY, JOHN, 'The Emergence of Evolutionary Psychology', in David Pines (ed.), *Emerging Synthesis in Science: Proceedings of the Founding Workshops of the Santa Fe Institute* (Redwood City, Calif.: Addison-Wesley, 1988).

—— 'On the Universality of Human Nature and the Uniqueness of the Individual: The Role of Genetics and Adaptation', *Journal of Personality*, 58 (1990), 17–67.

—— and COSMIDES, LEDA, 'Evolutionary Psychology and the Generation of Culture, Part I: Theoretical Considerations', *Ethology and Sociobiology*, 10 (1987), 29–49.

TVERSKY, AMOS, 'Features of Similarity', *Psychology Review*, 84 (1977), 327–52.

—— and KAHNEMAN, DANIEL, 'Extensional versus Intuitive Reasoning: The Conjunction Fallacy in Probability Judgment', *Psychology Review*, 90 (Oct. 1983), 293–315.

WALKER, STEPHEN, *Animal Thought* (Boston: Routledge, 1983).

WASON, PETER, 'Reasoning', in Brian Foss (ed.), *New Horizons in Psychology* (Harmondsworth: Penguin, 1966).

—— 'Reasoning about a Rule', *Quarterly Journal of Experimental Psychology*, 20 (1968), 273–81.

—— 'Regression in Reasoning?', *British Journal of Psychology*, 60 (1969), 471–80.

—— *Psychology of Reasoning: Structure and Content* (Cambridge, Mass.: Harvard University Press, 1972).

—— and JOHNSON-LAIRD, PHILIP, 'A Conflict between Selecting and Evaluating Information in an Inferential Task', *British Journal of Psychology*, 61 (1970), 509–15.

—— and SHAPIRO, D., 'Natural and Contrived Experience in a Reasoning Problem', *Quarterly Journal of Experimental Psychology*, 23 (1971), 63–71.

WEXLER, KEN, and CULICOVER, PETER, *Formal Principles of Language Acquisition* (Cambridge, Mass.: MIT Press, 1980).

WILLIAMS, GEORGE C., *Adaptation and Natural Selection* (Princeton: Princeton University Press, 1966).

WILSON, EDWARD O., *Sociobiology: The New Synthesis* (Cambridge, Mass.: Harvard University Press, 1975).

—— *Promethean Fire: Reflections on the Origins of Mind* (Cambridge, Mass.: Harvard University Press, 1983).

—— and LUMSDEN, CHARLES, *Genes, Minds and Culture: The Coevolutionary Process* (Cambridge, Mass.: Harvard University Press, 1981).

WILSON, N. L., 'Substances without Substrata', *Review of Metaphysics*, 12 (1959), 521–39.

WYNN, KAREN, 'Addition and Subtraction by Human Infants', *Nature*, 358 (1992), 749–50.

Index

INDEX